PLAYING HARD AT LIFE
A Relational Approach
To Treating Multiply
Traumatized Adolescents

Analysis should be regarded as a process of fluid development unfolding itself before our eyes rather than as a structure with a design pre-imposed upon it by an architect.

—Sándor Ferenczi

PLAYING HARD AT LIFE
A Relational Approach
To Treating Multiply
Traumatized Adolescents

Etty Cohen

THE ANALYTIC PRESS

2003   Hillsdale, NJ   London

Published by The Analytic Press, Inc.
101 West Street, Hillsdale, NJ 07642
www.analyticpress.com

Library of Congress Cataloging-in-Publication Data

Cohen, Etty, 1952–
    Playing hard at life: a relational approach to treating multiply traumatized adolescents/
    Etty Cohen
    p.   cm. Includes bibliographical references and index.
ISBN 0-88163-337-2
    1. Teenagers-Mental health. 2. Post-traumatic stress disorder in children—Treatment.
    3. Adolescent psychotherapy. 4. Abused children—Rehabilitation.
5. Child abuse—Treatment
    I. Title.

    RJ506.P55C64 2003
    616.89'140835—dc21

2003052458

Printed in the United States of America
10 9 8 7 6 5 4 3 2 1

Dedicated to the memory of my parents, Sally and Isaac Cohen.
Mom and Dad, it was too soon to lose both of you.

Contents

Acknowledgments

I wish to express deep gratitude to my patients—the subjects of this book—whose resilience and hope, despite multiple traumas and chaos in their lives, have been its source and inspiration. Their struggles affected me emotionally, and their unique participation in treatment led me to a new understanding of the psychoanalytic process in treating traumatized adolescents.

I am grateful to The Analytic Press, whose high standards every step of the way earned my appreciation and respect. I especially thank John Kerr, my extraordinary editor, whose compassionate comments on my book proposal moved me deeply. "Working with these kids is valuable simply as a human endeavor," he said. John validated my belief that the book is exploratory, experimental, and tentative since there are no definitive answers, as yet, to how to work with patients such as these, who often disrupt attempts at an orderly treatment. John's editorial suggestions deepened my thinking and writing.

My appreciation extends to Dr. Paul Stepansky, who expedited the progress of my book, and to Eleanor Starke Kobrin, who provided astute editorial guidance in addition to excellent copy-editing. John, Paul, and Lenni helped me with my English, which is not my native language.

To Dr. Charles Strozier, a friend and a remarkable editor, I offer my heartfelt gratitude. Chuck has been available at critical moments to help me develop theoretical constructs and to explore my clinical material. As he shared my enthusiasm, we became a special team. His rich, creative thinking and willingness to be a partner in this endeavor was a catalyst for the development of the "meat" of my book: the clinical illustrations.

Portions of this book are based on my Ph.D. dissertation at the New York University Shirley M. Ehrenkranz School of Social Work. I want to thank Dr. Judith Mishne, my dissertation advisor, teacher, and mentor. She has guided my professional footsteps from the beginning of the Ph.D. program, when I arrived from Israel. To Dr. Mishne, my respect, gratitude, and affection.

Dr. Jay Frankel carefully read and commented on most of the chapters. Many of the concepts discussed in this book were the result of conversations with Jay. He has a remarkable ability to reach into the depth of concepts, and I profited enormously from his feedback. His criticisms were direct and candid and influenced the shaping of my ideas. I also thank Dr. Neil Altman, who read a few chapters and gave me tremendously valuable feedback.

I am grateful to my dear friends Angela Molenar, Dr. Semra Coskuntuna, and Judy Shapiro for taking time out from their busy schedule to provide me with editorial assistance. They were always encouraging.

To Dr. Jody Davies, my deepest affection and gratitude for accompanying me through the painful and the joyful moments along the journey of writing this book.

To Professor Gilad Ben-Baruch, I also express my respect and appreciation. As I wrote this book, I experienced my own personal trauma. Professor Ben-Baruch was available to me all the way from Israel. I am forever grateful to him.

For the last 10 years, my professional home has been the Psychoanalytic Institute of the Postgraduate Center for Mental Health. I am grateful to my supervisors during my training: Stefany Gordon, Dr. Julie Marcus, Esther Savitz, Joan Schwartz, and Susannah Shopsin. I wish to thank especially Ms. Margory Slobetz, Director of the Child and Adolescent Psychoanalytic Training Program at the Postgraduate Center. Marge helped me to survive and even value the states of regression and turmoil these traumatized patients presented during the therapeutic work.

I feel privileged to be a training and supervising analyst at The American Institute of Psychoanalysis of the Karen Horney Psychoanalytic Center. I am deeply indebted to my colleagues and the candidates at this institute for stimulating my curiosity, which led to new ways of understanding the therapeutic process.

My clinical supervisors in the Israeli Defense Forces, Dr. Ben-Zion Cohen, Dr. Emanuel Berman, Ilan Madar, Dr. Shimshon Rubin, and Dr. Jerry Wolkinson, have most influenced my clinical growth. I thank them all from the bottom of my heart.

With deep appreciation, I thank my colleague-friends, Andrea, Hadassah, Rivka, and Kate for our unique study group. The experience of sharing friendship and intellectual stimulation has been extremely special and rewarding for me.

For deepening my understanding and appreciation of Ferenczi's theory and therapeutic techniques, I want to thank my European friends, Drs. Carlo Bonomi, Franco Borgogno, Judith Dupont, and Luis J. Martín Cabré, whose friendships and wisdom I value.

I am thankful also for the extraordinary support of my friends. To mention a few, my thanks go to Giselle, Liz, Marge, Noam, Michal, and Yardena. I feel fortunate to have them in my personal and professional life. I want to thank my lifelong friends in Israel: Boaz, Edna, Michal, Rali, Ruti, Shuli, and Tami for quieting my fears in moments of panic, buoying my spirit during moments of challenge, and celebrating with me in times of accomplishment (פירגנו לי).

Finally, I turn to my family: my brothers-in-law, Dani and Boaz, and my nephews, Asi and Avi. Though many miles separate us, they have always been an important source of support and joy. Above all, my deepest love is reserved for my three sisters, Rachel, Ronit, and Orna, whose unconditional caring was with me through all the pages of this book.

Prologue

> *It is not within the capacity of*
> *psycho-analysis entirely to spare the*
> *patient pain; indeed, one of the chief gains*
> *from psycho-analysis is the capacity to bear pain.*
> —Ferenczi

Finding ways to treat patients with multiple traumas touches on profound issues in human experience. My choosing to work with such patients was strongly influenced by my own experience with grief and loss. As an Israeli citizen, I grew up in a society in mourning in which repeated traumas were a familiar part of the landscape. I was raised on war. I was barely in school when my uncles fought in the war of 1967. Six years later, three good friends and two close neighbors fought and died in the Yom Kippur war. I was called up from the reserves during the fighting and was stationed near the front line. After college I joined the Israeli Defense Forces (IDF) as a major in the Mental Health Corps and served for 13 years. I counseled young men and women who had been deeply scarred by the Intifada's activities in Lebanon and Gaza. Through two more wars—the Lebanon War of 1982 and the Gulf War of 1991— I continued my work with traumatized patients and shared their grief over the loss of friends, family, and fellow officers.

My therapeutic approach took shape after more than 25 years of clinical work and entailed long struggles to develop a theoretical orientation consonant with my experience. My introduction to psychoanalytic theory came during my work as a mental health officer with vulnerable soldiers in the Israeli army. The problem was that initially I had been trained in classical techniques, which neither suited my temperament nor were appropriate for the needs of my patients. I was unaware of other clinical approaches. I had struggled over the years to reconcile the discrepancies between my own values (I felt more comfortable with mutuality) and the professional training I had received in the Israeli army, which was based on a hierarchical model of the doctor–patient relationship.

After I came to the United States, I found myself drawn to the battlefields of New York. The victims of the inner city are veterans and survivors of an urban war. They struggle to endure the violence that they witness in their families and on the streets. They grow up impoverished, abandoned, or neglected by their parents, surrounded by the temptations of substance abuse and criminal activity. As I had with the traumatized soldiers I worked with in the Israeli Defense Forces, I came to discover that little information was available to guide a clinician in treating traumatized inner-city adolescents. This book, based on more than 25 years of experience, is written to meet that important need.

After I became acquainted in New York with Ferenczi's theory and techniques, the paradigm I used was distinctly more intersubjective. The remote officer in me became an equal partner with my patients, and this kind of partnership suited me intellectually and emotionally. Ferenczi's writings became the main source for the theoretical framework of my doctoral dissertation, which was on the application of Ferenczi's theory and techniques to group psychotherapy with fragile, traumatized adolescents facing the loss of parents to AIDS (Cohen, 1997a).

Ferenczi inspired me. I read his works as though they were novels. The quality of Ferenczi's writing and the vitality of his engagement with his patients impressed me equally. I could not put the books down until I got to the last page. I was fascinated by the rationales for therapeutic approaches that fit my personality, my personal values, and my professional beliefs. Ferenczi's emphasis on mutuality informed my approach to my psychoanalytic control case (Cohen, 1997b). In this work I described in detail both the transference and the countertransference enactments that occurred in the treatment of a troubled youngster.

In recent years there has been a concerted effort to explore the impact of trauma on children (Green, 1983; Horovitz, 1985; James, 1989; Terr, 1990; Herman, 1992; Scharff and Scharff, 1994; Gil, 1996; Prior, 1996; Pearce and Pezzot-Pearce, 1997; Wolfe, McMahon, and Peters, 1997). The reaction of adolescents to trauma (Sugar, 1999; Anastasopulos, Laylou-Lignos, and Waddell, 1999), however, has received less attention, and adolescence as a distinct developmental stage has been largely ignored in trauma theory. A special issue of *The American Journal of Psychoanalysis* sets out to address the theoretical and clinical questions surrounding the ways adolescents deal with trauma and the ways trauma affects adolescent development. This special issue includes papers by Giovacchini, Cohen, the Novicks, Mishne, and Frankel (Cohen, 2001).

In *Playing Hard at Life* I seek to demonstrate how a relational approach can be applied to treating these fragile adolescents. Although this book illustrates theoretical concepts that I found useful in working in all modalities with boys and girls, the focus is on a group of six female adolescents who were facing parental loss through AIDS. Some of them had been sexually abused. I also focus on two soldiers suffering from war trauma who were seen in a military mental health clinic and a female patient I saw in an inpatient unit; she had been emotionally abused and suffered from an eating disorder. I chose to focus particularly on these traumatized adolescents because they had the most powerful effect on me with regard to my countertransference feelings—and because of my often painful experience as a failed therapist. My therapeutic experiences with these patients were instrumental in leading me to develop the orientation I use in working with other vulnerable youngsters. It was from these patients that I learned to tolerate the chaos and ambiguity of beginning treatment without a theoretical agenda. They fight against attachment and are difficult to engage, but I believe that each can be understood in a way that fits each of them uniquely.

Their particularity notwithstanding, I believe that the cases described in this book represent a wide variety of traumatized adolescents and the general issues that occupied them and me. The names, identifying characteristics, and other details about the patients presented in this book have been changed to protect their privacy and preserve their confidence and that of their families.

Part I of the book extends the context of trauma from relational theory to its clinical application in treating traumatized adolescents. Part I explores issues in therapeutic relationships. This section focuses on clinical examples; secrets and self-disclosure, enactments, dreams, and dissociation and cultural difference. Part II highlights the evolution of the transference–countertransference matrix and includes the engagement phase—resistance and antitherapeutic alliance; the safety-phase—mutual tenderness; and the erotic phase—the confusion between tenderness and passion. Part III focuses on treatment plans; gender in the dyad; individual, group, and family therapy; contact with parents; and termination.

I

ON THE ROAD TO SURVIVAL

Secrets and Self-Disclosure In The Therapeutic Relationship

Felicia [singer]

She's blind.
There are no colors in her world.
Only black always black.
She's beautiful and scared.[1]

This chapter illustrates how a relational-constructivist approach can be applied to the treatment of multiply traumatized adolescents. Let me begin with a proposition from Hoffman (1998), namely, that the patient's and the analyst's experience and understanding of each other are, in the first instance, constructions. These constructions are based on the individual histories and personalities of the two parties and their interpretations of their participation with the other.

Within the constructivist approach, such as Hoffman's, it is axiomatic that analysts cannot know the full meaning of their own or their patients' behavior. As a result, constructivists argue for a heightened sensitivity to, and a tolerance for, uncertainty and spontaneity. Such contemporary psychoanalytic theorists as Mitchell (1993) have attempted to integrate constructivism and hermeneutic principles into a relational model. Mitchell clearly stakes out the constructivist position on knowing:

It is impossible to envision a singular correct and complete understanding of any piece of human experience even as an ideal, because experience is fundamentally ambiguous . . . To say that experience is fundamentally ambiguous is to say that its meaning is not inherent or apparent in it but that it lends itself to multiple understandings, multiple interpretations [pp. 57–58].

---

[1] The poems at the beginnings of chapters were written by an adolescent patient and were published in her school newspaper. To ensure confidentiality, the name of her school is excluded.

From Mitchell's point of view, the construction of meanings in treatment necessarily occurs de nouveau and in an atmosphere of uncertainty. The analyst and the analysand are engaged in a continuous dance in which multiple meanings arise and are explored. Both parties in the dyad are capable of making correct interpretations: the rightness of fit of the therapist's view, when it occurs, corresponds to its match with the patient's core of experience. Balint (1968) referred to the usual disjunctions between the expectations of analysts and those of their patients:

> We analysts are often faced with the same experience. We give our patient an interpretation, clear, concise, well-founded, well-timed, and to the point, which—often to our surprise, dismay, irritation, and disappointment—either has no effect on the patient or has an effect quite different from that intended [p. 13].

Balint considered treatment failures to be the result of a "lack of fit between the analyst's otherwise correct technique and a particular patient's needs" (p. 22). He emphasized that a bad "fit" in treatment emerges out of an earlier relationship between the child and his or her caretakers.

Hoffman (1998) argues that the search for a rightness of fit and the making of good interpretations is a dialectical process. This dialectical process is, in his view, facilitated by maintaining an experiential openness to the tension between views that comprises a dynamic interplay between seemingly unrelated, opposing polarities, such as between discipline and personal responsiveness or between repetition and new experience.

To illustrate the application of the dialectical-constructivist view of the psychoanalytic process in treating a traumatized female adolescent, let us take the case of Keisha.

Keisha, an African American girl, was 14 years old at the time of referral to individual therapy. Her mother was concerned about her daughter's acting-out behavior, which literally risked her life. Keisha had lived with relatives since birth, because her mother was drug addicted and homeless and her father was in prison on robbery charges. She was an only child. After the mother discovered that she was HIV positive, she decided to raise her child before she died. Keisha, who did not know about her mother's illness, felt resentful toward her mother for taking her back. She felt a sense of loss over leaving her relatives. In the process, she also had to move to another neighborhood, which meant transfer to another school and separation from her friends. After the abrupt move, Keisha repeatedly ran away until she realized that, if she continued doing this, she would be placed in a group home.

The mother asked for help in finding the "right" timing to disclose to her daughter the news of her terminal illness. At the time of the referral, two of my other adolescent patients had recently lost their parents to AIDS without being able to say goodbye. I was worried that Keisha would have the same experience. I felt that it was important, before meeting Keisha, to help the mother disclose her HIV status as soon as possible. In the first session with Keisha, I found myself struggling with my presumptions about the goals of treatment. I felt that the only thing that mattered was for Keisha to learn about her mother's HIV-positive status and then work through the feelings of both of them about that information. I soon realized, however, that there were other issues to deal with.

Keisha: I don't want to live with my mother. For 14 years she forgot about me and suddenly she remembers me. I am not a toy.

Etty: You express your anger now, but maybe you feel very upset inside.

Keisha: Did I say that I am upset? I don't even know her. I don't care about her.

Etty: I said that you are upset. But after your response I realize that I am the one who is upset that you could not live with your own mother as a child.

Keisha: But I like my grandparents [that is how she identified her close relatives who acted like her grandparents].

Etty: I understand that your experience is different from what I thought. You feel very close to your grandparents and you miss them. Tell me, how was it to live with them?
[Keisha described in detail how caring her grandparents were toward her.]

Etty: Since you did not live with your mother, I am wondering how it is now living with her.

Keisha: How can I know?

Etty: Yes, maybe you can't know.

Keisha: She is the one who needs therapy, not me.

Etty: Why do you believe that she needs therapy?

Keisha: She always yells at me and is angry.

Etty: What is she yelling at you about?

Another therapist might well have made other choices in conversation with Keisha about secrets and traumas. I expressed empathy with Keisha's pain at the loss of her relatives. I felt ethically conflicted, however, since I had information about her mother that was not disclosed and it affected my feelings toward Keisha. I was caught in a devastating loyalty-bind: whether to betray either Keisha or her mother. I could have been silent in the hope of getting more orienting information so as to develop an understanding of what was going on. I could have offered to meet her mother so I could understand the "reality" of what was going on between them. At this point, I chose to learn only from Keisha about her experience.

Classical psychoanalytic theory holds that transference is a distortion in the mind of the analysand. Past experiences are displaced onto the analyst, who then develops countertransference feelings in reaction to the patient. The classical position presupposed a well-analyzed analyst who maintains an autonomous observing ego and who can monitor his or her countertransference feelings through self-analysis. One element that distinguishes the relational-constructivist from classical approaches is that, in the former, the therapist relies more on his or her own subjective responses as a creative source of information about the patient and the interaction. In this approach, instead of neutrality, the analyst's mood, feelings, fantasies, and thoughts are seen as the path to the patient's issues. Instead of analyzing the transference as a guide to unconscious truth, the analyst works to understand why the patient constructs an experience in such and such a way.

Relational analysts assume that in spite of having been analyzed intensively, analysts are unable to detach themselves from the therapeutic interaction with their patients so that perforce they must be able to observe and work through their own unconscious participation on the fly, as it were. The relational orientation has both the patient and the analyst mutually participating in the therapeutic process and therefore affecting each other. The goal of the collaboration, again, is to achieve a rightness of fit of interpretations and mutual understandings. Ferenczi (1932) discussed this mutual collaboration in terms that explicitly subverted the old approach, which left correcting the countertransference to the analyst's self-analysis: "We gladly allow the patients to have the pleasure of being able to help us, to become for a brief period our analyst, as it were, something that justifiably raises their self-esteem" (p. 65).

I feel that such an approach is necessary in working with traumatized adolescents. Listening to Keisha's life history provoked sadness in me. My "expressive participation" (as Hoffman, 1998, calls it) in my interaction with Keisha can be described by four factors: (1) my participation included an *affective connection, sadness, and tenderness,* in this case; (2) my participation was *immediate* and *unanticipated* rather than deliberate; (3) my experience came more from *within myself* than as a response to pressure from Keisha; (4) my participation offered Keisha a relatively new experience in the present rather than simply a repetition of something from her past.

I find a measure of relief in the constructivist approach in cases like Keisha's, since questions about reality versus fantasy are not focal issues. Instead, I could savor the ambiguities as emerging aspects of our coparticipation. This tolerance for ambiguity in the "truth" is significant in treating adolescents and even more so in treating traumatized adolescents. It enables one to find a measure of freedom from being ruled by a concern with what really happened.

Spence (1988) argues from a hermeneutic view that "narrative truth" is more central than "historical truth." Therefore, he sees truth in the analytic process as a matter of creation or construction rather than the slow accreation of "objective" data. Donnel Stern (1985), who has championed a constructivist approach to interpersonal psychoanalysis, argues that the epistemological questions in psychoanalysis have moved "from what we know to how and why we have the experience of knowing. The process of knowing is assuming as much importance as the content of knowledge" (p. 203). Mitchell (1993) notes that "psychoanalysis can no longer be a science in the way Freud thought about science. It is now a science that yields multiple truths, changing truths, truths that are embedded in particular interactive context of the analytic relationship" (p. 50).

These larger philosophical questions connect in many ways with current treatment issues. Writers who are part of "The False Memory Syndrome Movement" (e.g., Kihlstrom, Gliski, and Angiulo, 1994; Rauschenberger and Lynn, 1995; Brenneis, 1996) have suggested that certain traumatized patients are highly suggestive as well as fantasy prone. These writers believe that reports of events can result from a vivid imagination that is closely attuned to the implicit expectations of the analyst.

But Davies (1996), a leading spokesperson for the treatment of traumatized patients within the framework of relational theory, argues that what matters most is the pursuit of our patients' narrative truth. She questions the value of historical/objective truth.

> If we believe that there is, indeed, a newly emerging relational paradigm
> within psychoanalysis, a paradigm that stresses the multiple realities of each
> unique analytic pairing, as well as the multiple interpretive potentialities
> embodied in an essentially hermeneutic approach to analytic discourse, we

may well come to wonder about the formative significance of any single traumatic event within the life of an individual and how, as analysts, we can validate experiences about which we remain so uncertain [pp. 189–190].

Price's (1995) postmodernist attitude toward multiciplicity is important here because she argues that requests for certainty and objective truth create barriers within patients so that they are less able to conceive of multiple selves. These barriers also limit their access to dissociated experiences. However, let us not assume that it is advisable to undertake treatment with a traumatized adolescent, or a traumatized child for that matter, without attempting to get a developmental history from available informants, whether parents or grandparents or other involved adults. Therapists, I believe, underestimate the importance of a developmental history. In describing the adolescent patients in this book, I discuss crucial points in these patients' developmental histories. Paradoxically, having this kind of information helps to clarify rather than abrogate the importance of narrative truth. Some examples illustrate my point.

Nataline, a Caucasian girl, was 14 years old at the time she was referred for treatment. She is an attractive girl, tall and slim, with braces and brown hair pulled back in a high ponytail. At the time of the referral, her mother, Ms. B., was ill with liver cancer and AIDS and lived with her ex-husband, an alcoholic. Ms. B. desperately wanted to move out but had nowhere to go and had no one to care for her during her frequent illnesses. Feeling that she did not have much time left, Ms. B. strongly desired to repair her relationship with her daughter before she died. Nataline had been in a girls group for nearly two years before she joined my bereavement group. Even though Nataline announced that she "had no problems," she discussed feeling neglected by her mother and also having difficulty with girls in school who ignored her and left her out. Her mother expressed concern about unresolved mourning for Nataline's grandfather, who had died a year and a half before. In addition, Nataline's father was in prison because of his drug use.

Ms. B.'s childhood had been terribly traumatic. When she was six, her father, also an alcoholic, moved out (he returned after a few years) and her brother began molesting her. He was 12 at the time. Ms. B. complained to her mother, who did not believe her. When Ms. B. was seven, her sister caught the brother on top of Ms. B. No one discussed it, but the molestation ended. She became a member of a gang and later suffered a rape by six men. At 17 she began dating a man whom she really loved and hoped to marry. He suffered from depression and committed suicide. Soon after, Ms. B. began seeing Nataline's father.

A year after Nataline's mother began dating her father, she became pregnant with Nataline. Although the pregnancy was unplanned, the mother decided to keep the baby because her religious beliefs prohibited her from having an abortion. Although the father claimed he wanted the child, he never showed up in the hospital to sign the birth certificate, nor did he visit Nataline. He spent time in and out of jail for theft and drug possession. He and Nataline never lived together.

The mother stated that Nataline reached all the developmental milestones at the appropriate ages. At an early age Nataline developed asthma. The maternal grandmother described herself as Nataline's primary caretaker from birth. The mother lived with the child and both grandparents until Nataline was two years old. The mother moved twice before Nataline was five. At that time she started to use drugs and alcohol, so the grandmother threw her out. Nataline was very close to her grandfather. They spent time together, and she felt that he helped to ease communication between her grandmother and her mother. When he died she was very sad, and soon after she withdrew emotionally and refused to discuss the loss with family members.

The mother felt that Nataline had grown up "too fast." She explained that Nataline did not like to play the way other children did and preferred the company of adults. Nataline did well academically and described her teacher as her confidante, the person with whom she had the closest relationship. She felt like an outsider in her school, however, because most of the other students came from more affluent neighborhoods. Nataline lived with her maternal grandmother, uncle, and aunt. She had conflicted relationships with all of them. According to Nataline, her grandmother was never around and went to Atlantic City most weekends. Nataline complained that she did not have any privacy at home and expressed her wish to live with her mother.

Ms. B. was worried about Nataline's behavior; she misbehaved at home by cursing and lying, and she spread rumors that she was pregnant. The mother claimed that this pregnancy had never occurred. Almost two years later, this "story" on pregnancy came up in group therapy during the termination phase when Nataline suggested that the girls in the group play mothers who had babies and who came to see me as a social worker in order to be better parents than their own parents were. Nataline's story: "Before I had my baby I slept with my mother's boyfriend and got pregnant. My mother forced me to get an abortion."

I remember feeling struck by Nataline's story, not because of what she had shared with us but because of how she had told her story. She was very upset and did not make eye contact with us. I asked myself if the rumor she spread about being pregnant was a "true" story. Was it by coincidence that she chose a role play in which she was pregnant? And if the pregnancy had never occurred, as her mother suggested, what were the multiple meanings of her choice of a story?

Davies (1996) believes that traumatized patients and their analysts remain surrounded by doubt. She suggests that we must tolerate the ambiguities and be willing to exit sessions for long periods "not knowing." She notes that encoding traumatic and potentially fragmenting experiences in an empathic therapeutic atmosphere of relational stability represents a more essential piece of clinical work than does the veridical reconstruction of historical detail. Davies believes that by being freed from the obligation to know what really happened we are able to observe, in the moment, the immediacy of the transference-countertransference matrix.

From this vantage point, I found myself questioning what had been created in the analytic relationship that led to the interactive context between Nataline, the other girls, and myself? In the role play on "motherhood" the girls asked me to play the social worker whose function was to protect their babies, who, of course, might represent themselves. Each of them described in writing their role play. For Nataline, she was 27 years old, a twin sister to Michelle; her occupation was a doctor and she was a divorced mother. She made a list of all the expenses related to raising her child. Michelle was also a 27-year-old divorced mother; she was a successful journalist. Both girls brought to the session dolls that they had from childhood, pretending they were their babies. In reality, they were about to lose their parents to AIDS. They could not help but wish that their parents would do a better job taking care of them.

At this point in treatment, we had together created a holding environment (which I describe later in this book as the Tenderness Phase). I tried to fulfill their wishes by being a better parental figure, but I did not realize that, at the same time, my doing so would lead to resistance in someone like Nataline. She could not tolerate the experience she needed most, that of being cared for. Moreover, in the role play, getting pregnant by the mother's boyfriend may have represented Nataline's identification with the dysfunctional mother she was going to lose, a mother who risked her own life with drugs and promiscuous relationships. It may also have represented her remaking of herself. Trying to find the rightness of fit, I was continuously willing to abandon, as well as create, different constructions of her life stories.

Another important area lay in dealing with secrets, which for adolescents are always doubly complicated. First, at this developmental stage adolescents fight for their privacy and regularly carry secrets relating to their intimate relationships, their sexual activities, their school performance, and the like. Second, when they have experienced traumatic abuse, they carry the secrets of the abuse in the face of feeling shameful. There are many issues to explore. Why do adolescents need to have secrets? Is it our role to reveal their secrets? What are the meanings for adolescents when secrets are kept from them? Are the secrets really kept from them? What factors should be considered before we reveal secrets to adolescents? The following illustrates the role of a secret in its ambiguous aspects, its meanings, and its multiple understandings.

Nataline, who felt hurt as a child that her father did not visit her, did not know that he was in prison. When her mother was dying, her grandmother called me and told me that her mother had only a short time to live and asked me not to tell Nataline. I emphasized to the grandmother that I understood that this issue had to be dealt with very carefully but that I would like to discuss it with her. I told her I was concerned that hiding the information from Nataline would have a significant effect on her future and her relationship with her family. I added that withholding the information about her mother interfered with direct and open communication between them. Unfortunately, the grandmother did not want to discuss it further. I was again at the same crossroads as I had been with Keisha.

Another girl from group therapy, Carmen, whose father lived outside the United States, was upset because her father had not contacted her for three years. She had heard from a child in her neighborhood about an article in the newspaper reporting that Carmen's father had been murdered in connection with drugs. Carmen was devastated to find out this secret about her father accidentally, through a neighbor, who told her in a derogatory manner. As a result, Carmen displaced her anger onto her peers in school and felt isolated and rejected.

Likewise, another of the girls, Michelle, did not know much about her father, or so her mother thought. Her mother was wrong. During a therapy session, Michelle read from an essay in which she described how her parents had met: "He was the porter of our building. He would fix her house and fix other things as well, physical fixing"; that is, he had sexual relations with her mother. She also knew that her father wanted to raise her and that her maternal grandparents had rejected him. Trying unsuccessfully to avoid telling Michelle about her father might create distortions in her own belief about who he was and what his relationship was with her mother and the reasons for his disappearing.

I felt additionally upset when I learned from the mother that she had never told Michelle that she had a twin sister who had died after birth. My sense was that knowing this information might help provide Michelle with some understanding of her mother's reactions after she was born. The mother had blamed Michelle for her sister's death and as a result abandoned her in the hospital.

Michelle, who lived with her aunt because her mother physically abused her, told us in a group session that she had met with her mother without her aunt's permission. In another session she told us that her mother had a new boyfriend and asked us not to tell the foster care agency. She was planning to move from the city with her mother and siblings. She was afraid she would not be allowed to join them if the foster-care worker knew. At this time Michelle showed increasing anxiety as a result of keeping her secret. It created a tension between her and her aunt.

Secrecy was enacted in many ways in the therapeutic setting. During the beginning phase of the group, the girls spoke with a secret language. I had to use unusual interventions. I started to write on the blackboard. For example, I wrote, "You have many secrets in your life. You don't want others to know what they are about, but you let me know that they exist." Later, the girls taunted me by giving me clues to their secrets. Since in my own family I had struggled to discover secrets that were hidden, it took me some time to find a rightness of fit, that is, to appreciate and to explore the importance of their fantasies about my curiosity, about my reaction to their secrets, and about their unconscious desire that I would uncover their secrets, so that they might feel more protected.

The intensity of feeling surrounding a secret is difficult to disguise. The very act of keeping a secret generates anxiety in the patient or in family members, who must be constantly on guard against disclosure, avoiding particular subjects and distorting information. However, traumatized adolescents who are trying hard to keep their secrets from revelation may be trying to maintain a precarious balance in their inner object world in order to be able to tolerate their traumatizing experiences while living in the outside world. Their primitive, primary identification with the aggressive or abandoning aspects of the bad objects, and their ties to them (Fairbairn, 1952), may provide them with the motivation to maintain their secrets all the more steadfastly as a mean of protecting themselves from their pain.

There are other complicated moments within therapeutic settings when patients share secrets with their analysts. In situations where the patient's safety is involved, the therapist is faced with delicate and ethical struggles.

Yael was 17 years old when I saw her in Israel in a psychiatric inpatient unit. She was suffering from eating disorders. She had been physically abused by her father and was totally neglected by her mother. Two suicide attempts preceded treatment with me. Until that point I had worked for 10 years as a mental health officer in the Israeli army where soldiers carried guns. Suicidal ideations were part of our daily life in treating soldiers, and I dreaded losing a soldier under my care. Thus, when suicidal ideation became a central issue early in my treatment of Yael, I resented having to deal yet again with this tormenting issue. I felt the tension between keeping this "secret" between us (as Yael requested) and sharing the information with the director of the ward (as was required). Deciding that her safety was paramount, I did tell the director, who had Yael locked up on the ward.

From the start of treatment, Yael tested me. For example, she told me that she previously had gone to a hospital and informed the staff there that she had overdosed on pills so that she could have her stomach pumped. She had felt a great relief afterwards and asked me not to tell the staff about this incident. Since this behavior potentially entailed a risk to her health if it should be repeated, I told her that I had to share the information with the director of the ward in order to prevent her from damaging her body in this way in the future. She said that she would never be able to trust me. I felt I failed her. I was wondering, however, why she had chosen to share all this information with me.

In another session, Yael described past suicidal thoughts and behaviors, such as walking on the roof of her home with the intention of jumping off, her fantasies of stealing her brother's gun and using it on herself, or of collecting many pills from her father and swallowing them. I started to believe that she needed to worry me precisely so I would take actions to protect her. Again, my principal concern was for her safety. I told her that I had to call her parents and to inform them about her brother's gun and the pills she had collected. I emphasized my concerns and my willingness to protect her from her impulses to hurt herself. She reacted by not speaking with me for a few sessions. Nonetheless, I asked Yael to promise to tell me about her suicidal thoughts as they might come up so that we could build up some kind of mutual trust. I admitted to her that we had not yet established trust toward each other, that trust could be built up only as we got to know each other.

I believed that safety within the therapeutic setting could be established in this way, as Yael experienced me as actively protecting her from her destructive impulses. I saw her three to five times a week in addition to phone calls to the ward during weekends when she was not allowed to leave. Later in the treatment, she admitted that she would have had a difficult time sharing with me her suicidal ideation if she were truly serious about wanting to die. She believed that the only way suicide could be avoided was if she came to believe that I really could help her.

After a few months of intensive therapy, she told me of some more suicidal thoughts. Yael also started to share some childhood memories, as well as issues pertaining to sexual identity confusion. She was able to expose her vulnerable self to me. At that point, Yael stated that she knew she had gained my trust. Unfortunately, after she went on a series of eating binges, I had to have her locked up on the ward again. Although I explained to her what led to the joint decision of the ward director and me, she blamed me for torturing her and for not keeping her secret. Again, she tested my understanding of her suffering and how much she could rely on me. It was striking that after this incident she gave me the note she had written before a suicide attempt that had occurred before her treatment with me. No one knew about this note. It explored her deep despair at that time and her true feelings toward her family. It was a very emotional letter. After that in treatment she denied having any further suicidal ideation even though she had many more difficult moments. I believed her.

Skolnick and Davies (1992) discuss secrets in clinical work from a relational perspective:

> They [secrets] can be employed as an aid to the discovery and experience of intersubjective bonds, as transitional phenomena providing an opportunity to relinquish primitive omnipotence, and as a vehicle for the establishing of safe, secure boundaries between inner and outer, between self and others. In pathology, they can be adaptively erected to negotiate severe environmental trauma [p. 237].

Yael, who felt invisible growing up, wanted to make sure she was seen by me. Her eating disorder, as well as her suicidal ideations, gave her control over body, the only control that she believed she held in her own hands. In addition, the very intensity of her struggle suggested to me how traumatized her life had been. As a therapeutic alliance between us was established, she was willing to trust my ability to take care of her. Simultaneously she experienced her inner self as more in control.

Therapists who work with traumatized adolescents are often enlisted into colluding with their secrets. For Latisha, keeping her secrets meant being faithful, and disclosing the secrets meant betrayal.

Latisha was a 13-year-old African American at the time of referral to the clinic for individual therapy. She was a good looking girl of average weight and height. She was neatly dressed and well groomed in casual age-appropriate attire. She wore no makeup, and her hair was pulled back on the top of her head in a tight bun.

Latisha lived with her paternal grandmother and her aunt. She was not doing as well as she could in school, caused disruptions in the classroom, and antagonized other students. She obeyed her grandmother most of the time but could be disrespectful. Her family said that she stole money and other things at home and then lied about it. Latisha found it difficult to talk about these problems. She was "on punishment" most of the time because of her oppositional behavior. She acknowledged that she got into trouble when she was with friends and they cut classes together, but she felt that she liked these friends and that they stood up for her if she got into fights. Latisha was in a time-limited kinship foster-care program with her grandmother. The grandmother, who had been rearing her own children since she was 14 years old, was unwilling to adopt Latisha or take permanent custody.

Latisha's parents had known each other only a short time before they married. The couple frequently got into physical fights. Both parents started using drugs when Latisha was two years old, and they began cashing counterfeit money orders to pay for them. The father went to jail; the couple subsequently broke up after Latisha was removed from the home. After he got out of jail, the father said he would try to see Latisha on holidays, but her maternal grandmother would not permit it—so he would slip money under the door to her and she would cry on the other side. A few years later, the mother gave birth to two babies who were born addicted to crack and therefore were placed in foster homes.

Latisha was uprooted from one home to another several times in her life, twice by the Bureau of Child Welfare (BCW). She has often lived in an environment where drugs where being abused. When asked about any sexual trauma, Latisha's father said he had caught his older son, Arthur, when he was 14 years old, playing with Latisha's vagina when she was seven years old. The son said he was diapering her. The mother did not believe her husband until she herself later caught Arthur doing it. Then they stopped letting him watch her. Latisha came to live with her paternal grandmother, Ms. A., at age 10, after having lived with her maternal grandmother since age five. When she lived with her maternal grandmother she was profoundly neglected. She had to work in a supermarket packing bags, and the family would take her money and whatever people gave her. She was not enrolled in school, had no supervision, lived in a low-income "ghetto" neighborhood, and hung out in the streets until the wee hours of the morning.

When Latisha moved to her paternal grandmother's to live, Ms. A. spent time with her, making sure she did her homework. Her school grades improved—she was an honor student in the fourth grade. Later, when she moved to a new school, Latisha started doing less than she was capable of. Her grandmother reported that at this time she began to steal money and other things at home and then lie about it. Eventually, now 13 years of age, she was referred to treatment. She was seen in individual treatment twice a week for three years. After a few sessions into the course of treatment, we had the following dialogue:

Latisha: Hi, [Latisha was 20 minutes late] I want to call my grandmother and tell her I got here.

Etty: I called your grandmother already since I was worried about you.

Latisha: Can't you keep a secret?

Etty: What is your secret?

Latisha: My secret is that I come late because I like to see my friends after school.

Etty: Your grandmother does not want you to meet your friends after school.

Latisha: Don't you get it? My grandma does not want me to see my friends because she believes that they are bad news.

Etty: Why does she believe that they are bad news?

Latisha: So, can I call my grandma? [Without waiting for my response, she called her grandmother and told her that the subway had been late.]

Etty: Now we both share a secret and a lie.

Latisha: You are going to keep the secret. You told me that what we say here is confidential.

Etty: Yes, all we say here is confidential. However, if I believe that you are at risk, I am going to do all I can to keep you safe.

Latisha: What do you mean?

Etty: Last week you told me that you are afraid three girls want to harm you. When I called your grandma, I really was worried about you.

Latisha: Don't ever call my grandma when I am late!

Etty: I hope that you will be on time so we will have more time together. But maybe you can call me if you are late so I won't worry.

Latisha: You don't have to worry about me.

Etty: Maybe you need to experience me worrying about you.

Latisha: But if my grandma calls, don't tell her the truth.

Etty: I will suggest to your grandma that she ask you directly why you were late to session. By the way, you still did not tell me why your grandma believes that your friends are bad news.

Latisha: Did I say that I would tell you?

Etty: Now you are letting me know that you keep secrets from me as well.

Latisha: And you keep secrets from me also.

Etty: What do you mean?

Latisha: I asked you about your husband or boyfriend and you did not tell me. So, I am not going to tell you about mine.

The function of secrets depends in part on the family's ethnicity and beliefs about privacy. Adolescents are expected to keep some things secret in their lives, and it is considered part of the normal maturational process for them to do so. However, secrets such as hiding drugs at home, engaging in promiscuous relationships, or writing suicide notes in a diary are another matter. When a harmful secret is suspected, it is better for parents as well as therapists to err on the side of intrusion. When we openly express our concerns, the issue can at least be discussed. Imber-Black (1998) suggests reconsidering the lines between privacy and secrecy that so often are at the center of arguments between adolescents and their parents, teachers, therapists, and other caretakers. Imber-Black appeals to Bok's (1983) distinction between secrecy as "intentional concealment" and privacy as "being protected from unwanted access by others" (p. 10).

This issue was the basis of my struggle with Latisha in the foregoing vignette and remains my dilemma in treating many traumatized adolescents. Latisha's grandmother, for example, believed that her granddaughter hung out with bad friends and that she kept this behavior inappropriately secret, while Latisha regarded her social life as her private business. During later sessions I discussed with Latisha her fantasies of the potentially negative consequences—her grandmother's reactions—if she shared her secrets. After a long period of testing my dedication to her, Latisha was willing to share with me her very real struggles with her friends. She began to experience me as her ally and asked my help in inviting her grandmother to a few sessions with her so she would feel safer uncovering her secrets. Revealing secrets to parents has to be considered very carefully. Therapists should know the parents and their relationships with their children. There is a lot to consider before uncovering the secrets becomes therapeutically viable, and it is important to be prepared to work through a process that may be painful to the adolescents as well as to their parents. (This subject is discussed further in chapter 10.)

Another struggle that emerged in treatment with Latisha and with other adolescent patients lay in making choices about whether or not to disclose my countertransference feelings and whether or not to provide information about my personal life. For adolescents, nondisclosure by the therapist will typically be viewed as the therapist's keeping his or her own secrets—as in the previous dialogue with Latisha. As Latisha felt more comfortable with me, she started to bombard me with questions about myself, where I came from, what my age was, and so on. I must confess that, when I told her where I came from, it was not because I felt that doing so was responsive, but because I was exhausted with the process of frustrating her wishes and having her attack me.

Carmen told me that she would share with me what the girls discussed between themselves after the session only if I told them about my boyfriend or husband. Only then, she added, would they tell me about their relationships with boys. I asked the group what they wished to know about him; they asked his name and how long we had been together. This much I told them. I said that I would like to tell them more but that, when their parents had shared intimate information with them in the course of their growing up, they might have been overwhelmed so I wanted not to repeat this if possible. Later in the course of treatment, the girls asked me if I had children, how many siblings I had, and where my parents lived. They did not want to explore the meanings of these questions. They expected to get answers and were enraged when I made interpretations about why they had requested such information. I still feel that I may have been mistaken to withhold that information. On the other hand, as Aron (1996) has pointed out, for some patients who have experienced a lack of boundaries with parental figures, certain kinds of self-disclosure may close down rather than open up potential therapeutic space.

There are different schools of thought about countertransference disclosure. The traditional neutrality of classic psychoanalysis has been strongly challenged in the last 20 years. Beginning with Freud, the traditional view held that the analyst's self-disclosure was burdensome to the patient and self-indulgent for the therapist. For Freud, self-disclosure was not psychoanalytic (Greenberg, 1995). Although Freud (1912) was personally open with his patients, he established the rationale for analytic anonymity in no uncertain terms:

> But this technique [self-disclosure] achieves nothing toward the uncovering of what is unconscious to the patient. It makes him even more incapable of overcoming his deeper resistances, and in severe cases it invariably fails by encouraging the patient to be insatiable: he would like to reverse the situation, and finds the analysis of the doctor more interesting than his own. The resolution of the transference, too—one of the main tasks of the treatment—is made more difficult by an intimate attitude on the doctor's part, so that any gain there may be at the beginning is more than outweighed at the end. I have no hesitation, therefore, in condemning this kind of technique as incorrect. The doctor should be opaque to his patients and, like a mirror, show them nothing but what is shown to him [pp. 117–118].

Aron (1996) has suggested that this passage was written in response to Ferenczi, who longed for personal openness with Freud (see Freud-Ferenczi correspondence, Brabant, Falzeder, and Giampieri-Deutsch, 1993). Yet, is it possible to show our patients nothing? How about our office equipment? What about the analyst's pregnancy or illness? How about tone, facial expression, body gestures? Lynn and Vaillant (1998) found in their review of 43 of Freud's cases between 1907 and 1939 that Freud consistently deviated from his published recommendations on psychoanalytic techniques regarding anonymity, neutrality, and confidentiality:

> In all 43 cases Freud deviated from strict anonymity and expressed his own feelings, attitudes, and experiences. Freud's expressions included his feelings toward the analysands, his worries about issues in his own life and family, and his attitudes, tastes, and prejudices. Likewise, in 31 (72%) of the cases, Freud's participation in extra-analytic relations with analysands and/or his selection of analysands who already had important connections to himself or his family helped to eliminate anonymity. These various expressions and relations obviated the anonymity and opacity prescribed in Freud's published works and gave each analysand a rich view of the real Freud [p. 165].

Freud's actual self-disclosure may more closely resemble what contemporary psychoanalysts do than it does his recommended technique. For example, from unpublished autobiographical transcripts of Albert

Hirst's interviews with K. R. Eissler (Lynn, 1997) we learn from Freud's actual conduct in treating Hirst in the autumn of 1909 that Freud discussed with his analysand his role in the discovery of cocaine as a local anesthetic. Freud also discussed his views on sexual morality and marriage at length (Lynn and Vaillant, 1998).

Ferenczi challenged Freud's publicly recommended approach. Ferenczi (1933) called for analysts to open up the use of countertransference reactions to include the analyst's practice of self-disclosure to facilitate clinical technique.

> In reality, however, it may happen that we can only with difficulty tolerate certain external or internal features of the patient, or perhaps we feel unpleasantly disturbed in some professional or personal affair by the analytic session. Here, too, I cannot see any other way out than to make the source of the disturbance in us fully conscious and to discuss it with the patient, admitting it perhaps not only as a possibility but as a fact [p. 159].

Ferenczi saw the analyst's self-disclosure as essential in dealing with traumatized patients. If we grant that degree of self-disclosure is inevitable through the analyst's tone, facial expression, body gestures, and the like, we can readily appreciate the value of Ferenczi's stance. For example, a male adolescent patient played basketball with me during a few sessions. I felt frightened by his aggression. This boy, who had been physically abused, enjoyed watching me feeling scared when he threw the ball in a way that could have hurt me. As his play became more aggressive, I commented that I felt uncomfortable. "Are you afraid of me?" he asked with a smile on his face. "Yes," I said "I am afraid when you throw the ball forcefully toward my face." My fearfulness, and his seeing me be afraid, helped him to get in touch with his own feelings about his physically abusive father.

The analyst's disclosure of countertransference feelings to the patient is often an indispensable part of an attempt to acknowledge the patient's perceptions of reality. As well, it is a useful vehicle for admitting that the analyst contributes to the difficulties of the therapeutic relationship. Ferenczi (1933) believed that disclosure "instead of hurting the patient, led to a marked easing off in his condition" (p. 212) especially with patients whose parents may have denied their involvement in the trauma. Therefore, honesty and sincerity in the therapeutic relationship are integral to the curative process with traumatized patients, who will be able to have new experiences instead of repetition of the traumatic past.

As Ferenczi noted, the analysis allows the inevitable reenactment of trauma within the therapeutic setting and subsequent process of uncovering and validating the patient's subjective experience. Moreover, in a group setting the therapist's self-disclosure can serve the function of providing an interactive modeling of subjectivity for the patients. It is particularly powerful and encouraging for traumatized patients to watch the therapist validate the reality of a patient through self-disclosure and to take responsibility for contributing to the growth, as well as the failure, of the evolving therapeutic relationship. For example, Nataline confronted me during a group session when I was 10 minutes late. She pointed out that I had no right to talk to them about being late when I was not on time myself. I said that I was sorry that I had to be late. I had had an emergency phone call but acknowledged that I should be on time. I added that I understood that Nataline had good reasons for being angry with me, especially because she was the one who was usually on time. I reiterated that it was important for me to be on time and added that I hoped it would not happen again.

The kinds of cases for which selective, open communication of countertransference is most often recommended are those with preoedipal disorders. In a review of the literature, Gorkin (1987) finds the following arguments in favor of selective self-disclosure are most often given: 1) to confirm the patient's sense of reality; 2) to establish the therapist's honesty or genuineness; 3) to establish the therapist's humaneness; 4) to clarify both the fact and the nature of the patient's impact on the therapist and on people in general; and 5) to resolve a treatment impasse.

Psychotherapy with adolescents tends to have a built-in dimension of interaction in which there is a push for genuineness. Giovacchini (1974) argues that honesty is the best therapeutic approach with adolescents especially. As for the degree of self-examination required, he believes that "if the therapist is honest enough to admit that he might be having a countertransference problem, discovery of the problem is usually not too difficult" (p. 281).

Rachman and Ceccoli (1996), specifically addressing "analyst self-disclosure in adolescent groups," state that, because adolescents are preoccupied with self-definition, they bring a need for a role model to the therapeutic interchange. Thus, adolescents often bombard therapists with questions about their own values, feelings, behaviors, and experiences. These questions are expressions of the youngsters' struggles to form their own identity.

As I have mentioned, I did not usually answer my adolescent patients' questions about my personal life. I felt that it was not useful to disclose simply for the sake of honesty. Because I had doubts about disclosure, I wanted to wait until a clear picture of the transference–countertransference situation and the therapeutic alliance had become discernible. This expectation, however, is not always realistic, and I do not necessarily recommend waiting for such clarification when one is working with adolescents whose lives are tormented by multiple traumas and when the therapeutic relationship is so fragile. Maroda (1994) suggests that the optimal framework for effective use of countertransference is long-term psychoanalytic treatment with patients who have been coming at least twice a week and who are in the termination phase. These indications are not applicable to traumatized adolescents, who, more often than not, are willing and able to engage with us only within a fragmented framework. For example, they do not come to therapy regularly, and they terminate treatment without much working through.

Another adult analyst, Levenson (1996), recommends using self-disclosure in a limited fashion, and only with patients with whom one has a solid therapeutic alliance. In my own experience I could not consider the therapeutic alliance with my adolescent patients as ever being entirely solid; I have learned not to strive for this kind of alliance before I get to work. As I discuss later (in chapter 5), an oppositional therapeutic alliance is one way for such patients to become connected. Clearly, then, indications for self-disclosure in working with these patients must be unique to adolescents; they cannot be based on arguments derived from adult analysis.

In thinking about disclosure to adolescents, I find that my own sense of caution is mirrored by various caveats against disclosure in the contemporary relational-constructivist literature. Aron (1996) objects to the analyst's self-disclosure when it disrupts the transitional space of psychoanalysis, because it concretizes what ought to remain symbolic. He argues that children need not know some aspects of their parents' lives, and aspects of their parents' psyches should remain unknown to the children. Similarly, patients need to be given room not to know about aspects of their analysts' lives and also may need a private space in which their analysts may not know them. These arguments bear on my conflict about disclosing my personal life. The patients described in this book were overwhelmed and overstimulated by the information their parents had disclosed to them. A few girls knew that their mothers had been sexually abused by their family members or raped by strangers. Other patients were aware of their parents' drug use and criminal activities.

Stein (1997), reviewing Aron's (1996) book, observed that some traumatized patients desperately need to experience their therapists as strong and confident, even omnipotent, so they can sustain the hope of being helped even amidst deadly despair. It may be totally ruinous for a analyst to acknowledge his or her own anxiety or sense of helplessness in cases like these, where the patient's despair and helplessness are profound (and these are the very cases where the therapist may feel most anxious and despairing). Goldstein (1994) cautions that self-disclosure is contraindicated in certain situations: when the closeness that the patient seeks is very frightening to him or her, when the patient is trying to avoid experiencing intolerable affects, or when the therapist feels emotionally vulnerable.

For example, in one session, Michelle, of the girls group, read a letter in which she expressed her wish to find her dying father; she noticed that my eyes had become teary and asked me, "Please do not cry." The girls responded with silence and looked very upset. Lisa asked me if someone in my family had died. Laura commented that this was a silly question, because it was obvious that someone in my family had died. Nataline announced that she did not expect me to answer the question. Michelle stated that, because I had almost cried when I heard her reading her letter to her father, she believed that one of my parents had died. "Is it true?" she asked. "Yes," I answered spontaneously, "My father died." The girls did not ask more questions. I experienced their silence as their not being able to tolerate feeling that I had to be taken care of in my own grief. During this incident I felt emotionally vulnerable, and my grief was intolerable for the girls.

Aron (1996) writes, however, that a severe crisis in a patient's life that calls for an expression of human concern is an indication for disclosure, which here can be a means of entering the emotional life of a patient who defends against emotional growth by detachment from others. For instance, the girls I saw were facing the ongoing trauma of losing their parents to AIDS; when I announced my vacation, they became manifestly concerned. In response to their questions about where I would be spending my vacation, I chose to disclose that I was planning to visit my family and friends in Israel. While I was away, I sent them a postcard from my home city and reminded them of the date of our next session. After this interaction, there was a significant breakthrough in the girls' attachment to me. The disclosure related to my personal life and not to my countertransference feelings, but it nonetheless served an important function in letting the girls feel that I was being responsive to their anxiety.

Ehrenberg (1992) believes that sometimes it is best to respond immediately and spontaneously, without first processing one's reactions, and then to analyze with the patient what the impact on the therapeutic process has been. Bromberg (1998) suggests that self-disclosure must be an "act of freedom" in which analysts comfortably choose not to disclose or to disclose while feeling free to consider their own privacy and set their own boundaries. Opposing techniques that prescribe self-disclosure, he focuses on relational mutuality, valuing the spontaneity that creates the analytic growth. Similarly, Hoffman (1998) argues that overly specific technical principles threaten to interfere with the spontaneous personal authenticity that, from a relational viewpoint, has the greatest therapeutic potential. He suggests that the emphasis be less on discrete moments of choosing to disclose or not to disclose and more on an ongoing dialectic between personally expressive and personally restrained behavior.

In the course of my work with traumatized adolescents, I have struggled to find ways to utilize self-disclosure as a way of advancing our work. These adolescents challenged me right from the start of treatment, and persistently thereafter, by asking me about my personal life. I did not want to play "secrets" with them, but I did not want to burden them either. I learned that my trying to explore their fantasies about me made them feel that I was rejecting their attempts to achieve closeness with me. Their resistance was intensified. I changed my approach by trying to become more aware of the tension I experienced between being restrained and being expressive while retaining a sense of personal discretion in the choices I eventually made. For example, when the girls asked if I was a single mother, I shared my personal value about the importance of having a planned child raised by two parents. I told them, "I would not consider becoming a single mother. It would be too hard for me and too painful for the child." In response, the girls told of their own hardships of having been reared without parents or by a single parent.

Enactments
The Language of Therapy With
Traumatized Adolescents

Please don't go far.
You don't know how I feel for you
I can't show you but I do care
I know I went back with him.
But I don't know.
Please tell me you still want to be friends.
I guess I heard a lot and really did Not know what to believe.
So, I went back.
Please never go too.

Traumatized adolescents generally engage with us more through enactments than through words. These enactments take many forms but seem basically intended to express unconsciously, through action, dissociated aspects of self- and object representations (Davies and Frawley, 1994). In this chapter I discuss the meaning and evolution of various enactments by adolescent patients that allowed their traumatic past experiences to emerge. Let us take Carmen first.

Carmen, a Latina, was born in a Spanish-speaking country. She was 15 years old at the time of joining my group. She was tall and somewhat boyish and muscular, but attractive. Carmen lived with her AIDS-infected mother, Ms. N., and her younger half-sister. At the time of referral, according to the mother, Carmen was a compulsive liar and a petty thief who stole money. The school report disclosed that Carmen was aggressive in school; she threw chairs, tables, and in other ways was destructive. She was in a special education class, for which the other girls in school made fun of her and excluded her from their social group. The mother wanted to put Carmen in a boarding school.

25

Carmen's mother was multiply traumatized. The oldest of five children, she had three half-brothers. Her father was a drug addict and an alcoholic. Her parents divorced when she was quite young. She had seen her father only a few times. He was found stabbed and burned to death when Ms. N. was 17. Ms. N's mother had abandoned her when she was 9 years old. She stayed with her maternal grandparents, but used to steal from her grandmother. At the age of 11 she went to live with her mother, stepfather, and three younger half-brothers. She described being emotionally and physically abused by her mother and stepfather. Mrs. N. was placed in a group home where she was again physically abused. She ran away and lived on the streets. She became a prostitute, was raped three times, and used drugs. At that point she met Carmen's father and became pregnant with Carmen.

Ms. N. had used drugs on and off for the past several years. She was aware that her personal difficulties made it hard for her to discipline, control and most importantly, have a relationship with her children.

To understand Carmen's relational configurations, it will be helpful to describe the main points in her developmental history highlighting her multiple traumas. According to Ms. N., Carmen's father abused her throughout the nine months of her pregnancy with Carmen and thereafter until she left him when Carmen was a year and a half old. Carmen began to show behavioral difficulties early on. When she was one year old, she began to smear feces on herself. After Ms. N. left Carmen's father, she came to New York City, where she and her child lived in an apartment with no heat or hot water. At that time, Carmen developed asthma (as did her mother) and allergies. Most of Carmen's developmental milestones were achieved at the appropriate ages. Her speech, however, was delayed. She did not talk until she was four years old. Carmen began day care at the age of two: she had social and behavioral difficulties at this time and again during preschool. She was held back in the first grade because of learning and emotional problems.

Her mother reported in detail various traumatic and violent experiences suffered by Carmen at the age of nine. One day after school a group of boys pulled her pants down and "grabbed her breast," and on another occasion some boys "mugged her for eight dollars." Carmen was reported to the Bureau of Child Welfare (BCW) because she had been brought to the clinic for a vaginal discharge and the doctor suspected sexual abuse. The mother explained that Carmen got vaginal infections because of poor hygiene: "She did not like to bathe." On another occasion, a physician was concerned when she "fell on her head" and needed stitches. However, after a home visit, the child protection specialist felt that there was no reason to suspect abuse.

At the time of intake, Carmen's father was in jail. He had visited Carmen in the past, and she in her turn had seen him in jail, but their visits had never been consistent. However, she had good memories of her father, who, she said, spent more time with her than her mother did. Also, she mentioned that once, when she stayed with her mother in her father's house while he was away, her mother burned down his house. According to Carmen, she enjoyed the time that she spent with her father and his wife and her baby half-brother. Later, her father's wife and the baby died from AIDS complications. As noted in the previous chapter, Carmen heard from another child that her father had been killed.

In therapy, Carmen presented as a surprisingly bright and sensitive girl who masked her inner feelings of insecurity and self-doubt by "acting out" behaviors. She led a chaotic life in which something dreadful was always happening. She wanted to be accepted by others, but she did not have the socially appropriate means to achieve acceptance. Her interpersonal relationships were usually unstable and intense. She tended to be impulsive and was particularly prone to engage in activities that were potentially self-damaging.

Yet at times she could be extremely maternal, striving to provide for others some of the things that she and her friends had been unable to get for themselves. She would impulsively put herself in the middle of someone else's fight and was ever-ready to assume a "mothering" or "protector" role, indifferent to the risk of being hurt herself. Carmen's affective instability, irritability, and acting-out behavior at home and in school masked her intolerable feelings of loss and emptiness. Part of Carmen's developmental task was to separate from her mother, yet the traumatic experience of losing her mother to AIDS was reactivating other traumatic losses in her life that unfortunately also related to AIDS (her stepmother and her baby sister).

Carmen's mood during most of her treatment, though superficially cheerful, was anxious; she perennially seemed on the verge of anger. She was loud, talkative, and too impatient to listen to a conversation, often interrupting others in mid-sentence. During most of the beginning phase of the girls' group, Carmen was hyperactive and never stayed in her seat for long during the hour. She initiated playing basketball, liked to jump on the desks, sang, and danced. During these activities Carmen and the other girls would shout or laugh hysterically.

Carmen was unable to verbalize her feelings. Her actions and stories were what allowed access to her inner world. To one session (she was the only one who showed up) she brought an abandoned dog she had found on the street on her way to the session. As she entered my office, she said that she had already called her mother, who had forbidden her to bring the dog home. Carmen hoped that I would let her keep the dog in the session. To my question about what had led her to take the dog, she said that she wanted to take care of it so that the dog would look better. When the dog then urinated on the floor, however, she treated it aggressively, kicked it, and shouted at it, her tenderness shifting abruptly to aggression, as it often did with her peers and her family.

When I asked Carmen what she imagined the dog's life had been like before she found it, she became empathic and described how it was miserable, its parents had died, and there was no one in the world to take care of it. She added that she was worried that if she left the dog on the street it would die. Part of her wanted to take care of the dog, and another part of her was angry that the dog was sick and dysfunctional. She had similar feelings toward her mother. There were days when she refused to go to school because she wanted to stay at home to take care of her mother, while another part of her felt angry with her mother, who was too sick to take care of her.

Displaying her behavior toward the abandoned dog and discussing her feelings about it were Carmen's way of sharing with me how she experienced her life at that moment. Carmen's mother's health was dramatically deteriorating. She was hospitalized often for long periods, and there was the ongoing question of who would take care of Carmen. She did not have relatives in New York. Carmen was left each time with a different neighbor, whom she did not know, while her younger sister, a child from another father, stayed with the paternal grandparents. Carmen felt more abandoned than ever, and bringing the dog was a poignant communication about her own experience.

Ferenczi, who departed from traditional psychoanalytic techniques, devoted part of his career to developing the role of action in the analytic treatment of difficult patients. He recognized the equal significance of verbal and nonverbal communication in the therapeutic situation and believed that communication is itself a form of action (Ferenczi, 1920, 1931b). Indeed, Ferenczi (1920) argued that any interpretation was inherently active:

> Communicating such an interpretation is, however, in itself an active interference with the patient's psychic activity; it turns the thoughts in a given direction and facilitates the appearance of ideas that otherwise would have been prevented by the resistance from becoming conscious. The patient must comport himself passively during this "midwifery of thought" [p. 200].

Many years later, Levenson (1972) argued that "the language of speech and the language of action will be transforms of each other; that is, they will be, in musical terms, harmonic variations on the same theme" (p. 81). Sandler (1976), in his classic paper on the subject, suggested that the patient actively gets the analyst to play a role and thus actualize transference feelings through "role responsiveness" (p. 45), a phenomenon that Levenson (1972) also had noticed and termed "isomorphic transformation." Schafer (1992) reiterated Ferenczi's emphasis on the importance of actions as a form of communication in therapy: "Each line of action will be approached as a telling and a showing" (p. 228). Freedman (1994) believes that actions arise when verbal representations are felt to be insufficient: "Actions are a form of communication, a toss in the direction of realizing the transference. All intense moments of transference have motor components" (p. 95). He sees actions as potentially equivalent to fantasies, dreams, or free association.

Freedman's conceptualization captures well my experience with my adolescent girls' group. Nataline, for example, was excited to see all the signs and names she wrote on a familiar desk during the previous group she had attended. Similarly, although the wall had been painted, she could still see a word that she had written before on the wall. She could be in touch with her feelings of missing the girls in the previous group only by concrete reminders of her actions.

Action as a means of communicating inner struggles was also demonstrated during the termination phase, when sexuality became one of the main issues discussed. Nataline brought her girlfriend's toddler to one of the group session. While the girls took turns watching the baby, the discussion was focused on intercourse, abortion, love, and passion. Again, the girls needed a concrete reminder of their psychic conflicts. Nataline in particular was enabled to gain access to her struggles by the concrete action of bringing to the session a toddler to represent herself. She told us that the toddler's mother had a cold and there was no one to take care of the baby. She shared with us a story of another friend who had been abandoned by her family after she decided to give birth instead of having an abortion.

To my question about what they imagined the toddler's life to be like, the girls answered in a very depressing way. Carmen focused on the fact that, if the baby had only her mother to rely on, she might find herself alone in the world. I suspected that this was what Carmen was most frightened of since she did not have any relatives in New York aside from her terminally ill mother. During this session I felt upset as I watched

Nataline discipline the toddler in an aggressive way. When the toddler asked to get a toy, Nataline told her harshly to stay quiet. The baby looked scared. Nataline seemed to identify with the grandmother who had raised her and treated her in a similarly unresponsive, uncaring way.

The families of the adolescents described in this book show many forms of severe psychosocial pathology: alcoholism, neglect, brutality, illegitimacy, delinquency, and criminality. These adolescents grew up in environments in which impulses are not merely fantasies but are real because they are lived out. These youngsters exist in a recurrently hopeless, normless world where actions speak louder than words and impulsivity is dominant, where people live from day to day with weak ties to a meaningful past and little investment in the future. Their parents, though highly disturbed, inconsistent, neglectful, and seductive, and exhibit aggressive behavior toward their children, are nonetheless concerned and struggle to raise their children properly. The actions of these adolescents give us therapeutic access to their vulnerable selves.

Historically, acting out was originally seen as resistance to treatment. The conceptual model for that idea lay in Freud's (1914) trauma theory, which held that the "compulsion to repeat" had supplanted "the impulse to remember" (p. 151), particularly when aggressive feelings predominate. Fenichel (1945), however, emphasized that the action in acting out is mostly conscious, as opposed to other neurotic activity, and moreover that the action is generally a fairly organized activity, not merely a single movement, gesture, or mimicked expression. Fenichel further characterized acting out as being ego syntonic and as alloplastic (related to changes in the outside world) rather than autoplastic (related to changes in oneself). People who act out tend to change their environment rather than themselves; and, although their behavior seems appropriate to them, it seems implausible and inappropriate to others.

The idea that acting out relates to deficit and denial was long a staple of analytic theory. Greenacre (1950) proposed that, in the etiology of acting out, "the common genetic situation consists in a distortion in the relationship of action to speech and verbalized thought, arising most often from severe disturbances in the second year" (p. 211). She indicated that, in the early histories of patients who chronically act out, speech is inhibited or delayed. Jacobson (1957), writing on denial and repression, argued that the resistance against remembering entailed in acting out constitutes a form of denial. Thus, the function of acting out is denial through action.

On the importance of acting out, however, Boesky (1982) notes: "Psychoanalysis cannot take place without acting out, just as it cannot take place without transference" (p. 52). Winnicott (1958) pointed out that, in one case, "by acting out the patient informed herself of the bit of psychic reality which was difficult to get at the moment, but of which the patient so acutely needed to become aware" (p. 249).

Since adolescents have a heightened activity level stimulated by complex physiological and psychological changes, their behavior is more impulsive and more clearly revelatory of unconscious wishes and associated fears than that of any other age group (Chused, 1990). Chused believes that it is through action that the adolescent develops *self-definition:* "The adolescent feels compelled to act (or, conversely, to inhibit action) not only because of the urgency of his impulses, but also because of his intense wish to define himself" (p. 696).

Blos (1963) characterized the adolescent's use of action as a defense against fears of passivity, feelings of helplessness, and the danger of object loss. Further, he said, the maturational processes associated with adolescence tend to promote and favor the mechanism of acting out as a homeostatic device. He considered adolescents to be "addicted to action." He added that, through acting-out behavior, adolescents make contact with and communicate with external objects in a comparatively primitive way. To illustrate: during the first few individual sessions with me, one of the girls in the group, Dee, fell asleep. In discussing her feelings about falling asleep here, she complained that she was sleep deprived. Yet, after only a few sessions into treatment, she told me in detail how she had been sexually abused. Her mother's boyfriend and cousin used to come to her bed at night and sexually abuse her. Although there were no boys living in her foster family, she had difficulty falling asleep. She emphasized that what she needed most was to have some sleep, and she was happy to be able to fall asleep in my presence. In her action, she not only introduced me to the source of the terror, but also opened herself to explore what was otherwise so painful to put into words.

In such cases, treatment has to initiate the reconstruction of the dissociated, traumatic past and then support the ego in dealing with anxiety and integrating affects when confronting that past (Blos, 1963). Following Blos, Anastasopoulos (1988) believes that acting out during adolescence leads to a regression in symbol formation, which nonetheless may be seen as serving a supportive preparatory function. The regression sustains the completion of the self, while splitting off and discharging in the action regressed parts of the self, which otherwise would remain totally repressed and unsymbolized.

Bigras (1990), who treated sexually abused female adolescents, argues that, driven by the repetition compulsion, girls' promiscuous sexual activity enacts a search for a substitute sadistic partner; other acting-out behaviors—drug taking, leaving home—are scenes in the drama of living out a bad object world that has been internalized. Bigras remarks, "Acting out is the only recourse open to the adolescent sexually abused girl because she frequently cannot symbolize (in fantasy or symptom formation) her unstable or dead inner world" (p. 175).

For all the adolescents I discuss in this book, entry into adolescence brought a reenactment of early conflicts and trauma. The acting out of these themes occupied more and more of the adolescents' affective lives and became the dominant mode for the expression of feelings and the discharge of tension. These adolescents struggled to define and integrate their own sexuality while striving to find heterosexual relationships. Yet the process of object displacement led to their repeating past experiences over and over again in connection with current situations. For example, Michelle, who had had numerous promiscuous relationships with boys in the past, was now trying to establish a loving relationship with her boyfriend. She automatically felt that to be nurtured by him she would have to satisfy his sexual needs. At the same time her sense of deprivation was such that she was in a constant search for intimacy outside the relationship as well as in it and so was sexually active with other boys at the same time. Michelle was about to lose her father to AIDS.

As Michelle was relating her life history, it emerged that her mother had had a similar experience. Michelle's father, who was married to another woman, was their neighbor; he helped them out financially as long as Michelle's mother was willing to have sex with him. Michelle identified her boyfriend with her father. She could not forgive her father for having chosen his wife over her and her mother and abandoning them. The separation from her father was traumatic to her as a child, and now as a teenager she was about to separate from him forever. With her boyfriend, she gave what the father had wanted from her mother—sex—but Michelle was sure that sooner or later he would abandon her regardless.

There is some confusion in the psychoanalytic literature over the distinction between acting out and "enactment" in the therapeutic experience. Chused (1991) says that terms like "acting out" refer "only to the patient's behavior; they imply that the analyst is an observer, not a participant in it" (p. 628). Jacobs (1986) believes that the term acting out should be reserved for gross or impulsive behavior, while enactment relates to subtle interpersonal activity. Aron (1996) argues that acting out, an old, archaic term, was conceptualized in the context of a one-person psychology and deals only with individual activity. Enactment, a newer term, which has only recently emerged in the psychoanalytic literature, entails action as viewed within the context of a two-person interactional psychology that requires mutual participation.

Enactment, then, is arguably the more useful contemporary term than is acting out. One definition of the word enact is "to represent . . . as on a stage, to personate [a character] dramatically, play [a part]" (Compact Oxford English Dictionary, 1971). Clinical understanding of enactment follows this general dictionary definition. Freedman (1994) recognizes that the consequences of enactments may be progressive or facilitate a "broader process of transformations" (p. 94). One transformation entailed in enactment is the creation of the me/not-me space: "It is a physical rearrangement created by the condition of rearrangement of self and object experience" (p. 100). Nataline, who shouted at me during sessions, seemed to be saying, "Notice me, consider me, help me, fear me, or love me." Even if Nataline was not aware of her effort toward self-definition, or of trying to coerce my participation in finding it, she experienced greater cohesiveness and certainty in her shouting at me.

The work with Keisha started from the moment of her first call to me. She was in despair. After running away a few times she had been told by the judge that she had to be in therapy if she did not want to be placed in a group home. Keisha added that before she went to live with her mother, the school reported that she was cutting classes, and her teacher complained that her relatives, with whom she lived and who were old and sickly, did not interact with the school. Keisha said that she was tired of life because she was being forced to live with her mother. Tearfully, she described how her mother, without any notice, had moved her to a new neighborhood. She did not have a chance to say goodbye to her friends, and she missed her dog.

It happened that Keisha's first call to me came while another patient was waiting for me. I decided to stay on the phone with Keisha because I sensed her great urgency. I chose to engage Keisha in conversation on the phone instead of limiting the discussion by suggesting that she come in to talk with me in person. I felt that I should not miss this chance.

In line with Renik's (1994) observation about enactments in general, however, I became aware of the multiple meanings of my countertransference only after my enactment was well underway. I felt moved by the phone call because I too felt vulnerable—surviving in a foreign country and struggling with a new language, culture, and career. In fact, this level of mutual identification was later to prove beneficial in our subsequent work.

The case of Ben illustrates the emergence of transference–countertransference enactments, "dialogues of the unconscious" (Ferenczi, 1915, p. 109).

Ben, a Caucasian boy, was 16 years old at the time of referral to individual therapy. He had been living with his father and his stepmother for two years. His father, concerned about intense fights with him at home and about Ben's poor performance in school, had referred him to the clinic. The father attributed his son's difficulties at home and in school to the fact that Ben had been removed from his mother's custody in California and placed in his father's custody in New York. Ben, however, did not agree with his father's assessment. He attributed his problems to being lonely at home. His father and stepmother worked hard and returned home late in the evenings. "They don't have enough time for me, I don't feel that they care or love me." Ben complained that "we are two families, my dad and I, and Ms. Y. and my dad."

His mother's pregnancy with Ben had been planned. She was depressed during that time. Yet when Ben was born, without complications, his mother was very happy because she had wanted a son. The father described his son as a difficult toddler, crying a lot, breaking things, and very energetic. When Ben was four years old he was placed in private day care but was soon dismissed because he was aggressive, beat the other children, and would not nap. The mother could not tolerate Ben. The father was usually not at home, but, after he discovered that she was physically abusing their son, he sent five-year-old Ben to live with a retired couple for a year, a decision in which the mother concurred. The parents did not explain to Ben why they had made this decision. During the year Ben was living with the elderly couple, his parents visited him once every two weeks. At age six, Ben returned to live with his parents. During his childhood Ben witnessed his mother's breakdowns, her attacks of rage, and her suicide attempts. When Ben demonstrated his closeness toward his father, his mother would physically abuse him. When his older sister tried to protect him, the mother would pull her hair.

It was when Ben was six years old that his mother had her first breakdown. He then started to stutter and was placed in speech therapy. When Ben was nine years old, his parent's divorce proceedings began. He remembers the moment when his mother announced that she was going to get a divorce. He was in the kitchen and asked, again and again, "Why?" "Why?" "Why?" until his mother shouted at him to "shut up." He locked himself in his room for the whole day, refused food, and sobbed continuously.

Ben's mother often brought alcohol and cocaine with the household money that she had received from the father. The children frequently went without food and were threatened not to tell their father. When Ben was 12 years old his mother moved him with her to California—without any warning, in the middle of the school year. He was thus separated abruptly from his classmates and his father. Because his sister, who was 18 years old, refused to move, he did not have the benefit of her protection. During his first year in California he attended three different schools. He was denied any contact with his father. Finally, after he called his father from a public phone to let him know where he was, his father sent him an airline ticket through a friend, and Ben escaped. The way he left, without letting his mother know, left him with strong guilt feelings.

Ben struggled to improve his academic performance, but he never had difficulties making friends. At the time of therapy he still had two friends from elementary school. After the move to California he would call them, and they exchanged letters. He also spoke of a friend he had made in California: "He is like my brother. He helped me during the hard time with my mother. I shared everything with him." Now Ben was dating a girl.

From the very beginning of treatment, Ben's principal aim was to make of me an object to satisfy his aggressive wishes and needs. In sessions Ben behaved toward me in a most teasing and provocative manner. He imitated my accent, corrected my grammatical mistakes, and chose games to play with me that I was not familiar with. He taught me to play poker but changed the rules each session so that I became confused and was unable to follow the rules. I was so angry that I asked my friends to teach me the game's rules so he would not be able to fool me, although I did not want to believe that this young boy had so strongly affected me. My enactments with him helped me to become aware of my countertransference feelings of humiliation and shame. In one session, he "accidentally" knocked all the toys from the shelves. When I asked him to help me put the toys back in place at the end of the session, he moved so slowly that I had to tell him that I would finish the task myself so that I could see the next patient on time. In this incident, it became clear to me that Ben wished me to experience his helpless and frustrated feelings. By arousing these affects in me, he felt less alone (projective identification).

Renik (1994) identifies three stages in his formulation of enactment in the therapeutic process: by engaging in transference–countertransference reenactments, the analyst enters the patient's relational world; then, after the enactments emerge, the analyst becomes aware of the transference–

countertransference feelings; and, finally, with the hope that insight and change will ensue, the analyst interprets with the patient what has occurred between them.

Emergence of Mutual Enactments and Actualization of the Internal and External Relational Worlds

In one session Ben, spilled glue on my shoes because, he said, he wanted to leave signs on me that I would not be able to take off. (But he later expressed regret for dirtying my shoes.) I felt "frozen" at first, I worried about spreading the glue and worried about my anger; Ben had succeeded not only in treating me aggressively in his play but also in getting me to feel his sense of powerlessness and immobility.

Awareness of Transference–Countertransference Feelings

After I was able freely to engage in the enactments, I could disengage sufficiently to observe and be aware of the transference–counter-transference feelings of both of us. As Stern (1997) notes, through analysis of enactments and intersubjectivity, unconscious experience is formulated and created. In the incident I just described, there were multiple meanings to Ben's behavior. In addition to Ben's nascent erotic transference, that is, his wish to find some way to hold on to me and to leave his mark on me, his aggression also communicated his feelings that he was stuck with me. They operated as a defense against his erotic transference. I was hurt and enraged, but remained frozen (I did not move and could not find the words to stop him), but I was careful not to lose my control.

Interpretations of Ben's Internal and External Relational Worlds

After coming to an awareness of the transference and countertransference feelings involved, through the enactments, I could make interpretations of what was being revived. Among the theoretical formulations available to me to understand this pattern of aggressive behavior were (1) that Ben was testing my acceptance of him by watching me survive his destructiveness; (2) that he was identifying with his mother, who often was irritable and who made him feel victimized, a position in which I now joined him (what Racker, 1957, calls the "complementary identification"); (3) that he was watchful to see if my reaction would be similar to his mother's when she abused him (what Weiss and Sampson, 1993, term a "behavioral test" of the analyst).

There were many possible variations on this last theme. Did I resent his aggressiveness and his seductiveness? Was I trying to provoke a reaction by not responding and risk stirring up his anxiety about rejection? He also seemed to want some confirmation that his own feelings of being victimized and "stuck" were valid, confirmation that he could not get if I related to him without any emotional disclosure. But I think he also wanted me to notice that, despite his similarity to his mother, he could be tender and generous (as when he expressed his concern about dirtying my shoes). That discernment on my part constituted a new experience, one of helping Ben rework representational models, that is, to keep his models of relationships open to potentially positive experiences rather than approaching all new relationships with a negative bias.

In general, I found in my work with traumatized adolescents, that any attempts I made at interpretation during the beginning phase of treatment were mocked or met with furious, obstinate silence. I learned to let this aggression emerge naturally and not to intervene prematurely. Only this approach pushed my adolescent patients toward "benign regression" (Balint 1968), that is, allowed them to find a way of using the therapeutic environment to reach themselves. I tolerated expressions of anger in the form of destructive behaviors, but within limits so that they could not physically hurt themselves, or me, or damage the clinic's property. My stance represented recognition that some regression was inevitable. I stopped trying to control these young patients.

Both Jacobs and Mclaughlin conceptualize enactment as a two-way mutual participation between the analysand and analyst. Jacobs (1991) emphasizes the aspect of performance in enactment. He sees enactments as behavioral expressions of unconscious wish fulfillments and as a need to involve the analyst as witness and gratifier of the wish. From McLaughlin's (1987) point of view, these enactments are an "experiential dimension that actualizes and externalizes the patients' inner life of conflict and relation to objects" (p. 557).

White (1992) uses the term enactment to mean

the vivid reexperience of a childhood role played out on the stage of the analyst's consulting room. The analyst is assigned a part and is expected to join the play. Both parties lose their sense of distance and get swept up into the verbal and nonverbal interactions; both contribute intrapsychic dynamics to the shape of the interaction [p. 339].

Following White but focusing more specifically on adolescence, Markman (1997) believes that the treatment process with adolescents very much needs to be focused on the interaction considered as play. The process, Markman says, must make creative use of the highly charged drama that the adolescents live out in order to deal with their developmental conflicts around autonomy and the formation of solid identity. From Markman's point of view, when the interactive play breaks down, enactments take its place, and then the adolescent patient experiences a loss of autonomy. To create a collaborative experience for themselves in the therapeutic relationship, adolescents have to experience the analyst as free to play with them. Countertransference feelings emerge most strongly when analysts refuse to play the role their patients assign to them, refuse, that is, to allow the therapy to go the adolescents' way. (This point is elaborated further in chapter 5 on resistance.) When treating traumatized adolescents, thinking in terms of enactment is a way of constantly working, not resisting work. Further, for adolescents working in this way is the only way possible to discover their true selves through the analytic work.

Schafer (1992) describes the significance of enactments within the analytic relationship as "the analytic relationship itself" (p. 227). Moreover, he calls on therapists to free themselves from the tyranny of the spoken word and to think in terms of enactment. His advice on this matter can only be strongly seconded when one is dealing with adolescents. And this is true in general: what we find being argued in the contemporary analytic literature vis-à-vis enactment in adult patients acquires additional force when we apply it to our teenaged patients.

Relational analysts, more than traditional ones, hold that interaction leads directly to change and that most important for the patient is to build up a new experience that is based in a new relationship (Aron, 1996). In the relational model, interactions and enactments are considered as inevitable, continuous, and useful.

From a relational perspectivist position, there is no way to sort out which element in the analysis belongs to the patient and which belongs to the analyst. This is another way of saying that, since interaction is mutual and continual, it is never possible to say who initiated a particular sequence of interaction. . . If we agree that mutual enactment and mutual participation are inevitable, then we must pay serious attention to our patients' perceptions of our participation [p. 216].

Summarizing contemporary relational and interpersonal views on enactment, Stern (1997), from a hermeneutic point of view, believes that any new understanding that people arrive at in life is the result of an interpersonal negotiation with someone with a different perspective, coming from a different place, and looking for a different kind of interaction.

Hoffman (1998) similarly argues from a constructivist point of view, that enactments have the therapeutic potential to prompt the emergence of a "new understanding and new being in the analytic relationship in the world" (p. 73). He considers that a subtle blending of old and new occurs with all interactions in the therapeutic process, whether they are interpretive, reflective, exploratory, or noninterpretive and emotionally expressive. Hoffman (1992) points out that there is an interplay of repetition of old relations and enactment of new experience. Bromberg (1998), who has emphasized the link between trauma and dissociative processes, has made a strong case that enactments are best understood as dissociated self-states. He further suggests that the significance of enactments for the analyst lies in the opportunity to be involved with the traumatized patients in the process of reaching these dissociated self-states through the interlocking of the transference–countertransference.

> The process of enactment, in analysis, often occurs in a dissociated self-state that is designed to communicate the existence of a "truth" that the patient is experiencing about the analyst, and that cannot be thought or said within the context of the self-other representation that the relationship is based on at the moment [p. 171].

All these theoretical openings have relevance to what I experienced in my clinical work. In addition, in my work with the girls I had to contend with the complication that what constituted an enactment between an individual girl and myself, and that begged to be understood as such, might become embedded, through contagion, with the group's dynamics and thus acquire the apparent seal of interpersonal validation. These collective enactments also needed to be understood as symbolic interactions between the girls and myself that had unconscious meaning for both of us. This sort of complex enactment often happened in the case of Dee, who was seen both individually and in the group. Before we discuss Dee's transference enactments, it is useful to know something of her background.

Dee, a tall, strikingly attractive girl, was 15 years old at the time she was referred to treatment with her sister, Lisa. She looked older than her age and presented with a serious demeanor. When I interviewed her, she avoided eye contact. Her mood was initially somber with a superficial veneer of indifference that could change abruptly into an emotional outburst and sobbing.

Dee's foster mother described her as "real depressed sometimes, kind of going off into her own world about things, and she cries a lot and is sad and upset." During the intake interview, Dee reported not having an appetite, not being able to fall asleep, and being unable to concentrate in school. Dee's social life appeared to revolve around her sister and her foster mother's daughter. The foster mother (referred to as "Grandma") reported that Dee was depressed "for a number of reasons," one being "the fact that Dee had been sexually molested at the age of 13." Another "fact" that upset Dee was that her natural mother had AIDS, and Dee feared that her half-brother would also die of AIDS.

Dee was reluctant to visit her biological mother and had done so only on occasion since moving to her foster home. Dee was frankly ambivalent about her mother. Many times and in very strong language, she said that she did not want to return to living with her mother, with whom she had never been close. She did not feel safe with her mother and was afraid of having to watch her mother die. She recalled that, prior to going into foster care, she had had to care of her mother when her mother had pneumonia.

Dee also felt that her mother did not really want her back in the home and only wanted her youngest brother to return. Dee felt that, although her mother might feel guilty about the abuse Dee had been subjected to, she did not truly care about Dee's welfare. Dee had formed a strong attachment to her foster mother and expressed her hope that she would be able to stay with "Grandma." But this decision was "up in the air."

Dee had been born three months prematurely. The mother stated that at the time of the birth she had suffered from kidney problems as well as high blood pressure and that these health problems had induced the premature delivery. Dee's mother reportedly had had "medical problems" most of her life, and these had worsened over the course of the pregnancy. Dee remained in the hospital until her condition was stabilized. The mother recalled that Dee was always "moody," having been through "too many deaths"—the death of two significant females who had been close to the family (especially to the girls) and the disappearance and death of three out of four fathers.

Dee had been sexually molested by her mother's boyfriend and by a cousin when she was 13 years old, both apparently within the same year. Dee had wanted to talk about the abuse but was afraid that by doing so she might endanger her mother, the mother's boyfriend having threatened to harm the mother if Dee told. When Dee, much later, told her mother a little bit about what had happened, her mother asked the boyfriend to leave; as for the cousin, her mother asked Dee never to mention what had happened. The foster mother stated that at least once a week Dee would suddenly seem depressed and tearful. It was during these periods that Dee had flashbacks of the rapes. She became very upset if there was anything on television regarding the subject of rape.

She also had nightmares and routinely slept poorly. At times she had a poor appetite, though at other times she ate well. When she had a poor appetite, she drank a canned nutritional supplement to maintain her health. Dee was able to say that she sometimes felt like killing herself and that when she was living with her mother she had attempted suicide by trying to cut her wrists. She had never told her mother about these incidents.

During the intake interview Dee stated that she felt hopeful about the future. She felt very safe with her "Grandma" and was adamant about wishing to stay with her permanently. She also spoke of feeling guilty that she had changed in many ways. She was no longer as independent and helpful to others as she had once been. Prior to entering foster care she had been the primary caretaker of her younger brother, with whom she was very close. She was troubled now by a fear that she would have to watch him die.

I felt a lack of connectedness from the first moment Dee walked into the room. As I initiated interactions with her, she responded, but her responses seemed forced and she was unable to be spontaneous. During the initial individual sessions, Dee typically remained silent, and she remained profoundly withholding at a deeper level for a long period thereafter.

When Dee joined the group, she still responded only minimally to queries or overtures from me. She denied any emotional pain and accused me of "bothering" her, of demanding more than she was willing to give. She seemed bored, disdainful, and hostile to the interpersonal engagement sought by me and the other girls. I felt unwanted, unimportant, uninvolved, and unseen. Her haughty isolation expressed both a compromise between the wish for and the fear of intrusion and a defense against an awareness of the meaning of her actions. Dee's behavior outside sessions similarly reflected her tendency toward isolation.

I felt that in individual treatment Dee assumed the "cocoon" position (Modell, 1986): nothing leaves and nothing enters—a narcissistic state. In Dee's sessions I found myself struggling to get close without "hurting" or "being hurt." I worked very hard to reach her, and, when these efforts continued to fail, I felt frustrated, inadequate, enraged, and, ultimately, depressed. We developed a complementary process of enactments in which she withdrew or withheld her contribution to the therapy, and I responded by feeling anxious and on the brink of being abandoned. I found myself also inhabiting a "cocoon." I felt bored, was unusually quiet, and could not concentrate.

After the mutual nature of the enactment emerged more clearly for me, I began to be aware of Dee's transference and my countertransference feelings. Unconsciously Dee wanted me to join her in her boredom so that we could avoid our excessive anxiety and vulnerability and remain connected through a nonthreatening emotional inertness. By joining in her enactment I fed hers and kept it going until I became aware of our mutual involvement. After Dee joined the group she gradually moved out of her cocoon position and began to verbalize her resistance more directly. I too moved out of my cocoon position and actively tried to reach out to her to persuade her to continue therapy, as I did with the other girls.

There were ongoing enactments, of course, with the other girls as well. During the two years of treatment, the girls repeatedly asked why they had to continue to come. The girls tested my responses by threatening to leave therapy. I believe that they wanted to know whether or not I was adequately attached and committed to the treatment. They seemed to test the degree of my involvement so they would feel safe.

As I struggled to find some ways to engage the girls, I was struck by the difficulty of my task and by a sense of my reluctance to admit to my fears of being abandoned by these young girls. But, I asked myself, how could it be possible that I feared being left by them? This level of experience was denied by my sense of improbability and absurdity. I was more than once tempted to retaliate by withdrawing interest and empathy. On a few occasions I even let myself consciously wish that the girls would cancel sessions or just go away.

Meanwhile, I was becoming more and more acquiescent to their concrete demands. They asked me to bring a different snack each session and I complied, becoming increasingly submissive to their endless demands. Although it was not convenient, I agreed to buy them French fries. They asked me to have them hot, which meant I had to arrange my time so I would have a 20-minute break before the group session. I felt that I was constantly *giving* to these needy girls, only to be asked for more and all the while receiving no expressions of gratitude from them.

In short, in ways large and small, verbal and otherwise, the girls were enacting with me their nonverbal experiences of abandonment; they all felt unwanted and not loved unconditionally by their parents or caretakers. Despite the differences in our childhood experiences, similar anxieties were evoked in both me and the girls when it came to experiencing fear of abandonment. Yet we could not share a common feeling.

Because I was emotionally involved with the girls, I felt their threat of abandonment only as a wish to leave *my* therapy. *My* fear of the girls' leaving therapy set up the ongoing enactment in which I *gave* something belonging to me, my time, that is, the 20 minutes needed to buy the French fries, a gratifying enactment for them. But this enactment cast me in the countertransference position of *giving* something to the girls only in response to an implicit *threat*. My repetition of this pattern of giving when I feel the threat of abandonment related to my personal life: by giving, I have fought my whole life against separation. By giving I can show how much I care. During the beginning phase my experience of the girls' actions was that they essentially were saying: "We will hurt you before your tenderness hurts us." And my participation in my countertransference enactment set the stage for: "I feel hurt and impotent with you but I will still give." Eventually I shared with the girls my understanding of the meanings of our enactments. Although they did not respond, they listened and were able to accept my bringing in cold snacks that could be bought in advance.

The therapeutic work with my adolescent patients was aimed at relieving the anxieties that had resulted from their traumatic experiences. We were not trying to find better solutions to their characterological problems. In the first stage of work with the girls I quickly moved to control the chaos by putting their enactments into words. In a sense, I was responding to them as if they were "acting out." I eventually realized that I needed to deal with the chaos differently, as an enactment that many traumatized adolescents engage in; and I began to attend more closely to the countertransference feelings as they emerged.

I stopped being so attached to verbal expression. For these girls activity was a major line of defense because it made them feel in charge of both their internal and their external worlds while, at the same time, it helped them discharge some of their tensions. Because the girls treated me as an extension of themselves, my emotional experience now reflected more closely what they were struggling with internally, and thus my ongoing countertransference reactions were particularly revealing in treating them.

It is important to appreciate the intensity of the response that these traumatized adolescents could produce. I was constantly pulled into and pushed away from their transference enactments. During the course of their treatment, they and I lived with a high degree of mutual participation in continuing enactments in addition to other analytic interactions. I differed from them only in having better control over and insight into my own countertransference.

Traumatized patients may be able to verbalize what has happened to them only if they are convinced that their analysts are "taking in their horror, holding it for them, responding to it emotionally [reenacting] and giving it back in more modulated and containable form" (Davies, 1997, p. 244). These patients can get in touch with their feelings only as they see the affective states of their analysts in the analysts' eyes and faces, what Davies calls *therapeutic enactment*. Davies points out that there is a difference between *traumatic listening* and *psychoanalytic listening:* in traumatic listening, we engage in a kind of *therapeutic enactment*: "You are no longer alone in this horror. You can watch me feel it for you, and you can begin to know some of what maybe you felt" (p. 245). This kind of listening is explored in the next chapter.

Dreams
The Royal Road to Trauma

Sixteen

I want to be older,
I want to be younger,
Why isn't life simple?
Why can't I make wishes?
Knowing they'll come true.

Dreams are ambiguous. They are an amalgam of repetitions from the past and new experiences in the present, fantasy and reality, construction and discovery. Dream interpretations in therapy are not an archeological dig or a library search for symbols, but a creative process between two collaborators searching for meaning in the present. Traumatized patients guard against the emergence of terror in their conscious verbalizations. The regressive thinking implicated in fantasy, daydreams, and dreams allows for a less anxiety-provoking entry into the terror that is at the root of the trauma. The regression in dream work is more temporary, limited, and reversible than when terror is experienced in reality and in the transference.

This chapter focuses on the traumatic dreams of two adolescent patients, Joseph and Chanelle, who experienced different kinds of traumas: war trauma and sexual trauma, respectively. I chose to discuss these patients, who were in individual therapy with me, because both of them were curious to explore the meanings of their dreams to the point where dreams became the center of our therapeutic work, which led to the exploration of their past traumas.

Joseph

Joseph was 21 years old when the Combat Stress Unit of the Israeli Defense Forces (IDF) referred him to me for treatment. This unit is composed of mental health officers in regular or reserve service who have acquired sufficient knowledge and experience in treating Israelis soldiers who are suffering from Combat Stress Reaction (CSR). My experience qualified me to become a therapist in this unit. I was then working as a mental health officer in an outpatient clinic.

Joseph was a civilian serving as a reservist. He was suffering from delayed combat stress reaction (DCSR) dating from the Lebanese War of 1982. DCSR is prevalent partially because regular or reserve soldiers returning to civilian life after having participated in war or other combat activity have no opportunity to share their traumatic experience because such discussion is not encouraged in the civilian environment.

At the time of his referral, Joseph's complaints included having nightmares of amputated limbs, becoming depressed after watching an Israeli documentary movie on combat stress reaction, insomnia, losing 25 pounds within three months, being on the verge of expulsion from university because he had failed his tests, and feeling hopeless after a recent separation from a woman whom he deeply loved. To support himself financially, Joseph worked as a waiter. He became worried after he began experiencing dissociated states in his job. He imagined heads of strangers on bodies of people in the restaurant, and he heard talking as buzzes. He was able to hear what people said only after they shouted at him to pay attention to them.

Joseph had completed his compulsory service in the army only a few months before I saw him. He served as a noncommissioned religious officer in northern Israel during the 1982 Lebanon War waged by Israel to counter the presence of Palestinian guerrillas in Lebanon, Israel's northern neighbor.

At the beginning of his service Joseph coordinated soldiers' funerals. Only 19 years old, he had to evacuate dead bodies. Jewish tradition requires that the body be buried intact. If a body part has become separated as a result of some form of violence, that part must be recovered and buried with the rest of the corpse. Only after the whole body is buried will its soul leave the body and ascend to the sky. Burying a body without all its parts will lead to suffering for the soul. Joseph's work was considered the most sacred in the army. He was taking a course in which he was taught a procedure for identifying bodies through cross-identifying information such as items found in a soldier's pockets and information gleaned from interviewing friends who were with the soldier in the battlefield. All Israeli Defense Forces (IDF) units were available to him and provided any means that was needed to carry out this mission.

Joseph felt that he was a very important figure who got whatever he asked for to fulfill his mission. Part of his job was to take care of the body before it was buried. On one occasion, he had to prepare a dead officer for his funeral and found him to be without his head. Immediately, Joseph's commander arranged for a helicopter to fly him with other soldiers to find the officer's head in the battlefield. Many volunteers joined them, including the soldier's friends from his unit, and they searched for two days and two nights. Eventually, they found the head and were very proud of themselves. Then they drove the head to the pathology unit.

Joseph was proud to have served in this prestigious unit. He did not have any nightmares during his service in the army and was surprised at his unemotional reaction; his family and friends with whom he shared his experiences were distraught at hearing his stories. People even wondered how it was possible for him not to have nightmares. Because he felt uncomfortable with these reactions, he stopped sharing his stories. His one worry was that, if by coincidence he identified the dead body of one his friends, he would lose his mental balance.

Joseph was the fourth child among ten. His parents came from different cultures. His father was born in France and emigrated to Israel at age 18 for ideological, Zionist reasons. The mother emigrated from Tunisia and met her husband in a religious village. Joseph described his father as an intelligent man, an individualist, a loner but the dominant parent at home, who used to say: "You can think whatever you want, but you should do whatever I want." He was afraid of his father but was confident that in bad times his father would be there for him. The father physically abused all his children, while the mother remained uninvolved. The mother was described as a beautiful, intelligent woman, fanatic in her religious beliefs, but submissive and uninvolved in the children's education.

When Joseph was seven years old he saw his parents having sex. He was not able to explore his feelings when he first told me this, but his description of his relations with his mother suggested she had conflicted feelings toward him and he, in turn, struggled with his own sexual feelings toward her. He enjoyed telling me that he was his mother's favorite son, but at the same time he told me about having had extreme reactions to her touching him. His mother liked to touch him physically. From the age of 10 onward he did not let her touch him any more since "I felt that by letting her touch me I wouldn't be perceived as a man." Later in life, however, he altered his stance. After he realized that hugging softened his mother, he sometimes demanded that she hug him.

Joseph had been educated in yeshivas. When he did not do his homework, disrupted the class, or did not come to the prayers, the rabbi beat him. He resented having to follow the rules of the yeshiva as not reading newspapers or listening to the radio. His father requested from the rabbi a report each day of how Joseph was doing. At that time Joseph had suicidal ideation, although without specific plans. Joseph struggled with his religion. He wanted to break his ties with religion and to experience the secular world. He would cut classes and spend time on the beach; he met girls and fell in love with one. He smoked on Saturday. While his siblings were exempted from the army because they were orthodox Jewish, he decided to join the army as a bridge to secular life. He was the only one in his family to do so. Indeed, after he completed his service in the army, he adopted a secular lifestyle in spite of family pressure.

In the army, Joseph was considered a dedicated soldier. His commander, a rabbi, treated him as a son. This rabbi brought him food from home and invited him to spend the weekend with his family. Joseph called him "Baba" (father). With regard to his work as a noncommissioned religious officer, he never talked about his feelings to his commander or anyone else. However, he readily described to me his feelings of anger and resentment when a soldier was killed "at a time that was not convenient for me." And he was particularly furious at soldiers who committed suicide at night, when he would have preferred to have slept, and he felt angry that they did not wait at least until morning. Even so, when terrorists killed Israeli soldiers, he made sure that they were buried in a respectful way.

One month after Joseph completed his military service, he moved out of his family home to a rented apartment and began his studies in art history. When he moved to the new apartment, his symptoms started and he felt overwhelmed by his nightmares. He tried to deal with his emotional breakdown by himself, but the nightmares became a nightly routine.

As early as the beginning of last century, during the time of World War I, Freud became aware that his theory of dreams needed revision in light of reports from young colleagues about soldiers who suffered from repetitive dreams of battlefield traumas. Freud (1920) came up with his idea that ego mastery involved repetition and reexperiencing of past traumatic situations. Although Freud did not support his arguments with clinical examples, he noted that dreams of war replay traumatic events, and thus he brought into question the distinction between manifest and latent content. Freud's differentiation between manifest and latent content had been based on drive theory, in which original latent impulses or wishes were disguised and transformed into the manifest dream. The manifest content of the dream was sufficiently disguised as to enable discharge of unconscious impulses without rousing the dreamer: thus dreams served as the "guardian of sleep."

In addition, Freud observed that the traumatic dream increases anxiety rather than decreases it. This observation contradicted the dream's theoretical function of keeping the apparatus in equilibrium. Most important, traumatic dreams seemed to contradict the established theory that dreams are generally characterized by wish fulfillment. Freud thus considered traumatic dreams to be more like true memories than like true dreams, given the absence of the dream work that disguises the latent dream-thoughts and the lack of wish-fulfillment: "It is impossible to classify as wish-fulfillments the dreams we have been discussing which occur in traumatic neuroses or the dreams, during psychoanalysis, which bring back to memory the psychical traumas of childhood" (p. 32).

In the decades following Freud's revision of his dream theory, both sexual trauma and war trauma were subjected to a degree of cultural and theoretical denial that made treatment and recovery very difficult. Generally, there was a tendency to deny the long-term effects of trauma. Because of intense cultural and political controversy, the psychological study of trauma itself seemed to suffer from "episodic amnesia," as Herman (1992) puts it. Men in war as well as women in the family suffered literally unspeakable pain. Understanding of war trauma could be achieved only as traumatized soldiers established their own political movement to counter the social tendency to stigmatize their suffering, their struggles, and silence. Herman points to the periodic revival of public consciousness of the psychological sequellae of war trauma during World War I, World War II, and the Vietnam War. Between these wars, however, trauma studies were abandoned because they seemed to have a demoralizing effect on the public and were a source of embarrassment to civilian societies in peacetime. Traumatized soldiers were considered to be "moral invalids," "malingerers," "cowards."

This history of denial was repeated in Israel. Elizur (1999), a psychologist and a member of an Israeli team that investigated combat stress reaction in Israel, summarized the findings of a series of studies on Israel's wars. During the War for Independence, psychiatrists treating soldiers who broke down emotionally labeled them as "timid," "hypochondriacs," "psychopaths," and "losers." During the next two wars, the Sinai War in 1956 and the Six Days War in 1967, mental health officers lacked a theory on which to rely; and, in order to identify and treat those soldiers who were traumatized, therapists were forced to proceed on the basis of their own personal perceptions. This lack of theory went hand in hand with official denial. There was a belief that, if people were less invested in theorizing and documenting psychological trauma in these wars, the effect of the problem would decrease. It was also thought that formal acknowledgment of the problem would trigger others to pretend to be traumatized in order to escape the battlefield. Finally, memories of the Holocaust echoed in the background and put added pressure on soldiers to deny any emotional struggle, doubt, or confusion.

There are specific similarities between the history of Israel's wars and the American experience. The Mental Health Unit of the IDF, after the 1967 War, started to develop a few therapeutic plans for treating soldiers who suffered from combat stress reaction. At the same time, in 1970, the peak period of the Vietnam War, psychiatrists Robert Jay Lifton and Chaim Chaten helped soldiers in Vietnam Veterans Against the War to voice their war experiences publicly in "rap groups" (Herman, 1992). Research work was initiated to investigate the effect of wartime on the lives of returning veterans. In 1980, this work led to the creation and formal recognition of posttraumatic stress disorder (PSTD) as a diagnosis in the new edition of the Diagnostic and Statistical Manual (DSM-III) (American Psychiatric Association, 1994).

It was found that soldiers who had been traumatized as children and had repressed those unbearable memories were likely to relive these memories in the course of being retraumatized again in war. Often, those early traumatic memories appeared first in symbolic forms, which might be unraveled through dream analysis in a way that would open the door for the analytic dyad to work through these painful experiences instead of covering them up. This realization returned knowledge to where it had previously stood. Fairbairn (1952), acting as a visiting psychiatrist to a special hospital in the Emergency Medical Service during World War II, had treated traumatized soldiers on the basis of a similar insight. He pointed out the importance of dream work with these patients, whose witnessing of the horrors of war had led to their being flooded with forgotten memories of childhood.

> The effect of such traumatic situations and traumatic experiences in releasing bad objects from the unconscious is demonstrated nowhere better than in the wartime dreams of military patients. The appearance of such dreams is sometimes accompanied by a revival of repressed memories of childhood [p. 77].

Fairbairn believed that the goal of treating traumatized soldiers was to release them from internalized bad objects (the abusive parent) arising newly from the unconscious so the patients would be able to cope with the objectively bad objects of army life. Fairbairn argued that it is the soldiers who were physically abused who could not bear shouting by their commanders, and soldiers who were deprived of food as children who could not eat army food. These experiences evoked in these soldiers traumatic childhood memories.

For many years after the Vietnam War, veterans still struggled to work through the horrific experiences of the war. Lansky and Bley (1995), studying combat veterans in a VA hospital, found that traumatic dreams transformed shame into fear and rage. The authors suggest that nightmares are infiltrated with material from childhood or adolescence or with current concerns. Years earlier, Lidz (1946) similarly argued that patients who suffered from repeated nightmares often had long histories of unstable relationships permeated by early terror and insecurity.

During the beginning phase of treatment, Joseph insisted that his nightmares had nothing to do with his life experience. The nightmares may have served to concretize his state of mind, the helplessness and terror that he had experienced during his childhood, living with an abusive father and an avoidant mother; again, in the yeshivas where he got his education; and, yet again, in the army. Yet Joseph dissociated the dream experience from any continuity with his life, his childhood, his military experience, or his current personal difficulties. This severing of meaning left his waking life impoverished. He felt totally blocked emotionally. He did not remember a moment in his life when he was pleased or felt passion about something he did.

Joseph could minimally identify the appearance of the nightmares as coinciding with his moving to his rental apartment. A few months into treatment, we found out that he had reacted to the smell of moths in his apartment with an intensity that approached a reliving of his experience of his work in evacuating dead soldiers. This smell reawakened the smell in the morgue when he brought the bodies in from the battlefield. The smell of his apartment also triggered a flashback memory to the smell of the dead bodies he delivered all over the country for burial. It is important to note that his nightmares occurred after he had "escaped" his family home. (I return to this point later in this chapter.)

There were significant differences between Joseph's actual experience and his traumatic dreams.

Actuality/Dream #1

Actual experience "There was a terrorist attack, and a soldier died from a bullet in his neck. He lost a lot of blood and was wrapped in a blanket. I forgot to put a sponge under his neck to stop the flow of the blood. [In Jewish tradition, blood represents the soul. Therefore, it is very important to stop the blood from pouring from the dead body.] The blood was all over the car. The driver and I cleaned the car and emptied the soldier's pockets, in which we found sweets. The dead soldier was a son of a colonel. This colonel asked to speak with me in order to get information about the last moments of his son's life and how I found him. This was the first time that I met the father of a dead soldier. I was in shock watching the colonel sobbing as I described the situation of his son's death."

Traumatic Dream, First Version: "I found the dead soldier with his eyes open, looking at me. His body was whole. Then his eyes were closed. Then I met the soldier's father in his office. The father asked many questions. I felt uncomfortable and fearful that they would find out that I did not put the sponge under his neck. Later, I went to sleep and woke up to meet the rabbi. I washed my face and talked with the rabbi with a shaky voice. I left the rabbi's office with heavy feelings. Then I woke up."

Traumatic Dream, Second Version: "In the dream, I lay down and saw only the soldier's head above my bed, his eyes looking at me. A few seconds later, the living head became dead. The face was white, and blood poured from the neck. Again there was a head without a body. Then I opened the back door of the car, and I saw a lot of blood. I understood that I had messed up and immediately cleaned the blood with a blanket.

"Then there was the meeting with the soldier's father. The father asked how his son looked after he was killed. I said that his son's body was whole, his face was without any injuries, and he had one bullet in his neck that caused him to lose a lot of blood. I hid my mistake. The soldier's father asked many more questions that irritated me. The father asked what his son had in his pockets. I did not know where the chocolate was that I found in his pockets. The father asked if his son had a watch and where it was. I did not remember. The father was sobbing. He thanked me, shook my hand, and left the room. I watched the father sobbing and felt a pain in my chest. With this pain I woke up. I was in a cold sweat. During the next day I felt chest pain and could not push away my dream. Pictures of the dream came up repeatedly."

I felt traumatized upon hearing Joseph's actual traumatic memories and nightmares. I myself started to have nightmares, which dealt with wars, illness of my close family and friends, death, and losses. I felt angry at the army that had exposed this young man to such horrible experiences. I could not concentrate during sessions. There were other times I felt somewhat dissociated when Joseph was talking. The notes from one session illustrate this sequence.

Joseph: You are very quiet.

Etty: I feel sad [long silence} . When I feel sad I am quiet. How do you react when you are sad?

Joseph: I don't know about this, but I know that when I feel fear I become angry or depressed. Fear is the worst for me.

Etty: Can you tell me about moments that you felt fear?

Joseph: No, I cannot tell you.

Etty: Now you are angry with me.

Joseph: Yes, I am angry with you for the questions that you are asking me about my feelings. I am tired of this.

Etty: What are you tired about?

Joseph: I am tired of my whole life.

Etty: I am wondering if you are tired of trying so hard to keep your struggle inside yourself.

Joseph: You also keep things to yourself.

Etty: What do you think I keep to myself?

Joseph: Before, you were quiet and told me only that you are sad.

Etty: What would you like to know more about?

Joseph: I want to know what you think about what I was telling you about my job in the army?

Etty: You did very important work in the army. There were times that it was so painful for me to hear your stories that I was unable to listen to you. I was thinking that in order to do this work you might have to distance yourself from your feelings.

Joseph: Again, feelings [laughing and not angry].

Ironically, it was the army that helped me deal with my crisis. I was given high-quality supervision and advanced training in how to deal with situations of war. I was fortunate to have the personal support and professional help in the form of my individual supervisor, Professor Emanuel Berman, and my group supervisor, Dr. Jerry Wolkinson. My colleagues in the outpatient unit also were available any time I needed them. In supervision I was embarrassed to admit that I could not listen to Joseph's memories. I felt shame about bringing to supervision my process notes because they showed how unresponsive I was during sessions. At that time I did not have the understanding of dissociation that I have today, and I could not understand the meaning of my withdrawal.

After many hours of work in supervision and in my own analysis, I realized that the raw memories Joseph described overwhelmed me with intense feelings of terror. I uncovered my childhood fantasies of mutilation and of being dead and buried. For years I had succeeded in dissociating those unbearable feelings. I could not run away any more; fortunately I had this help available in working through my own feelings. I remember that there were other moments when I felt on the edge of crying for the soldiers who were killed in a brutal way. I pictured my own friends who had been killed in the war and imagined how they might have been left mutilated on the battlefield.

Unconsciously, Joseph wanted me to join him in his dissociated states so that we would avoid our anxieties and vulnerabilities and yet remain connected through a state of mutual dissociation. There were moments when I could not hear Joseph's voice or what he was saying. As Joseph described his nightmares over and over again, I was able to keep in my memory more and more of the details of his traumatic dreams. From being dissociated, disturbed, and frozen, I moved to a place where I was able to take in Joseph's horror, holding on to the feelings when he could not let himself feel them, responding to them and reflecting them to him in a more integrated form. Only then was Joseph able to connect his affect with his stories and associate his recent traumatic memories with his childhood traumatic experiences.

To summarize our work on dreams: Joseph associated the first dream to his own experience of himself as a "dead child," as dead as the dead soldier in the dream. He did not feel enjoyment in his life and experienced himself as a "robot." He felt jealous of the soldier whose father sobbed over his death. No one cried for him. He described a memory of being thrown out of a school and not being accepted at another school he wished to go to. He cried for two days, and no one in his family showed compassion toward him.

During another session devoted to the first dream, Joseph associated to the "final" and painful separation between the father and his son and his final separation from his parents when he left home and abandoned the religion. From his childhood experience he learned that his parents' not saying a word about his becoming secular did not mean that they accepted his decision. He remembered that when he was 12 years old his parents found a pornographic magazine in his room. After the magazine disappeared Joseph suspected that his parents had taken it. A month later his parents mentioned that they had found the magazine, but they did not say more. Their facial expressions indicated to Joseph how angry they were. The only way Joseph got attention from his father was when his father was enraged and hit him. His father would take off Joseph's underwear and beat his bottom with a belt.

Joseph stated that there are children whose parents are poor and cannot help them financially but nevertheless are good friends to them. There are other parents who cannot be their children's friends but who support them financially. "My parents" Joseph said, "do neither."

After this session, Joseph told me that when he went to catch the bus he was unable to stop crying. Then, for a few sessions, he left the door open when he got to my office. When discussing the meaning of keeping the door open he expressed a feeling of safety in having more noise. Silence overwhelmed him. In further discussion he expressed his wish that I were distracted and unable to "touch" him emotionally. He added that he wanted to have the control to open or close the door; I suggested that he needed to have the control of opening or closing his memories and the associated feelings.

Joseph associated the father in the dream who asked many questions with me and emphasized that I was trying too hard to get him to speak about issues that he did not want to open up. He felt ashamed that he had forgotten to put the sponge under the bloody neck of the dead soldier. He dreamed the first version of his traumatic experience before he started therapy. After a few months of discussing his nightmares, he dreamed the second version. At this stage of our work he responded emotionally— but not in my presence. He felt chest pain after he awakened from the dream, and for a whole day he was unable to forget it. Yet only after leaving the session could he feel and be vulnerable.

I tried to focus on the differences between the versions and mentioned the sweets and the watch that he had taken from the pockets of the dead soldier. Teasingly, Joseph asked me not to try too hard. I felt that as I was trying to reach out to him he was distancing himself from me. I shared with Joseph my understanding of the emergence of the enactments in the transference–countertransference. One of the dream themes we coconstructed was that of a patient who felt "dead" but was guilty at being revived and nurtured (getting sweets or a valuable watch) by a caretaker who did not understand his deeper experience.

Actuality/Dream #2

Actual Experience: "There was a bombed car. Two soldiers and a female terrorist were killed. We could not identify the bodies since they were distorted. The terrorist was in a body bag, and I remember putting my hands on her body. We transferred her body to a hospital."

Traumatic Dream: "I saw the female terrorist's face. She was with her eyes open. She was beautiful. I did not see the explosion. I saw her private parts and two amputated legs. I woke up at the point when I saw amputated legs all over the place."

Like the previous dream, this was another repeated dream occurring both before and during the course of treatment. However, Joseph did not remember that there were different versions of the first dream. When I asked about his feeling, he was annoyed because I was behaving like his family and friends, who assumed that he felt something. He emphasized that he was used to seeing dead bodies and that's why he was not affected by the dreams. When I asked him about the difference between the actual event and his nightmare about the female terrorist, he did not notice that in the dream he saw her face and her private parts. He added that he knew that he was not allowed to touch her or look at her private parts. I commented that he might have had warm feelings toward the terrorist, just as he might have had warm feelings toward others who had harmed him. Joseph described his relationship with women who behaved sadistically toward him. The more they rejected him, the more he felt attracted to them.

Later in treatment we explored further his relationships with women. If I asked if there was something in a dream that was related to us, especially to me as a woman, he answered laughingly that my being a woman did not make any difference. He added that what happened with other women was not going to be repeated with me, since he was not going to be dependent on me. When I commented that perhaps he felt he would like to "touch" me without me being able to feel or being aware, his laugh disappeared and he looked sad.

Actuality/Dream #3

Actual Experience: "Two reserve soldiers stepped on a mine. There were amputated limbs for over 100 meters all around. We were four soldiers working very hard for 10 hours to collect all the body parts. It was the first time in my life that I saw a human brain. We took the body parts to an institute where they would be able to identify the bodies."

Traumatic Dream: "We got a message that a few soldiers had stepped on a mine. We got to the battlefield with the information that the soldiers were still alive. I saw one of the soldiers looking at me; then he exploded. I could identify the body parts [in the actual event he was unable to identify the body parts]. I collected the soldier's brain with its blood pouring through the blanket. I continued to collect his amputated limbs and wrapped them in nylon. I put on black nylon sandals, as protection against mines, in the car and I woke up."

Out of my own anxiety I went to the facts and commented on repeated themes in Joseph's dreams, such as the dead soldiers looking at him, the outpouring of blood, the amputated limbs, the mutilated bodies. "So what?" he responded. Then he began to talk about his daily routine. When I asked him to go back to the scene in his dream and focus on sounds, visual images, smell, and other physical sensations, he was quiet for a few seconds. Then he said that, even though in the dream he heard the explosion, generally, in many other events he recalled, it was the silence that was very much present. He hated this "silence of death."

I commented on the extreme situations he had faced in real life and suggested that his dreams might represent the fragmentation of his self into pieces that he wished to "collect." Or one could understand the theme of amputated limbs in his dream as his multiple self-states and their contradictions, which were unconscious to him. He struggled to tolerate the multiplicity in his life experiences. I suggested that he bury parts of himself that he was struggling with. He said that he was tired of his mood swings.

When I asked what his mood had been during the actual trauma, and also in the dream, he answered that he could not remember. But he remembered the strong smell of the dead bodies. This smell would not leave him, and he preferred not to talk about it so the smell would perhaps disappear. To my question about what the smell had made him feel, he made a face and covered his face with his arms. He said, "I cannot believe that I tolerated smelling it." I answered, "The smell has been more traumatic than what you have seen." I attempted to explore further memories of smell but he did not respond.

It is clear that there were meaningful differences between the actual traumas and the nightmares Joseph explored. When describing the actual traumas, he evidenced no affect at all; but he described the nightmares in a frankly terrified way; there were expressions of guilt, shame, pain, forbidden passion, and fear. The frequency of the dreams' occurrence decreased as we explored them to the point where he eventually no longer had these nightmares. They were replaced by dreams that led to an exploration of Joseph's traumatic childhood.

Joseph began to bring his paintings to the sessions. Although it was obvious that he painted the portraits of the dead soldiers seen in his dreams, he was surprised when I pointed this out to him. In his paintings, the figures were depicted with fearful eyes and open mouths. They wore army uniforms against black backgrounds pocked with smudges of red paint. He told me that, although previously he did not have colors in his paintings, he was now using colors. He associated this change to the change in himself—now he was able to feel, though only when he was alone. He had shed a few internal layers, but he was not sure that he would be able to deepen his work.

A few months later Joseph associated to his experience with me as having many drawers. He had learned only about the contents of a few. The others remained closed to him. He thought he might even prefer not to know their contents; he hoped they might be empty. He reported leaving one session feeling so physically weak that he had difficulty walking.

At times he experienced himself as a lost child. At these moments he believed that, if someone asked him a question, he would not be able either to understand the question or to answer it. Joseph told me a dream that he characterized as Talmudic. Initially he said that he did not remember much of it, but as he told it, its details came back to him. He reported: "In the dream I saw a child. I ordered the child to sing in Latin and Aramaic. When people told me that I had behaved badly, I saw that they wore biblical clothes. I think the dream took place in an orthodox neighborhood of Jerusalem. The streets were narrow. I drove a car and broke the mirror on one of the parked cars. I remember a BMW that had a big trunk."

Joseph identified with the boy in the dream, who was scared but was forced to sing. He described his own "songs" as secrets and lies. He remembered being a manipulative child who would lie to protect himself from others when they were angry or disappointed in him. He admitted that he had lied to me because he was afraid that, if he opened all his "drawers," both of us would be horrified. Although I again tried to explore his experience of our relationship he dismissed it.

The biblical clothes on the men made him think that these people might be women. Joseph's sexual confusion came up more fully later in treatment. The narrow streets that interfered with his driving also represented for him the lies and rationalizations that interfered in his life. He laughed when he described some of his daily tricks in dealing with people. Just as he did not feel guilty about breaking the car's mirror, he did not feel guilty about hurting others. His main concern was that he not be injured. He added that he was not interested in looking at himself in the mirror and that he would have liked to hide in the trunk of the car. (I wondered if his avoidance of the mirror in the dream might symbolize his lack of curiosity about himself.) I was unable to find helpful ways of construing his experience, and he was not ready to examine how he experienced my ideas about him.

The next dream followed: "I was in the pub where I worked. There was a woman whom I had the sense that I knew, but I could not identify her. Someone threw a tequila bottle in the air that exploded near me. Then another tequila bottle was thrown toward my face, and I woke up before it exploded in my face."

Relating to the dream, Joseph was aware that he often did not protect himself and even put himself in risky situations. When I pointed out that in the dream it was his face that was exposed to injury, he remembered two traumatic experiences. The first occurred when he was 12. His father slapped his face and accidentally broke his eyeglasses. Pieces of glass got into his eyes, and for a few seconds he lost consciousness. He was frightened. The second incident happened when he was 14 years old. His friend kicked his face, and, again, his eyeglasses were broken. This time his face was injured, and he was left with some scars. He experienced himself as having been an ugly boy. He was teased because of his thick glasses. As an adult, he did not go out wearing his glasses, which he wore only when he was with people who had known him for a long time.

Joseph remembered that he and his siblings had enjoyed teasing their mother, who would then tell on them to his father. The father reacted by hitting the children. The mother then felt guilty and tried unsuccessfully to stop the father. Out of such experiences, Joseph seemed to identify with his aggressive father and became sadistic toward women. Joseph was ashamed to tell me that he had stolen money from his parents and bought sweets and food. Later, he used the stolen money for entertainment. He did not feel guilty as much as he did disrespectful.

As an adult, he was essentially poor, whereas his parents were able to buy expensive electronics and often went on trips to Europe. They never helped him financially, even though they were aware of his struggle to study and support himself. Once, after he had not visited his parents for a long time, his mother called and asked him why. When he told her that he did not have enough money for a visit, rather than offering help, she suggested that he hitchhike home. He felt alone, without a family. He said, "Whatever was missing in my life I will never get." He added that not only did his parents not nurture him, they also drained energy from him. His parents did not exhibit his art at home and never complimented him when he showed them his portfolio. They never asked to have one of his paintings and in general were not proud of his choice of career.

In a paradigmatic dream, Joseph saw his parents lying dead on the floor while he and his siblings sat around blaming each other for their parents' death. He saw the images of the dream in his head all day long; he could not get rid of them. That evening he attended an Independence Day party but could not enjoy himself. He was thinking about his dream: What would he feel when his parents were dead? Would he feel different toward his mother and father? Did he want them to be dead? How did his siblings feel about his parents? He felt deeply depressed and could not tolerate being with others. He left the party and went up to the roof, where he could be alone. He looked down at the street and asked himself why he did not jump. He did not have an answer. He sobbed for an hour and then went home.

He could not fall asleep for a long time but finally did, although he woke up suddenly from another dream. He tried to calm himself by drawing the dream. He brought his drawing to the next session. In the drawing he drew himself in the shape of a penis; his arms covering his head "protecting me from being hit," but his body and head were covered with blood from being hit. On one side of the drawing, his father looked like a blue amoeba; his mother was on his other side in the shape of a yellow amoeba. In the corners of the page were his siblings in vague and small shapes, while he was the biggest. By the time he completed this drawing he had calmed down. "The drawing replaced my crying" Joseph said. He felt very disappointed that none of his friends had called him, even though they were aware that he was very depressed.

He remembered that when he was 18 years old, before joining the army, he told his parents that he did not want to be religious any more. His mother had cried, saying that she would never forgive him and that his renunciation of orthodoxy would kill her. He felt at times that he had, indeed, killed his parents.

In another session he described problems with his bowels. For many years he had suffered from constipation. He never felt comfortable in the bathroom at home, for he was ashamed that he needed a long time to discharge his bowels. As a child he thought that maybe his feces disgusted him and that this was why he had constipation. He tried to explore his feelings by touching the feces, but he did not feel disgusted. He called his feces the "black things" that he liked to empty.

When Joseph shared with me these experiences from the past, he began to feel that he was not at war with me anymore. He was, so to speak, ready to discharge his "feces" in my presence. During this period he reported that he was capable of being alone and enjoying himself. He did not "run" to call his friends when he was alone, and he was able to concentrate on reading his books, as he had liked to do in the past. He felt more energized in his artwork, and he did not have nightmares.

This work led to another fragment dream in which, as Joseph described it, "I was about to eat up a black guy." His peers used to call him a "dirty Sephardi" [a Jew from northern Africa] and a negro because of his dark skin and his black curly hair. As a child he worried that no woman would want to marry him because of his background. Associating to the dream, he said that he felt that he would like to force his "black things" inside so they would disappear. When I pointed out the intensity of the aggression in the dream, he expressed his fears about his own aggression. He noted that he was afraid to raise his hand to a woman because he was terrified that he would not be able to stop himself. He mentioned intense aggression in his erotic fantasies, but he felt too ashamed to share them with me. Another dream followed:

"I dreamed that I returned to live at home, and I was there for a few days. I was in the living room. My father confronted me and said that, since I know what religion is but don't believe in it and don't pray, I have to leave home. I was conflicted about what to do. I went to my room and packed my things. I knew that I didn't want to pray, and I told that to my father, who shouted at me while my mother stood by and did not say a word. Then I shouted back at my father. I asked him how he could want me to pray if I ate bacon and did not observe the sabbath. I continued shouting and blaming him for always being so logical. I blamed my mother for her neglect. I also blamed my father for the miscommunication with my siblings. I shouted that all of us were lonely and isolated socially because of him. While I was shouting my mother tried to calm me down but unsuccessfully. I woke up to a telephone ring. I felt very relaxed."

Joseph reported that generally he expressed anger more easily towards his peers than toward his parents. The shouting in the dream reminded him how rebellious he was in art school. He understood the timing of this dream as related to his recently leaving his apartment, the one in which he had smelled moths and that had been the trigger for reliving his past traumas.

Joseph noted that as a child all the important events of his life had happened in the living room. The living room was also the place where he was physically abused. Joseph felt proud of himself that, at least in the dream, he had told his father what he really felt. None of his siblings stood up to his father. They all were scared of him. His siblings also had difficulties in relationships. Joseph remembered his father denigrating his mother by saying, "I have told you this 2000 times and you still don't get it." He described his father as a loner.

Joseph remembered the day he left home. He had waited until Saturday evening, trying to respect the end of the sabbath. His family did not even notice that he had done them this courtesy. For years, praying in the mornings had been a struggle for him.

In the next session Joseph told me a dream that was similar to the previous one:

"There was a mess in the living room. After a few minutes all my family members disappeared, and I was left alone with my father. He told me that if I did not want to pray I had to leave home. I don't remember that there was shouting or that I went to my room. I left home."

When I asked how he understood this dream without the shouting, he focused on his depression. He also said that he characteristically went from one extreme to another, either shouting or being totally blocked. Internally, his shouting could be very loud but he had difficulty expressing it verbally. His façade of a relaxed man was the opposite of his internal turmoil. Later he brought up two short dreams. In the first, a refrigerator fell on him; in the second, a gravestone fell on him. He felt heavy, he said, without energy, "internally dead."

A few months passed and Joseph started to describe how aggression was central to his sexual pleasure. As a teenager he had experienced orgasm only after masturbating to the point of pain. The only women he enjoyed sex with were those he hit and who hit him back, inflicting physical injury. He could stimulate himself sexually through recourse to erotic fantasy, but he did not feel aroused when he was with women in real life.

As an adult, he evolved a routine toward women that he described as sadistic. He would invite them to stay with him at his apartment and then ask them to clean the house and cook for him. At bedtime he would say he was too tired to have sex. He did not feel passion toward these women; it simply was convenient to him to have them around. The women in his life were more or less frankly mother substitutes, and he routinely displaced onto them the anger that he felt toward his mother. There was a significant gap between his erotic fantasies and dreams and his low libidinal energy when he was actually with a woman.

Joseph was his mother's favorite son. But he felt betrayed by her when she reported to his father about his bad behavior. As he put it, the "drawer" about women was sometimes open and sometimes closed. In the beginning of a relationship with a woman he would get excited and believed that that this new relationship was what he needed. A short time later, however, he would feel disgusted and confused, and the drawer would close again. He went out with a few women at the same time so that he would never be alone.

After this discussion another dream followed: "The place was after an atomic bomb and only a few people survived. Two men raped a woman. I was the woman who was raped. I was also someone watching the rape."

A second dream, the same night: "An optimistic woman met two men. They raped her without words. After the rape she ran away with me and then I saw another woman who was also raped. I woke up with unpleasant feelings."

Joseph tentatively expressed his homosexual fantasies in his associations to the dream. He described a number of incidents in which gay men had tried to seduce him. He felt anxious about acting on his homosexual desires. He told of memories of sexual play with boys in the yeshiva when he behaved in a sadistic way.

At this critical point in therapy, Joseph asked to end treatment. He felt that I had helped him stop his "emotional deterioration." The work with dreams was very significant to him, he said, and he would miss this part of the therapy. We reviewed the process that he had gone through in analyzing his dreams as we terminated. A few relational configurations were explored again: from the terror of others (soldiers), through being a victim physically and verbally abused by his parents and peers, to being the abuser in sexual interactions with women as well as with men. He was too ashamed to explore his struggles about his own aggression and sexuality. In the last session he brought me a gift, a self-portrait depicting his fearful self. He described his treatment with me as an intense war in the beginning, then as a ceasefire, and finally as a return to the war zone, since, in his words, he still was "unwilling to surrender."

Although his therapy was incomplete in many ways, Joseph could now tolerate in his life a degree of uncertainty and ambiguity that would have been unthinkable before. He decided to move to another city, where he started a promising job in a gallery despite his anxiety and fears of being found out to be a fraud. He could not, however, sustain a view of multiple aspects of himself or others; he preferred to latch on to one aspect or another out of an array of possibilities. He could be charming and feel appreciated by his teachers, while keeping this self-experience totally sequestered from his feeling of being rejected by his friends. He was unable to acknowledge his different self-states that led him to interact differently in different situations. He continued to use splitting as the defense of choice in his relationship with others.

The function of traumatic nightmares has been of enduring concern for psychoanalytic theorists. Beginning with Freud, traditional analytic theory held that dreams serve to lower anxiety, modulate disruption, and diminish unpleasure. Yet, in the wake of experiences gained in World War I, it became obvious that trauma-related nightmares generated anxiety by repeating the traumatic scenes.

Freud (1920) eventually came to the view that the ego's wish for mastery instigates traumatic dreams. Lansky (1991), who has written extensively on posttraumatic nightmares, believes that the explanatory force of Freud's concept is limited. While he concedes that posttraumatic nightmares seem "inescapably to challenge the notion that dreams function to move the dreamer's psyche from greater to somewhat lesser unpleasure" (p. 470), his own hypothesis is that posttraumatic nightmares transform shame into other affects, such as fear and rage.

> The dream, therefore, despite the overt discomfort that it seems to generate, is attempting to minimize the experience of shame by changing circumstances and by transforming it into rage and consequent anxiety of fear of attack. The attempt is to modulate the disturbance caused by shame in the contemporaneous narcissistic wounding in the dream [p. 487].

This is exactly what happened in the work with Joseph. He never described his shame or humiliation to me. To do so would have been too overwhelming for him. Rather, after the emergence of his memories through the dreams, he articulated feelings of fear and rage, both relevant to his identification with his father (the abuser).

As Herman (1992) points out, survivors of war and survivors of rape and domestic battery manifest similar psychological syndromes. Rape victims and sexually abused children are casualties, no less than those who have suffered in war. In this realm, too, political development preceded therapeutic innovation. As veterans did with their rap groups, the women's movement established consciousness-raising groups for telling victims' stories. Out of that movement came a new understanding of abused women, along with a heightened consciousness in society. In other words, feminism enabled an advance in the psychological study of sexual trauma.

Chanelle

My clinic patient Chanelle was a sexually and physically abused 16-year-old white girl. She had lived with her aunt for the past several years because her mother was in a rehabilitation clinic and her father had left the country a few years before. After she reported to the school counselor that her uncle had raped her, a police dossier was opened and she was referred for therapy. Her uncle ran away to avoid trial. Chanelle complained of having nightmares, did poorly in school, experienced changes in her mood and lack of appetite, and stated she wanted to die. But she was not actively suicidal.

Chanelle was not a planned child. Her mother was in and out of the hospital during the pregnancy and continued to use drugs. Chanelle was born addicted to heroin and stayed in the hospital during the first two months of her life. She was born underweight and was bottle fed throughout her infancy. Baby Chanelle was left alone for hours at a time on numerous occasions until Child Protection Services took her and her brother, two years older than she, out of the home when Chanelle was three years old. For the first five years of her life her hair literally did not grow, and the other children routinely made fun of her. Eventually, when Chanelle was five years old, her aunt was asked to take care of her and her brother. Over the course of her childhood until that time, Chanelle was cared for by many babysitters and by her father when he was out of jail.

Chanelle was described as having been a withdrawn child, who did not talk much, was always afraid, looked dirty, and seemed perpetually hungry. Her mother seldom picked her up from school, and the teacher had to phone the aunt to come get her. Chanelle always admired her brother even though he called her "retarded." When Chanelle started school at age five, coordination problems were noted. She was tested and diagnosed as learning disabled. Chanelle had a history of physically fighting with her classmates. Once she hid for a whole day under the desk, where she felt safer. The aunt reported that Chanelle always had trouble making friends: "She seeks friends, but they do not seek her."

During the first few therapy sessions, Chanelle cried. Her greatest fear was that her uncle would appear. Though she reported having had nightmares, she could not remember them. She stated very clearly that she did not want to talk about the rape and that she believed that it was her fault. We were in the sixth month of treatment when she first shared with me that she had been writing a journal. I suggested that, when she felt ready to share her writing with me, she was welcome to bring it into therapy. Two months later she brought me one page of her journal; on it she had written two poems and described a dream.

"I was in my bedroom, and my uncle came in threatening me with a knife and asked me to take off my clothes. I begged him to leave me alone, but he ignored me. I wanted to shout, but no voice came out of me. I was running to the window to reach it and to jump out but changed my mind. At that point I woke up."

Chanelle did not tell me the dream but asked me to read it by myself from her journal during the session. She said the dream reminded her of being threatened by her father with a knife. It was the first time she had ever mentioned her father. It was clearly a highly traumatic memory for her, but she did not elaborate.

In the dream, as in her life experiences, the alternative that Chanelle chose for survival was to comply. The dream also represented her feelings toward her mother and the transferential feelings toward me: No one was there when she needed help. She was alone. Her mother was in a rehabilitation program, and I saw Chanelle only two hours a week (as she repeatedly complained). One of the dream themes we pursued was about a caretaker who was not there for her when she was in danger. She did not respond to my reflection that memories about her abusive father seemed associated with the memories of her abusive uncle.

By giving me her journal to read instead of facing me while describing the dream during the session, Chanelle was able to avoid the full impact of her feelings of shame at having been passive in abusive interactions in the past. Chanelle was not ready at this point to have me be a fuller witness to her trauma. Chanelle could not tolerate looking at me face to face and sensing my affective response to her dreams. Her affective experience relating to her nightmares would, however, become clear later when we reached the point when she could watch me feel.

Another dream followed a few months later. Chanelle described it with strong feelings: "My father beat me up with his belt and my mother watched and said nothing. It was in my school. Weird I remembered that he beat me without any reason. I felt pain but did not cry."

This dream brought up a memory from when she was seven years old. She remembered that there was a boy who used to bully her. She was afraid to go to school. To my question if she was afraid to go home as well, she became sad and silent. I thought to myself that it was strange that dreaming about her uncle evoked memories about her father and dreaming about her father evoked memories of her peers.

Sharing the pain of Chanelle's still largely unformulated experiences even for a few moments opened the way for our rapport and stimulated a series of dreams in which her father's abusive nature was prominent. Over time, I believe, she could allow herself to witness my helplessness in the face of her terror. This new willingness fueled a sharper crystalization of these dreams into traumatic memories, since the traumatic tableaux typically included the figure of a helpless caretaker. The extent of abuse that Chanelle suffered became more and more apparent as she continued to explore her dreams.

Yet until this point, Chanelle had described only physical abuse in the dreams, not sexual abuse. The sexual nature of the abuse was revealed only gradually: "In the dream I was in the bathtub. I lit a few candles and turned on my radio. I closed my eyes and felt relaxed. Suddenly, I heard noises as someone tried to open the door. I was scared. I woke up."

Chanelle began to cry as she said that she could never enjoy taking a bath. She always was worried that her father and later her uncle would be able to open the locked door. To my asking what made her to think that, she answered that her room did not have a lock and that was how her uncle was able to rape her. She refused to tell me more about the rape; she mentioned only that it happened at noon, when her aunt was at work and she had come home from school for lunch. She added that she was afraid of her father when he was drunk. She remembered that, if she were taking a bath when he wanted to use the toilet, she would have to get out or he would have broken down the door. Once he had actually broken down the door, and she felt embarrassed that he saw her naked.

Traumatic dreams of sexual or physical abuse represent a special challenge in psychoanalysis. Different models of dream formation have described the function of integration, synthesis, and mastery. Ferenczi (1931a) defined the traumatic dream as the unconscious road to the patient's unmastered trauma that still cries out for solution. Fairbairn (1944), in his elaboration of object relations theory, stated that dreams are representations of endopsychic situations in which the dreamer has got stuck. Describing the "state of affairs" dream as essentially a traumatic one, Fairbairn argued that it represents relationships exciting between endopsychic structures—parts of the ego—and internalized bad objects that were the sources of traumatic experiences. One type of internal objects—exciting or libidinal objects—represents the seducing parents continuing to stimulate the child's libidinal ego but never satisfying the child's needs for love and caring. The second type—rejecting or antilibidinal objects—represents the depriving mother who continues to disappoint, and fails to gratify the child.

Traumatic dreams were described similarly by Kohut (1977) as "self-state" dreams in which an overwhelmed and fragmented person sees himself or herself as unable to complete meaningful actions because of the disorganization and disintegration resulting from trauma. Self-state dreams aim to bind, sometimes with the assistance of the subsequent verbalization of dream imagery, the nonverbal tension of traumatic states. Thus these dreams attempt to deal with an "uncontrollable tension-increase" or "a dread of dissolution of the self" (p. 109). Kohut argued that, since self-state dreams do not yield deeper unconscious meaning nor do they entail a regression to primitive modes of drive discharge, they are most appropriately interpreted from the perspective of the patient's vulnerabilities. Most of all, self-state dreams directly involve undisguised childhood events and help maintain a cohesive self-structure.

From a contemporary relational-interpersonal perspective (Levenson, 1983, 2000), dream analysis is mutually constructed; moreover, a dream is never simply talked about but is always enacted as it is being discussed.

I asked myself while treating traumatized adolescent patients whether or not the events depicted in their dreams "really" happened. What could I make of the fact that they had traumatic dreams? Should I assume that the patients actually had been abused as they were in the dreams? Or did their dreams echo our current interactions? Mitchell's (1997) relational-constructivist view of dream work cautions analysts:

> to be occupied primarily with figuring out what the dream "really means" is to miss the point. Dream interpretation must facilitate the analytic process. . . . Arriving at a "best guess" decoding of the dream is neither possible nor desirable; what is important is engaging him [her] about the dream in a way that sparks and quickens his own analytic interest in himself [herself] [p. 225].

The dreams discussed in this chapter were analyzed as being reflective of more than current real experience. Rather, the current traumatic events in Joseph's and Chanelle's lives were linked, in my view, with earlier traumatic situations dating back to their early childhood. The common feature of the dreams was an expression of the youngsters' experience of helplessness in the face of overwhelming danger.

People who have experienced severe trauma have reason to feel tremendous fear of introspection, for they do not wish to become aware of their dissociated states. Moreover, traumatized patients in general, and traumatized adolescents in particular, will, as a final line of defense against being flooded with affect, guard against the inadvertent emergence of their terror in their verbalization of their dreams. They may tell us their dreams on the phone, ask us to read the dreams from their journal, or draw them. But generally traumatized adolescent patients are not open to understanding the meanings of their dreams, especially those that revive their traumatic experiences.

Traumatized adolescents need space to distance themselves—from the therapist's "helpfulness" above all—not only because of the real social distance that exists in class, culture, and language, but also because their first and foremost agenda is to avoid the humiliation and shame inherent in the traumatic memory. It falls to the therapist to empathize, in the first instance, with their need to avoid this kind of retraumatization.

4

Dissociation and Cultural–Social Difference

Life Today

Today was just another day.
Just another day of drugs
Just another day of shooting, fighting,
Racial problem, homeless people.
Criminals, fire, someone died.
A baby being beaten, a women
being abused by her lover,
Young people dying, AIDS, TB
Some say we don't live in a war.
But in my eyes we all are in war
A different war from Vietnam,
A struggle of life in the 90s.
So when will another day change?

One of the curious facts of psychotherapy is that radical cultural differences between therapist and patient may become part and parcel of traumatic residues in their own way and may lead to dissociation for either or both partners in the dyad. Bromberg (1996) vividly illustrates dissociation as an interpersonal process between patient and therapist and as a dynamic element in the therapeutic relationship. I know that in my own work I have experienced this kind of interlocking dissociation as a direct consequence of cultural differences between my patients and me.

Once, after several sessions in which my girls engaged in speaking in Spanish or cursing me in Spanish so that I would not understand them, I found myself unwittingly speaking Hebrew to them. Amazingly enough, I was not aware that I was speaking Hebrew until the girls brought it to my attention. I do not remember the content of what I said, but I remember very well what I felt: I felt angry, humiliated, and helpless at being ridiculed by the girls.

I had dissociated for a few seconds and lost track of where I was and with whom I was communicating. The intensity of the girls' aggression had traumatized me. I dissociated in order to preserve my selfhood. Interestingly enough, my speaking in Hebrew created a dramatic shift in my relationship with the girls. In keeping with the dictates of "adolescent culture," the girls were very concerned with presenting themselves to me as "tough" and they tried very hard to show serious, not to say hardened, façades.

Yet, during the incident of my speaking in Hebrew, they laughed until their eyes filled with tears. When I realized why they were so amused, I joined them in their laughter. One might say my momentary countertransference dissociation (Davies, 1999) created a bridge to disparate self-experiences that the girls had tried so hard to bury. This was one of the few moments of real tenderness between us. It turned frozen space into "potential space" and created something new. After a short time, however, the girls became aware of their laughter and returned to being "tough." They were unable to tolerate the newly revealed multiplicity of self-states and allow communication between different self-states of themselves. As a result of this event, the girls and I unconsciously joined in a momentary mutual identification with one another surrounding being different and not being recognized—our shared trauma. This became the basis for a mutual healing experience for myself and the girls.

Therapeutic styles can also subtly create trauma and foster dissociation. The remoteness that is promoted by some classical theorists has the potential to retraumatize some patients. Such retraumatization is particularly likely to occur among multiple traumatized inner-city patients. Relational psychoanalysis, it can be argued, provides a theoretical basis for a more democratic and antiauthoritarian approach generally, which is an especially valuable approach with these patients. During the two years of treatment with the girls, I went through changes in my professional beliefs. For the first six months of therapy I used a classical psychoanalytic approach. But girls, whose early lives had been marked by deprivation, could not tolerate my neutrality and abstinence. They experienced my remoteness as a recapitulation of the neglect by their uninvolved parents. In search of a means to achieve greater mutuality within the therapeutic space, I turned to a relational framework. I found that relational concepts buttressed my freedom to be a coparticipant in the therapeutic process and reduced the impact of the differences that my authority created. I believe that creation of such spontaneous relationships with these patients functioned as a way of preventing retraumatizing. For example, when the girls asked me if I colored my hair, and if so what my natural color was, I answered spontaneously. After that we continued to engage in girl-talk about makeup and such things.

Cultural attitudes can also lead to the experience of difference. In my struggle to achieve a degree of spontaneity with the girls, I found that "being real," in their terms, and being reserved, in mine, have personal significance for me. In Israel, I grew up genuinely appreciating spontaneous expression. Spontaneous confrontations were familiar to me in my interactions with my supervisors, teachers, and my students. Accordingly, although I had brought with me the tolerance and ability I needed to survive my adolescent patients' aggression toward me—this was not new—I found it terribly difficult to deal with the girls' emotional distancing. In response, I became impatient, expecting them to be expressive and spontaneous. At times I may well have provoked their aggression as a means of actualizing an aspect of my own sense of self that was identified with my Israeli culture. I do know that I was more responsive to the adolescents who were expressive than to those who were guarded.

My awareness of the differences between my interactions with American friends and colleagues and my interactions with those I had left behind in Israel helped me to reinternalize my own struggle. In America I reacted as I had in Israel. But here people responded to me differently. They accused me of being aggressive and impolite, while from my point of view I was only being direct. I often felt misunderstood, attacked, and rejected for being different. From my own painful experience, I became very much aware of the multiple meanings that cultural differences had for my patients. To a limited extent this awareness helped us acknowledge our mutual struggle in terms of not being free from our cultural backgrounds. We all experience cultural conflicts that become part of our unformulated, unconscious experience.

How can therapists best address potentially traumatizing cultural differences? Gibbs (1989), writing about the treatment of African American adolescents, recommends that a therapist be especially attentive to cues that the patient is testing the therapist for signs of prejudice, feelings of superiority, disapproval, or rejection. It is also important to recognize different cultural styles in creating and maintaining the formality that regulates social distance and, among other things, helps govern the sense of safety.

To illustrate: even though I introduced myself to the group by my first name, Etty, Dee and Lisa, the two African American sisters, called me Ms. Cohen for several months. On many occasions I asked them to call me Etty, but they kept addressing me formally as Ms. Cohen. Persisting in my efforts to create more equality, I failed to understand that African American girls might have different reasons, based on their culture and family background, for calling me Ms. Cohen. My efforts to encourage the sisters to be active collaborators in the treatment actually clashed with their deeply held hierarchic norms. A change occurred only after a few sessions during which the sisters became more connected to the other girls and to me. They joined the other girls in expressing their anger. At about the same time, they asked if they could celebrate their birthdays in the group session. I realized then that the sisters did not experience me as a stranger anymore, and they felt comfortable from then on calling me Etty.

We must also be aware of the potential dangers inherent in denying cultural differences. I became aware of the full extent of my cultural denial only by rereading the group progress notes. I had kept detailed progress notes for my dissertation. When I first arrived in New York, I felt overwhelmed by all the new things I was exposed to. After two years, however, by the time the girls terminated treatment, I had arrived at the point of reanalyzing the progress notes for the discussion chapter of my dissertation. It was only then, after two years of working with a diverse population in a public clinic, that I became truly aware of the vast cultural differences between myself and the girls and the effect of those differences on the therapeutic relationship. I realized, upon reading my notes, that I had fairly consistently failed to comment on cultural issues among the girls and, with only rare exception, had failed to bring up the cultural factors in any of my comments on the transference–countertransference matrix. My patients and I were all engaged in mutual enactments, pretending that cultural differences did not exist. That I was white, from a different country, with a different religion, and had an accent intensified our cultural differences.

Therapists coming from the more privileged sectors of society may deny cultural differences because of guilt. Such feelings may prevent us from engaging with our less advantaged patients' experience of envy, anger, and neediness toward us. We may also have our own feelings and attitudes about these differences, and, insofar as these attitudes remain sequestered, we are that much more prone to engage in certain kinds of dissociated enactments. There were times, for example, when toys or art supplies "disappeared" after my sessions with the girls. I was surprised to find myself pleased to think that they had taken some toys from me, since they could not get them from their parents. I was in a compromised situation, however, since I was aware that the toys were clinic property. Looking back to this experience, I can see that, by not responding to their behavior, I was avoiding discussing their experiences of material deprivation, which had not been a part of my life growing up. Willy-nilly, my sense of guilt keeping me from working through the issue at a conscious level, I became part of their dissociative process.

Adolescents from deprived backgrounds may be open about their sense of entitlement, and this openess may intensify a therapist's guilt feelings. Economic differences were raised readily by some of the adolescent patients whom I saw individually. This level of difference was more recognizable by me.

Among my patients outside the girls' group, Ben stated that, because I was different, I could not understand him. Jane explained that, from my clothes, it was clear that I had a lot of money because I came in each week with another "nice outfit." Barbara assumed that I had a "regular" family with two parents. David wanted to know where I lived so he could figure out if I lived in "an expensive neighborhood." Joe insisted on knowing how big my TV was.

I asked my adolescent patients if they felt that I was different because I had a foreign accent. Franco said that I was different, not because of my accent, but because I was "gringo." He enjoyed refusing to explain to me what the word meant. After I played "Monopoly" with Arlene and the money became the center of our discussion, she asked me to give her $5 for real. She added that she believed I had so much money that I would not miss the money I gave to her.

Guilt reactions toward these patients became a dominant motif for me. After Jane remarked about my "expensive outfits," I found myself dressing differently. I was not only reacting but overreacting, and not only identifying but overidentifying (above all, as a victim). I acted out by attempting to compensate my patients. I did this in different ways. Every few weeks, for instance, some of the girls from the group would loudly complain about the food I brought. I found myself trying unusually hard to gratify the girls and experienced tremendous guilt when I had to frustrate them. My fears of becoming the oppressive white woman led me to feel under pressure to avoid confrontations or negatively tinged interactions. I was unable to avoid negative interactions with them, however, since they repeatedly attempted to arouse my guilt. It became a sadomasochistic interaction in which owing to my guilt feelings, I allowed them to dominate me.

It may be, of course, as Ferenczi (1932) clarified, that trauma is an inevitable part of the therapeutic process. No matter how hard a therapist may try to be a caring figure, there will be moments of emotional disconnection that will retraumatize the patient. Ferenczi added, though, that the only way to work through a patient's traumatic experience is to relive the trauma within the analytic dyad. What distinguishes the therapist from the patient's abuser is that the therapist will admit to a misunderstanding. Rather than disrupting the analytic process, this disclosure, "instead of hurting the patient," can lead to "a marked easing of his condition" (p. 212), especially with patients whose parents may have denied their involvement in the trauma. Honesty and sincerity in the therapeutic relationship are integral to the curative process if the traumatized patient is to be able to have a new experience instead of repeating the traumatic past.

One final comment about the possibility of productive work cross-culturally: as a bilingual therapist, I find myself disagreeing with Pérez-Foster (1998) that English work with my bilingual traumatized adolescent patients was "pseudotherapy" (patients' resist the mother tongue) or "quasitherapy" (patients lose the essential meanings of their experience through translation). On the contrary, my listening to the trauma of these patients involved a "therapeutic enactment" in which they were able to get in touch with their feelings through a variety of nonverbal channels, like my facial expression and gestures, that mirrored back to them their own feelings.

I acknowledge the significance of expressing in therapy one's feelings, fantasies, memories, and dreams in one's own native language. However, focusing exclusively on verbal encoding through language misses the point in many cases when verbalization is not available. I believe that the richness of our analytic work depends on many factors. My ability to grasp the meaning of my patients' associations, feelings, and dissociations was not necessarily compromised because I did not speak their language. Moreover, there were many moments when I asked my patients to explain to me what they meant since they were using words unfamiliar to me. By explaining to me, they explained things to themselves. For example, one of the girls used the word slut. Asking them to explain this word to me brought up a discussion on the girls' different views on "slut". I learned from this discussion not to take anything for granted—not to assume that the girls' perceptions were consonant with my own.

I do agree with Pérez-Foster (1998) that native phrasing can sometimes stimulate affective arousal and can be considered significant within the relational space of the analytical dyad. For example, when Ben asked me how to curse in Hebrew, I found myself really struggling to curse in my native language even though I felt comfortable saying the same things in English. For me, cursing in Hebrew evoked feelings of rage and shame that were intolerable, whereas cursing in English detached me from these feelings. Moreover, since cursing is not as acceptable in Israel as it is in New York, it does not come naturally to me. It was a revelation for me to realize that I could easily and comfortably curse in English. Later, I learned that this is a common experience: cursing in a foreign language comes easily.

Before discussing value differences and how they influence the analytic dyad, I would like to describe Dee's dissociation in the therapeutic setting. This will provide the framework for discussion of different levels of dissociative states later in this chapter.

Dee

Dee had been multiply traumatized. (Dee, who participated in group therapy and in a few individual sessions, was described in chapter two.) We recall that her mother's boyfriend and her cousin had both sexually abused her. Her mother, who had AIDS, was in a drug recovery program. Together with her sister and brother, Dee had been placed in a foster care. During the intake interview with Dee and her foster mother, Dee told me, "Grandma (foster mother) says I behave like 'three different people.'" When I asked her to describe these three different people, her foster mother explained that Dee talked like a three-year-old, a 10-year-old, and a 15-year-old (her actual age). The foster mother added that, as the three-year-old, Dee cried and spoke in a small voice. She was unable to get words out to express her requests, and the foster mother had to guess whether she was tired or hungry. Dee as the 10-year-old was quiet and did not say a word for days, and Dee as the 15-year-old was dominant and critical of her sister Lisa. Interestingly the foster mother was describing some typical characteristics of these three developmental stages.

Dee's three disparate selves were enacted during the group sessions when different issues concerned her. She began one session by sobbing, "I want to see my mommy." When I asked her what prevented her from seeing her mother, she ignored me and kept on crying and asking to see her "mommy." Lisa informed us that it was their mother's birthday but that the foster agency had not arranged a meeting with their mother because this was not the day of the week for their regular meeting. The other girls expressed their anger about the demeaning attitude of the foster agency and suggested that we call the mother at her recovery program, which we later did. During the group discussion, Dee kept crying and could not be comforted.

Later I learned that Dee was the one among her siblings who was assertive about refusing to live with her mother; since she was worried that her mother would abandon them as she had a few times before. She also found different excuses for not coming to the regular meetings with her mother at the foster care agency. Beneath all this was her anger and the feeling of betrayal because her mother had not protected her and prevented the abuse. She also blamed her mother for her brother's AIDS. I therefore wondered about the multiple meanings of her sobbing because she could not see her mother on her mother's birthday. Was Dee overwhelmed with tremendous guilt? Was she afraid of losing her mother? Did she identify with her mother since no one celebrated Dee's birthday? Was her cry a reaction formation to feeling so enraged toward her mother?

As for the reactions of 10-year-old Dee, there were sessions in which she sat curled up in the corner of the room, withdrawn and not responding to my and the girls' attempts to interact with her. She would not say a word and looked only at the floor. The only sound she made was the sound of her foot tapping on the floor. She would stay this way until the end of the session. When in the next session I tried to bring up this reaction, she would ask me to leave her alone. Then the other girls would jump in, attacking me and shouting at me to "shut up."

From this withdrawn state Dee would shift to the other extreme reactions, being aggressive mostly toward her sister. In one session the girls chose to play "Monopoly." Lisa, who was the banker, tried to cheat all of us. When Dee found out, she yelled at Lisa and tried to slap her when Lisa yelled back. I stopped her by holding her hand and reminded her of our contract not to hurt anyone physically.

Dee had never had a stable home; she did not know her father; even knowing that her daughter had been sexually abused, her mother did not protect her; and she was about to lose her mother to AIDS. Dee was unable to bridge her disparate self-experiences and was not ready to negotiate them in the therapeutic setting. She saw me individually only before joining the group. Her refusal to see me individually later was problematic given that it was difficult to create a safe environment for her in a group with other girls who were determined to preserve their own selfhood by their resistance to joining me in an exploration of their feelings. Then, too, Dee needed all my attention without sharing me with the other girls.

During one session Dee connected two chairs so she could lie down away from the other girls. I did not say a word as I watched her. She closed her eyes. The other girls, as they did at the beginning of each session, shared their experiences during the previous week. Nataline described her fights with her grandmother; Michelle updated the girls about her relationship with her boyfriend; and Carmen complained that her mother spent too much time in bed. Dee did not join the girls in the discussions, and the girls avoided her.

About 10 minutes into the session, I asked Dee if she was tired; she did not respond. The girls shouted at me to leave her alone. I battled with myself about what to do. Was the girls' shouting at me to leave Dee alone a message that they wanted me to join them? Or was Dee at a point of needing me to be there for her, even though she did not communicate with me verbally? Because Dee's behavior was unusual, I chose to sit next to her. After about another 10 minutes, while her eyes were still closed she angrily whispered, "Don't tell me to stay quiet, I don't want to stay quiet." Her body was shaking. While they listened to the radio, the girls in the group were busy arguing over who was their favorite singer and did not pay attention to what was going on with Dee. Trying to whisper as Dee had done, I said, "I want to shout so someone will save me." She was crying and said nothing. The girls then heard Dee crying and angrily shouted at me, "You always make us upset with your stupid questions." The girls asked Dee to tell them what made her upset, and she answered that she did not know. She stayed quiet until the end of the session.

Before joining the group Dee had told me that she would tell the other girls about her sexual abuse only if they were open about their own experiences. Therefore, I could not intervene freely with Dee during this session. Inviting her to have an individual session with me did not seem like a good idea either, for it would suggest that we were keeping secrets from the girls, which was a very sensitive point for them. Thus, as we had agreed, I reminded the girls that, if any of them wanted to see me individually I would be free in my office for 15 minutes before the next group session. Unfortunately, Dee did not come to see me individually, and I did not bring up her reaction in the previous session, since I was not sure that she was ready to work with me on her sexual abuse in the presence of the other girls. I believed that the girls' refusal to see me individually was a way of avoiding painful traumatic experiences.

Danny

Although the differences between the girls and me were seemingly very clear and radical, more subtle cultural and economic differences can also make it difficult to approach trauma in the therapeutic dyad. Working as a therapist with multiply traumatized soldiers in Israel, where I treated the soldiers in my native language, and shared class and economic status with them, highlighted differences different from those just discussed. Being unaware of these differences and thus misunderstanding the patient's subjective experience can lead to empathic failure. I have chosen Danny to illustrate this point because working with him traumatized me the most.

On the surface, Danny, a 19-year-old soldier, might seem to have a common baseline with me. We both shared the same culture, we came from the same social class, and we served in the same army. We had different values, however, and different military experiences that retraumatized both of us.

Danny served in a prestigious unit in the Israeli army (IDF). After a few months as a soldier, stationed in the occupied territories, he reacted in an extreme way: he was found at his post stripped to his underwear and sobbing uncontrollably. Danny had been diagnosed as suffering from borderline personality disorder and was transferred to a unit close to his home. Danny, who felt acutely that his troubles stemmed from his having been traumatized during his service in the occupied territories, asked for therapeutic help to "repair" what was "damaged" in him. He felt shaken emotionally and was worried that he had lost his sanity. Then, too, the transfer added to his difficulties. With tears in his eyes he expressed how much he missed his friends in his previous unit and how much he wanted to return to them.

Danny, the youngest of six siblings, all boys, was the son of divorced parents. He described his mother as physically abusive toward him and neglectful. Violence between his parents and among his siblings was common in their household. Danny described his father, however, as a warm man with whom he had a good relationship. Danny was very successful in school but was bullied by his classmates. He was teased about being short and physically weak, and for wearing torn clothes. At 17 years of age his self-esteem improved, and he developed close relationships with some friends with whom he has kept in touch. He also had a girlfriend, but he described himself as behaving sadistically toward her, threatening repeatedly to leave her, and not answering her phone messages when he felt tired of her. He was the one in the relationship who decided how they would spend their time together.

Identifying with his brothers, Danny had asked to join the prestigious military unit a few of them were already in. A very good soldier, he was admired by his fellow soldiers and by his officers.

I saw Danny twice a week for a year. Very early in the therapy we came to focus on what was the main theme for him: what had happened to him in the army. "Until joining the army," he told me, "I was a humanistic, sensitive, and unique individual. In the army I felt ashamed and fearful of the aggression that exploded in me."

We identified a chain of events during his time in the occupied territories that led to what we later understood as his dissociative reaction. For two weeks, the period of time his unit was stationed in the occupied territories, he had witnessed violence by his fellow soldiers and officers against Arabs. These attacks took place during the first Intifada (Arabic for "uprising"), a series of demonstrations, strikes, riots, and violence led by Palestinians and directed against the rule of Israel in Gaza and the West Bank. That Intifada began in late 1987 in the Gaza Strip and spread rapidly across the occupied territories. It was characterized by civil disobedience and demonstrations during which Palestinian youths frequently stoned Israeli security forces and civilians.

At first, Danny's peers attempted to be civil to the Palestinians; they felt uncomfortable when they had to search the Palestinians' homes and would apologize for intruding on their privacy. After a few months dealing with the violence of Palestinians, however, a shift occurred. Danny felt like an outsider, too soft; he questioned his manhood. He admired his friends, whom he perceived as strong, masculine, and competent.

These soldiers were multiply traumatized watching their friends being killed by terrorists; some of them were injured themselves by terrorists. Daily they were taunted by young Arabs, who threw stones at them. Israeli soldiers themselves are only 18 years old when they join the army. Danny's friends who were encountering violence became numb and violent themselves. Danny, also numbed, dissociated and eventually collapsed.

I had a difficult time listening to those stories. I felt traumatized by his words and watching Danny's pained facial expressions. I could not imagine being there. I was frozen. I had done my compulsory service in the same area as Danny. I knew the territory. That was the best time in my life. I was excited to leave home and start my journey as an independent woman. I felt proud of my job as a radio communicator in an area that prestigious units served. The occupied territories were very quiet then, and I used to walk freely and safely with my friends in the same places where Danny served. I did not come home for weeks on end and had a great time. Until meeting Danny, I was not aware how difficult it was to meet this kind of violence.

In my last year as an undergraduate, after my compulsory service, I did my field work in the army's mental health services. This placement suited my growing professional curiosity and offered an excellent chance to explore a wide range of possibilities and specializations. Having had a most fulfilling experience in the Israeli army, I began my professional career as a military mental health officer, work that lasted for 13 years. My first job was in a field unit numbering approximately 2,000 soldiers. My role was defined on several levels. The first was primary prevention, focusing on minimizing the incidence of emotional disturbance by providing consultation to officers, medical, and welfare staff. Secondary prevention involved the direct treatment of soldiers experiencing difficulty. I made use of a regional mental health clinic that had a full professional staff of psychiatrists, psychologists, and senior social workers.

After three years as a mental health officer assigned to the field unit, a period during which I learned the pressures and demands of the military community, I began a new assignment in a draft office. This position primarily involved evaluation, diagnosis, and service classification of adolescents with psychopathological disturbances; my job entailed evaluating teenagers' mental states and appropriateness for military service, and determining their placement so as to prevent harm, either to them or others.

I spent two years diagnosing adolescents on the eve of their induction into the army and then was chosen to serve as a senior mental health officer in a military psychiatric clinic. Regional military mental health clinics are the highest level professional facilities offering diagnosis and treatment in the area of mental health in the military. Only for the purpose of psychiatric hospitalization does the army use the civilian health system. These clinics also serve as teaching facilities for the military mental health system and provide support and backup services for mental health officers and medical support in the field units. It was at this point of my career that I treated Danny (and Joseph, described earlier).

During the first few sessions with Danny I was very quiet, which was unlike my usual self. Danny felt that I did not believe the story he had told. On the contrary, it was my reaction of horror to his story that had so deeply affected me. It seemed to me useful that he should know my feelings, so I shared with him my shock at hearing his story. I added that, even though I had not responded verbally as I usually do, I was trying to be fully attuned to him emotionally. Danny challenged my comfortable idealization of the army. Our dialogue led to mutually fruitful sessions.

We began by discussing two of Danny's self-state experiences, his passive self and his active self. When he became too active, his passive self protected him through "internal brakes." When he became too passive, his active self woke him up. After a period in which Danny was withdrawn and out of touch from his affect, he would turn to being actively aggressive. He chose to participate only in activities in which there was "action."

This was a very difficult time. There were many terrorist attacks. Danny and his friends did not sleep, they did not have time to talk with each other, and their officers were too busy to take care of them. He felt angry that, while the Palestinians slept in bed in their homes, he and his friends had to deal with such nonsense as making sure that the Arabs who had written and pasted up defamatary posters would wash them off and repaint the wall. "I was tired of being the good boy, obeying, and constantly controlling myself," Danny said. Danny found himself shifting from feeling that he was only defending a position to becoming involved in "the action" of finding terrorists, "being poisoned," which might be translated as "selling one's soul." One evening, Danny recounted, he began to feel "emotionally frozen." He explained that this sudden switch to emotional passivity helped him defend against his own aggression. Later, he was able to concede to his emotional vulnerability and cried incessantly. As he put it, he "melted" (dissociated), thereby necessitating his removal from the occupied territories.

What was so traumatic for Danny that he finally snapped? One night he came to a prison cell and saw 20 Palestinian adults facing the wall, along with a few Arab children who had been accused of throwing stones. A 10-year-old child caught his eyes. Danny described the child: the boy wore a torn tee shirt that exposed his stomach, and he had no shoes. Yet the boy had a look that expressed not only "fear, and degradation, but also a sense of victory." Watching this child shook him but he didn't understand why.

In treatment Danny explored the similarities and differences between him and the Arab child. His association to the fearful Arab child aroused in him childhood memories. Danny started to describe how much he feared his mother and brothers, who used to beat him up while he cried. He remembered that often they would become angry at him for disobeying them, but there were other times when he could not understand why they beat him. Danny admired the Arab child who, despite his fear, could hold disparaging feelings toward the Israeli soldiers, who, in fact, felt helpless before the Arab children who threw stones at them. Danny admired the child who did not cry even though he was hungry and cold. In that state of self-denial, the child expressed his sense of victory. Danny, on the other hand, felt ashamed that, as a child, he often used to cry when he was physically abused or when he felt humiliated.

The Israeli soldiers had to return the boy so his parents would pay the fine for his behavior, presumably to discourage such behavior in the future. When they arrived at the child's home, his mother refused to pay because, she claimed, she did not have the money. Danny emphasized that this was a very upsetting moment for him, since he believed that his own mother probably would have reacted the same way. The Israeli soldiers returned the child to their unit. Danny wrapped the child with a blanket to warm him, convinced him to eat, and stayed with him until he fell asleep. Taking care of the child, however, was terribly conflictual. He was caring for someone who had the potential to hurt him and his fellows. The boy's throwing stones also reminded Danny of his own childhood and his brothers stoning him. Yet Danny admired this young revolutionary child who tried to fight against the big Israeli army. He was happy that the child eventually succeeded in escaping. Danny remembered himself as a child running away from home for a whole night and being tired and hungry. When he returned home the next day no one paid attention to him. They were concerned only that he had not washed the dishes the night before.

The next day, Danny could not stop thinking of the child. "As I became close to the Arab child, I became closer to myself. The child unmasked me." On the morning after this incident, Danny had guard duty on a building roof. After a period of quiet reflection about the child and his own childhood, he found himself sobbing and shouting, over and over again, that he hated the army and wanted to quit. Then Danny took off his uniform, left his gun on top of his clothes, and stood in his underwear; he could not remember now the moment he took his clothes off. For at least an hour he could not stop crying. His commander, who tried to soothe him, told him later how "weird" his reaction had seemed. Fluid seemed to be pouring out of his body; he was flooded with tears, a runny nose, and perspiration, even though he was wearing only his underwear in very cold weather.

Working through his reaction in session, Danny associated to his inner emotional experience in equally dramatic terms. "The iceberg started to melt. I heard the noises of the breaks inside of me." Danny associated his "uncontrolled" crying to crying when he was 15 years old and felt lonely, desperate, and hopeless. He rode his horse toward the sea and, sobbing, felt that something had changed in him. He was shaken. He did not feel his hands, nor could he use them to dry his tears.

Danny recalled, long after his breakdown, he had felt ashamed of himself, lying on his cot while his friends risked their lives. For three days he slept, read books, and listened to music. He felt that he had cleansed himself of his "internal poison." His friends, however, were worried about him, comforted him, and forced him to eat. Danny, who had taken care of the Arab child, now was taken care of by others. His friends tried to convince him to stay in the unit, but he felt too fragile.

Danny identified the Arab boy's facial expression as the breaking point for him, since it enabled Danny to be in touch with traumatic memories. Compassion toward the child replaced the hate Danny felt toward the Palestinians. His internal conflict intensified, however, because his compassion was for someone who represented his enemy. His tiredness and the loosening of his defenses also played some part in his dissociative state. As his intense feelings were exposed in therapy, Danny began to experience me as his abusive mother. "I feel there is a camera here in the room filming each move I make, I cannot hide," Danny stated angrily at one point. We explored his anger when Danny was ashamed to discuss his struggles about his masculinity. He said that our relationship reminded him of the one he had had with his ex-girlfriend, who required him to be more open emotionally. He left her because of this demand. He considered leaving treatment many times but he wanted to keep the promise to his father to continue treatment at least for a year. He kept this promise.

Danny said that, if his commander had known how to talk with him the way I did, and if he could get help in learning to express his feelings, he probably would be able to remain with his unit. He asked for my "professional opinion" since he questioned his emotional stability. I validated his feelings that service in the occupied territories was a traumatic experience for all soldiers but more so for him since it reactivated painful childhood memories. He spoke about his "insane self" and his "nerd self." His only way to express his feelings and ask for attention was to act out his "insane self." His "insane self" was constituted by his openness to expressing his feelings at "full volume" but without being able to balance them. He remembered yelling and cursing at his mother as he got older. Most of the time it was the "nerd self" that he felt more comfortable with. This self was described as a good boy, obedient, passive, and submissive to those who abused him. Danny had experienced these disparate selves while serving in the occupied territories.

Although Danny had access to both selves, he did not have the sense of a comfortable containment of them. As a result of his past traumatic experiences, his self-states were taken as agonizing and discontinuous, and Danny had a difficult time connecting his various self-states. His "insane self" was not known before his dissociated reaction. We also discussed the meaning of his "weird behavior" in saving him from breaking down further. I emphasized that being aware of his different selves and working through the traumatic experiences in treatment would prepare him to be able to tolerate violence charged situations without acting out. During the termination phase, Danny chose to stay in his new unit and gave up his wish to return to his previous, more prestigious unit. Although he felt disappointed with the army, he kept saying that he was still proud of serving in the Israeli army. We shared this pride.

Danny's dissociative reaction functioned as a proactive, defensive response to the potential repetition of trauma (Bromberg, 1996) by enabling him to avoid returning to the occupied territories. Relational analysts argue that dissociative self-states cannot be verbalized and can reach awareness only through their impact on the therapist–patient interaction (Davies and Frawley, 1994; Bromberg, 1996; Stern, 1996; Pizer, 1998). At the beginning of therapy, when I was less responsive than later because of my own feeling of traumatization in listening to Danny's story, I evoked for Danny his childhood experience of being abandoned by his mother. Later, as therapy proceeded and Danny got in touch with his traumatic childhood memories, he experienced me as the abuser. As Danny ultimately began to enjoy life, he started to experience me as the rescuer.

A brief summary of relational ideas about dissociation may help explain the function of Danny's dissociative state, his states of feeling "frozen," and his dramatic, "weird" breakdown. Bromberg (1996) points out that "dissociation is primarily a means through which a human being maintains personal continuity, coherence, and integrity of the sense of self" (p. 515). Pizer (1998) argues that for a patient who is traumatized "the effort to bridge intolerable paradox places a demand on the mind to work on overload" (p. 71) and thus forces his mind to deploy a defensive dissociation. From Stern's (1997) point of view, dissociation represents an "inability" to reflect on unformulated experience, an active defensive process, and becomes a means of survival and a psychological necessity. In an atmosphere of safety, Danny was able to uncover his earlier experiences of being physically abused, experiences that had remained unformulated for so many years. Danny's interaction with the Arab child reenacted self- and object-relational scenarios from his traumatic childhood (Davies and Frawley, 1994). Our ongoing collaboration helped Danny articulate his conflictual identifications with his mother and siblings, who had betrayed him. He stopped trying to put the blame on himself.

Pizer (1998) has discussed Winnicott's distinction between "disintegration" and "unintegration" in terms that can help us understand the different levels of Dee's and Danny's dissociative states. Dee was not lucky to have the "good-enough/ego-coverage" (Winnicott, 1962) that a mother provides to help her child deal with her "unthinkable anxiety" or to develop her capacity to tolerate paradox (Pizer, 1998). Dee's "disintegrated" self functioned as a defensive dissociation to gain internal mastery in the face of external assault and object impingement; Dee's mother, after all, had repeatedly abandoned her to homelessness and had not protected her from sexual abuse. Dee's "disintegrated" self can be explained by her frequent inability to move from one self-state to another. Danny, however, had a "good-enough" father, who compensated for Danny's mother's abusive behavior; he developed an "unintegrated" self that still was not truly organized into a psychic unity but was a means for bridging the multiplicity within his self.

Analysts offer different distinctions among types of dissociation. Bromberg (1996) suggests a distinction between two kinds of dissociations: "normal" versus "pathological dissociation." Davies (1998) argues for "therapeutic dissociation" versus "traumatic dissociation." She believes that, while traumatic dissociation is accompanied by a disorganizing fragmentation of experience (as we saw in Dee's and Danny's cases), therapeutic dissociation is accompanied by work with multiple self-organizations in the clinical process. Davies suggests, instead of "simple binary distinction between normal and traumatic dissociation . . . a psychic continuum, a nonlinear and nonhierarchical mode of organization" (pp. 205–206).

Pizer (1998) distinguishes between dissociation as "adaptational talent" and dissociation as a defensive reaction. Whereas he views defensive dissociation as "an organization of unlinked mental structure persisting over time," dissociation as an adaptational talent is perceived as a "process of selectively focusing attention" (p. 74). This kind of dissociation was evident in the episode with the girls when I found myself unwittingly speaking in Hebrew. Dissociation, even though it is always the same psychological phenomenon, is quantitatively different. In all cases there are experiences of fragmentation and dissociation, but the adaptive and defensive levels of these mental processes can be very different and these differences will lead to dysfunctions of different intensity and duration.

We all share dissociative states of different intensity and duration. Living in a multicultural society may intensify these mental states. Cultural acclimation entails making routine the moment-to-moment employment of certain commonplace judgments and (largely stereotyped) perceptions. Experiences and perceptions that do not fit the cultural pattern (or the economic prejudices, or the particular value system) go unattended. Thus they create their own potential for creating communicative mismatches. These mismatches, in turn, are fertile ground for traumatic enactments' going unattended (which, at a sufficient level of intensity can lead straightaway to retraumatization). It is not merely that having one's cultural assumptions challenged leads directly to anxiety and fears of ostracism. It is also germane that cultural embeddedness contains a degree of "normal" dissociation, which becomes potentially problematic when one is dealing with traumatized patients in general and especially when dealing with traumatized adolescents, who are bringing their own sense of cultural dislocation to the encounter.

To conclude, differences in therapists' values, experiences, and cultural biases are as powerful in fostering the countertransference—and thus promoting traumatic reenactments—as are those more directly produced by encounters with our traumatized adolescent patients, whose world so markedly differs from ours in so many different ways. Avoiding such feelings will prevent us from processing them therapeutically. The goal of knowing how we differ culturally from our patients is to create a collaborative dialogue through which both members of the analytic dyad can work together to understand and parcel out the effects on each other of different relational dynamics and styles of communication. Exploring differences can be a key to grasping more fully a patient's experience and undoing dissociation. By finding common humanity and exploring the patient's experience in detail, the therapist creates the potential space for the patient to begin to relinguish his or her dissociations.

THE EVOLUTION OF THE TRANSFERENCE-COUNTERTRANSFERENCE
ENGAGEMENT, SAFETY, AND EROTIC PHASES

*The listening process becomes more complex as
the analyst feels freer to use himself interactively.*
—Bromberg

In traumatized patients, transference and countertransference matrices related to reliving the trauma uniquely manifest themselves within the analytic dyad. For traumatized adolescents, there seem to be three phases in reliving traumatic experiences within the therapeutic setting.

The beginning phase of my work with the girls was characterized by their transference as enraged victims, I being the helpless parent (Davies and Frawley, 1994), a role that I was compelled to play insofar as they experienced my repeated attempts to engage them as intrusive. The beginning phase lasted about nine months, by which time all six girls had joined the group. During this phase (described in chapter 5) an intense resistance and an "antitherapeutic alliance" emerged.

Later in treatment, during the middle phase, which lasted about five months, I was better able to tolerate their destructive behavior, and a good deal of mutual tenderness emerged. In this middle phase, the girls experienced me as the idealized, omnipotent rescuer (Davies and Frawley, 1994), while they allowed themselves the prerogatives of entitled children. In turn, the pressures pertaining to their traumatization shifted, and tenderness began to evolve into passion (Ferenczi, 1933).

The third phase, termination, lasted 11 months. Under the pressure of reliving past traumatic events, my traumatized patients and I engaged in a complicated dance around sexuality. In this erotic phase, a few of my patients experienced me as a seducer, and, one by one, they left treatment.

Engagement Phase
Resistance and the Antitherapeutic Alliance

My opinion is you had the pleasure of the penis inside
so take the responsibility for it.
Having sex is saying let me have the fun now And I
will deal with the responsibility later.
This attitude is wrong because as soon as that sperm
hits that egg a heart beat begins.
Once a heart beat begins a life has started.
That life has a right to grow and enjoy life
In the outer world and not die in the fallopian tubes.
You had a chance to live.
Your mother could have gotten an abortion,
but she did not. She gave you a chance to live,
So let this little heart get a chance at life.

Resistance as an Attempt to Preserve Selfhood

Therapists working with adolescents, especially traumatized ones, are faced with intense resistances that have significant and multiple functions, including an attempt to preserve selfhood. Understanding and acknowledging this and other dynamics may prepare us for the adolescents' intense resistance, especially during the beginning phase, when they are questioning our sincerity and commitment to caring for them. The girls in the group struggled with coming to therapy at traumatic moments in their lives when their parents' health was deteriorating and losing them became a real threat. To be in touch with their parents' pain and anger was a traumatizing experience. Their resistance to facing fearful reality can be seen as a dissociated aspect of their selves that had to be negotiated with me (Bromberg, 1998).

91

Carmen and Nataline missed sessions when they were most vulnerable. Nataline did not show up a few times because she had asthma attacks and "had to" stay home. She phoned at other times and acknowledged that she was too upset to come and that she did not want to talk about what had upset her. She believed that talking would make her feel worse. She typically promised to show up for the next session. I told Nataline that she was going through a difficult time by herself and that she might feel some relief to share it with us and not feel so alone. All she did was to ask me to send Carmen her regards.

Carmen was more direct. She usually called when she was not coming to therapy. Her reason might be that her mother had been hospitalized and she was too upset. Once she neither called nor came. When I called her, she asked me to hang up because her mother was about to call her from the hospital and she wanted to keep the line free. I suggested that she call me later if she wanted to talk. She did not call.

Finally, when Carmen did come to session and Nataline was absent, she asked to call Nataline. In another session, when Nataline did not show up, Carmen called and begged Nataline to join her in the day's meeting. Nataline, who lived close to the clinic, arrived 10 minutes later. For her part, Nataline tried to deal with Carmen's habitual lateness by asking me to tell Carmen that the session started earlier than it actually did so that Carmen would arrive on time.

The girls could tolerate only small doses of being in touch with their feelings. They told me in different ways how much they could handle. Nataline and Carmen, who had known each other before the group, were very close. They dealt with each other's resistance more successfully than I did. Overwhelmed with internal turmoil from their past and from current traumatic experiences, the girls resisted the therapeutic work to keep themselves from breaking down.

Traumatized adolescents tend to preserve the dissociative structure and to fight against the threat of a destabilizing new experience; they avoid further retraumatization and try to keep the "safety" of old structures (Fairbairn, 1952). Within the possibly adaptive aspects of their resistance, they fear that therapy will destroy their defenses against the terror or will deny them the developmental achievement of saying no (Spitz, 1959) that will enable them to exercise their autonomy. Adolescents like Carmen and Nataline need the analyst's affirmation of their needs for self-definition, but they can present real difficulties for the therapist.

Conceptualizing a therapeutic impasse as a relational event, we can attend more closely to how much resistance occurs in the space between analyst and patient (Aron, 1996; Bromberg, 1998). Ferenczi (1931b) long ago argued that a patient's resistance is a response to the analyst's countertransference.

The girls' unwillingness to acknowledge my wish to connect with them and their insistence that they had nothing to say constituted an ongoing narcissistic injury to me. These girls complained that they were wasting their time by coming to sessions. I felt useless, and the girls strove to reinforce this feeling. During one session when I felt especially useless, I looked repeatedly at my clock. Nataline caught me looking and had a tantrum. She screamed and paced around the room. She shouted that I was a liar to tell them that I was interested in knowing about their lives. She said that I was just like the others, pretending to be nice but thinking only about getting money from seeing them. I apologized for not paying attention and expressed my sorrow and my chagrin. All the girls came to the next session, and Nataline opened by turning the clock away from me and saying with a smile, "I dare you to bring it [the subject of the clock] up today."

Before illustrating a manifestation of resistance that I experienced with another girl in the group, Lisa, I believe a brief summary of her background will help clarify the interaction between us.

Lisa, a dark-skinned African American girl, 14 years old at the time of intake, lives with her sister, Dee (described in chapter 2), her younger brother, and her foster mother. Lisa's mother, Ms. X., was suffering from AIDS. Because of her mother's medical and emotional instability, Lisa and her siblings were enrolled in different schools and thus had to endure separations from friends and other loved ones. Eventually they were placed with the same foster family after having lived in a shelter with their natural mother.

Ms. X. had conceived each child with a different father. Three of these men died. Ms. X. herself had used drugs and alcohol since she was 12. She had been raped once. She had tried unsuccessfully to enter drug rehabilitation programs. The sisters' two-year-old half-brother tested HIV-positive. Because the family moved many times, the children had not had the opportunity to build peer relationships. As a result, they were tightly bonded to one another. The sisters, Lisa and Dee, insisted on joining the group together.

Even though the family moved frequently, Lisa earned above-average grades. She maintained a good grade point average and was in an advanced program for gifted teenagers. She appeared to like school, although she felt that it was too strict. She did not attend class regularly and caused trouble at school. She reportedly disrupted class by trying to attract attention by joking or talking out of turn. Although academically Lisa was a candidate for a prestigious high school, her school counselor said that, unless she settled down, she would be asked to leave school.

Ms. X. was on drugs when she was pregnant both with Dee and with Lisa. Lisa was born prematurely on the sidewalk outside the hospital. Ms. X. was ill after this pregnancy but did not state in the intake interview how Lisa had fared. At 18 months Lisa was hospitalized. Her mother would not elaborate on this experience either but described it as traumatic; Lisa had needed transfusions. The mother was mistrustful of "the system"—meaning me—and did not want to disclose information that might compromise her ability to regain custody. Lisa was conflicted about her mother's illness and did not want to leave her foster mother for fear that she and her siblings would be abandoned again or would have to observe their mother dying.

During the course of treatment, when all the girls were exploring their grief about losing their parents, Lisa and Dee were the most resistant to this exploration. While initially they came to therapy regularly and were always on time, now they started to miss sessions; they said that they did not have subway tokens. They always came together and joined each other in their resistance by missing sessions together. I suggested that I meet them individually, but they refused. Although I tried in many different ways, it was impossible to separate them so as to understand their individual dynamics. Being together served a safety function for them.

While Dee expressed her needs to be helped and connected with me, Lisa struggled and pushed her sister to join her in resisting my attempts to establish an alliance with them. Lisa would argue repeatedly that I was going to leave the clinic anyway as other therapists had, "So why bother?" One summer, when I was about to go on vacation, Lisa, surprisingly, was the one who asked where I was going to spend it. The girls asked if I planned to leave the city. Before disclosing my vacation plans, I wanted to explore their feelings, but they insisted on getting an answer first. Aware of their traumatic experiences associated with separations, I decided to postpone an exploration of their feelings. I told them I would be going to Israel for a couple of weeks. Lisa wanted to know how far Israel is from the United States, whom I was going to visit, how long the flight would be, and so on. I tried carefully to explore her concerns. Lisa said that she believed I might stay in Israel, but in the same breath she added, "I want to be clear. I don't care if you don't come back."

By enacting their intense resistance during the beginning engagement phase, the girls assumed the role of enraged victim, while I played the helpless parent. And, in fact, the girls' parents were helpless to deal with their children's anger. Each girl in my group expressed her anger in relation to different issues that came up in sessions. Lisa reacted mostly to my impending vacation. Her traumatic past experiences with her mother, who had repeatedly abandoned her and her siblings, increased her anxiety when she faced a situation entailing even the briefest separation. Lisa's mother used to leave her children alone for days and nights while she partied and used drugs with her addict friends. Recall that it was Lisa who was concerned about how far away from her I would be physically. My going across the ocean meant, for her, concretely abandoning and disappearing.

Of all the girls, Lisa was the most sensitive to my foreign accent and asked me early on where I was from. Letting them know that I was Israeli brought up issues I could not have predicted. The girls were interested in my country of origin, and I felt that my sharing made for a tender moment between us. On the other hand, this information about me also worried Lisa and other girls as well. They feared I would not return from Israel and would be yet another person to leave them.

A Typically Difficult Session

The girls knew that a new girl was going to join our group. They had seen her in the waiting room. It was Michelle, whom Nataline had invited to join the group. When I came to pick up the girls, I saw only Nataline and Michelle, both of whom ignored my comment that the group session was about to start. The girls were talking quietly and did not look at me. I told them that I would be in my office and that it was time to start the group session.

After five minutes, Carmen came directly to my office and asked if the other girls had left messages about missing the session. She added that she had finally succeeded in coming on time, and now the others were late. Therefore, she would come late to the next session. I told her how I happy I was that she had come on time, because now she would have enough time to bring up everything that was troubling her. I added that probably she had come on time because she had a lot to share. She responded that she had come only because she knew that today a new member was going to join the group. I mentioned that she seemed upset, but she ignored this observation.

Nataline entered my office with Michelle. Carmen asked about the sisters, Dee and Lisa. She added that she hoped they would not show up. When I asked Carmen to explain, she said that I ask too many questions that were none of my business.

Michelle took out of her school bag a few pictures of her family and started to tell us about the family members who were pictured. She spoke especially about her anger and her longing to see those whom she had not seen for a long time. While we were looking at Michelle's pictures and listening to her stories, Laura arrived, 10 minutes late. She turned on the tape player and put in a cassette that she had brought from home.

Laura asked me why I had not brought the cookies she had asked for. Carmen complained that I hadn't brought enough food and that she was hungry. Laura and Nataline asked if they could have the missing girls' snacks since the girls would be late or weren't going to show up. Carmen suggested waiting 15 minutes for them. I interpreted that the girls had feelings about not getting what they wished to get from me and were as well not getting enough at home either. They angrily responded, "You think you know everything."

Laura interrupted the girls' discussion and started to ask Michelle questions about her school, how old she was, and why she had joined the group. Michelle answered that she had come to the clinic because she was upset that she had to live with her aunt, that her mother abused her physically, and that she could not concentrate in school.

I asked the other girls to share with Michelle their reasons for being referred to the clinic. Carmen and Nataline were quiet. Laura said that she could not get along with her mother. When Michelle asked Laura where her father was, Laura answered that her father was in jail and had AIDS. Michelle said that her father also had AIDS but that she did not know where he was. When I told Carmen and Nataline that I was wondering about their silence, Nataline shouted at me that they would talk if they wanted to and that she wanted me to leave her alone. Carmen asked if she could later call her mother in the hospital. I said that she could and later she asked to call.

Dee and Lisa came in, 20 minutes late, with their cousin and her baby. I asked the cousin to stay in the waiting room and reminded the sisters that, under our group contract, if anyone wanted to bring a guest to the group, she would have to discuss this with the group in advance. I also noted that we shared very personal information in the sessions and that it was important to keep the information confidential. Now that all the group members were present for the first time, I took the opportunity to restate the group agreements. There was a discussion involving violation of the group contract, a subject we had talked about a few times.

I told the sisters that I was happy to see them but that I was very sorry they had been late. Lisa said that her subway had been delayed. Dee asked the other girls if they minded their cousin joining us, but the other girls remained quiet. I interpreted that the girls might have feelings about having a "stranger" in the group as they might have feelings about the "strangers" that come and go in their homes. The girls listened but did not respond. Dee said that she would leave the session if I would not allow her cousin to come in. I said that I would like to know more about why it was important for them to introduce their cousin to us but that first I would like to let Carmen call her mother in the hospital.

Dee asked Carmen to tell her what was going on with her mother and Carmen told her that her mother had been in the hospital for a week. The girls became quiet, and Carmen called her mother. Laura turned the radio louder. Carmen told her mother about school.

Carmen's mother asked to speak to me. She wanted to have a session with me after her discharge from the hospital, and I told her that I would discuss her request with Carmen. Then the group discussed the possibility of having sessions with parents. The girls not only gave me permission but actually encouraged me to meet their parents.

While Michelle put her pictures back in her bag, Nataline said that during the next session she would like to show us pictures from her school trip to Chicago.

Lisa asked Dee to go with her to see their cousin in the waiting room. I reminded them that we had only five minutes remaining, but Lisa left anyway. Dee wanted to stay, but her sister pushed her out the door. During these last five minutes the girls listened to a cassette we had made of the girls' favorite songs. We ended the session on time, and Nataline threw potato chips all over my office.

In that session I seemed to be a remote therapist, more concerned with interpretations than with my relationships with the girls. These girls, whose early lives were marked by deprivation, doubtless experienced me as yet one more unresponsive authority figure. They seemed to require a new and different experience in the course of treatment. They had few reliable psychological tools to fall back on in a stressful situation, such as when reminded not to bring a friend without first discussing it with the other girls. Alternatively, they just played tough, as they had learned they must do to survive.

For me an extremely difficult aspect of sessions such as that was the girls' repeatedly announcing that they had nothing to say. Giovacchini (1985) argues that difficult adolescents are in a developmental phase in which their character is still unconsolidated and fragmented and has not achieved the cohesion that comes with a unified self-representation. Their inability to talk may be related to the various parts of their psyche being unconnected to each other. It may be that these patients are not resistant but are simply unable to explore their feelings. A different possibility is that, as traumatized adolescents who have been abandoned, abused, or rejected, they relive the traumatic experience in the therapeutic setting. They try to reproduce the experience of maternal failure, lack of empathy, and lack of gratification. The girls tried to force me to abandon my therapeutic stance, and at times I did. I reacted as if I were rejecting them by withdrawing and by making interpretations instead of being with them emotionally.

The aggressive resistance of these girls was a signal to me to renegotiate our relationship. The girls repeatedly and in different ways asked me to leave them alone. By their intense resistance they tested my capacity to survive their destructiveness. The more each girl insisted that I leave her alone, the more she showed the vulnerability that arose from her dependence and longing for care by a maternal figure. It is striking that even Nataline, who was the most direct in pronouncing that I should leave her alone, was the one who stayed in therapy for the longest time and who returned, a year and a half later, to the clinic.

At the outset of the group—as in the session I just described—the girls were controlling and bossy, acted omnipotent, and defended against feelings of helplessness and need. The overwhelming frustration of their early infantile omnipotence, their needs to control their own experience (see Ferenczi, 1913, and Winnicott, 1956), had left them with a need to control others. When this need to control was threatened, they reacted with rage. The girls could remain with me only if they could maintain the fantasy of being in total control. Their active aim in this session was to make me an object, the target of their aggressive wishes and needs. I struggled to allow myself to be "used" (Winnicott, 1969) as an object and to be "destroyed" without being abused. Thus, I hoped, the girls' static "frozen space," resistance, might turn to potential space (Bromberg, 1998). In this phase of the evolution of the group's process, the girls attempted to achieve a feeling of mastery. Their aggressive aims and acts facilitated this mastery, and, toward the end of the beginning phase, several of the girls began to report improvement in their academic performance.

The positions of these girls were "nonnegotiable" (Pizer, 1998) during most of the treatment. Their way of alienating me frequently led straightaway to moments of empathic failure when I resorted to attacking their resistance. I would find myself saying, "I am wondering if your anger toward me has something to do with your feelings toward your sick mother." Such a comment only intensified the girls' nonnegotiable positions and prevented me from sustaining a therapeutic dialogue with them. Their nonnegotiable attitude toward me made me fail. They needed me to fail so they could enact hated aspects of themselves and of their object representations with me.

Nataline and Carmen, the first to join the group, met with me alone for four months until the third girl, Laura, joined them. At the beginning of therapy Nataline and Carmen presented intense resistance. They cursed at me, shouted at me to keep quiet, and spoke in a secret language or in Spanish. Carmen and Nataline liked to jump on the desks. They enjoyed looking at me from above and would talk as I sat while they stood on the desk. They sometimes brought a basketball, which they would throw at me to scare me. They threw pieces of paper with glue at the wall because they wanted to leave signs of themselves. Both Nataline and Carmen described how much fun it had been to torture their previous therapist.

Carmen arrived for one session with an aggressive air about her and confronted me with a direct and challenging look. It was rather warm in the office, and she asked me to open the window wide (which was out of the question, in view of the cold weather outside). Carmen got up and belligerently yanked open the window herself. Then, approaching my chair, she said that she wanted to sit in my place, which was near the window, and told me to take hers. My look did not convey cooperation, and she furiously ordered me to do as I was told. Seeing that the girls had calmed down enough to listen to me, I interpreted to Carmen that the wish to command, to occupy my chair, corresponded to her wish that I would suffer the fear, humiliation, and pain that she had endured. She did not respond.

Later, after all the other girls had joined the group, three girls, Nataline, Carmen, and Lisa, behaved toward me in a most teasing and provocative manner. Laura, who at the beginning of treatment had been nice to me, was called "brown nose" by the other girls. When I asked the girls to explain the meaning of the term, they were amused and proud to have something to teach me.

The girls would do destructive things such as marking up the walls (I learned to keep a good cleaning liquid in my office). The girls knew, though, that, if they marked up the walls, damaged anything, or spilled something on the floor, they would have to fix the damage before they left, with my assistance if necessary. Often, Nataline and Carmen would not let the other girls repair the damage, and I had to do it before the end of the session. They threw Play-Doh on the walls as high as they could so that I would be unable to remove it. After I cleaned up the day's mess, Nataline enjoyed knocking some toys from the shelves while she was leaving my office at the end of the session. I noticed that the girls became more aggressive when I controlled myself.

Because of the girls' sadistic behavior, I feared that I would be physically assaulted by certain of them (Nataline, Carmen, Lisa, and, toward the end of the group, Dee). I had more than a few moments of doubt about my ability to help the girls, who were so angry and ambivalent toward me. I felt frustrated when I experienced our alliance as fragile; I even came to wonder if there was a relationship at all. Although intellectually I grasped that the girls' erratic mode of relating to me was related to their childhood and present traumatic experiences, I nevertheless found it difficult to endure. I felt intruded on by the girls and experienced great discomfort and dread.

The girls and I experienced what can only be called mutual hate. Epstein (1988) remarked that hate can restore ego equilibrium and can provide an ongoing sense of ego identity. The girls experienced the world mostly as full of enemies. When the girls felt their sense of self weaken, they could easily recover by provoking me to attack them. When I interacted with them positively, they experienced me as inauthentic and reacted in rage. The girls' sense of self-worth and self-esteem was extremely low. They experienced me as powerful and as having all the things they did not have. They were envious, and their envy elicited in them feelings of rage and hate toward me. The contrast between us in personality style, economic status, and ethnicity was so great that the girls felt inferior and envious. Their feelings of spite, hate, and envy were unbearable to them. To reverse the imbalance, they tried to make of me someone worse than they were.

As the therapy with the girls progressed, though, the hateful interactions decreased in intensity and frequency. The hateful attacks were less generalized and more specifically related to feelings about my empathic failure. It took me a while to become aware of my countertransference hate and even longer to acknowledge its potential value and recognize those moments when the girls needed to receive it.

Resistance during the beginning phase took such passive forms as not coming to sessions, not leaving messages, coming late, as well as such active forms as shouting when interpretations were made. Nataline would listen to her Walkman and ignore me. She and Carmen were excited by this passively defiant behavior. A negative response to an adult was their source of strength. All the girls, in different ways, stated that they did not trust my ability to be helpful; at one time or another they all asked me to leave them alone or to be quiet. An adolescent's protestation to leave her alone often masks dependency longings and yearning for a meaningful attachment to a significant, consistent, caring adult (Mishne, 1984).

Adolescents use action as a defense against fears of passivity, feelings of helplessness, and the danger of object loss (Blos, 1963). The adolescent process tends to promote and favor the mechanism of acting out as a homeostatic device. Blos considered adolescents "addicted to action." He added that, through acting-out behavior, an adolescent makes contact with and communicates with people.

The girls in my group also manifested identification with the aggressor. Anna Freud (1936) described the dynamic of this defense from an intrapsychic perspective, whereas, from Ferenczi's (1933) point of view, this defense serves a relational function and is a focal response to parental dysfunction. Ferenczi defined identification with the aggressor as a child's immediate adaptation to trauma whose consequences, he felt, could be long-standing. My adolescent patients learned to behave and feel as their abusive parents expected them to. Not surprisingly, they behaved like their parents. To master their anxiety, these abused youngsters wished to be powerful and inflict harm on me. At the same time, they wanted my empathic understanding of what they felt.

While some of the girls were experiencing rejection from parents who were themselves struggling to survive with AIDS or who had long been absent from the girls' lives, I was struggling internally with the loss of my father a few years before. He had been the inspiration for the pursuit of my educational goals. I experienced his absence as a missed opportunity to share with him my career growth. In a similar way, the girls had no chance to have their parents accompany them through their life journeys. I identified with their despair and anger at losing their parents. This identification enabled me to feel compassion for them and gave me a high tolerance for their aggression toward me.

Even at the peak of their positive transference toward me, my girls did not give up their resistance to the awareness of that transference (Gill, 1982). Such an awareness might have led, in turn, to an awareness of their feelings (anger, shame, envy, tenderness, sadness) toward their parents, teachers, friends, and other significant others, which might have led to fragmentation. Therefore, the girls consistently held on to their resistance, which I tried to respect. I kept negotiating with them to express their feelings but did not expect them to reveal their dissociative self-experiences. In contrast to the classical perception of resistance, the relational conceptualization of resistance is a dyadic, rather than a unitary, one. The girls and I mutually engaged in a process of opposing and being opposed, confirming and being confirmed.

The parent–adolescent relationship is similar to the therapy situation: the adolescents' negativism and oppositional behavior are their efforts to practice autonomy and self-definition, efforts that need to be acknowledged by the therapist. These adolescents engage with us in their "anti" behavior. Adolescents who are "not anti" may not establish as deep a therapeutic alliance as those who are "anti."

The Antitherapeutic Alliance

All of us who treat adolescents are faced with their often noncommunicative stance. They may express their alliance indirectly (by referring their friends to us) or by engaging us through enactment (by bringing their friends to session), but not often do they articulate their ambivalent relationship with us. They become negatively engaged, and they need us to respect and maintain this stance of self-determination. With each of my adolescent patients I could acknowledge a therapeutic alliance only at a level she could tolerate.

The therapeutic alliance is critical to work with adolescents, especially in the beginning phase of treatment, because the majority of adolescents withdraw early from treatment (Novick, 1982). Adolescents seldom, if ever, come for a first appointment with an accurate conception of the analyst's role (Harley, 1970). They often deny that they need to see a therapist; they do not believe they have any problems needing attention. Moreover, they are usually referred by the people with whom they have difficulties—their parents, a teacher, or another adult—and who chose the therapist. The initial contact is characterized by the adolescent's anxiety, as well as his shame and guilt about revealing his inner life.

The therapist must be able to tolerate ambiguity in the process of engaging with adolescent patients by negotiating in a different way with each patient. This capacity to negotiate with patients was conceived by Ferenczi (1928) in his paper, "The Elasticity of Psycho-Analytic Techniques." By elasticity he meant, "the analyst, like an elastic band, must yield to the patient's pull, but without ceasing to pull in his own direction, so long as one position or the other has not been conclusively demonstrated to be untenable" (p. 95).

My first task—and a difficult one—was to convince the girls to come to the first session with me. To build the necessary holding environment (Winnicott, 1960), I had to demonstrate a high level of elasticity. The girls' willingness to participate a therapeutic alliance was always unclear. It was Nataline's and Carmen's idea to form a specialized group of teenaged girls who were losing their parents to AIDS. They also were the first girls to join the bereavement group. I was planning to have a phone conversation with each girl to let her make her own decision about whether or not to meet with me. I first contacted Nataline and Carmen two months after their previous group therapy fell apart because their therapist had left the clinic and the other girls showed no motivation to continue therapy.

Nataline: In the phone conversation, Nataline announced that she had changed her mind and did not want to continue therapy. I suggested that she meet with me once, that she would be free to make her own decision about joining the group. She refused to meet me with her mother present. She said that she was "too tired to listen to her mother's problems." She did, however, agree to meet me with her grandmother present and also agreed to my meeting alone with her mother. (After we met, I learned that her mother's health had dramatically deteriorated.)

Before joining the group, Nataline had refused to see me individually. Even so, at the beginning, when only she and Carmen were in the group, there were times when she was alone because Carmen did not show up. During these sessions Nataline was cooperative and interactive with me. She left her art work with me; later, in the group, she tore up her art work so that nothing was left with me. Although we two often seemed not to have a therapeutic alliance, she did state to the group, without explanation, that she knew that I would always keep confidentiality.

Lisa: During the screening interview, Lisa denied having any problems or need to be in therapy. After I reiterated that girls should join this group only if they felt the need for help for some problem, she admitted that she had "reacted before thinking."

Dee: During the first intake interview Dee agreed to enter my office on the condition that her foster mother and her sister be in the room. She insisted that she did not want to talk and would only nod "yes" or shake her head "no." She cried without explanation. After I met with the three of them, Dee agreed to see me individually in addition to joining a bereavement group.

Dee did not, however, show up for her initial individual session. I called her and told her that I was concerned about her and looked forward to meeting with her. I emphasized that I would like to hear her suggestions about what would be the best way for her to get help. Later, she was resistant to having 45-minute sessions and was willing to have only 20-minute individual sessions. She agreed to my suggestion that we schedule 45-minute sessions and, if she wanted to leave before the time was up, she could. Although she denied that she had any reason to be in therapy, she became depressed after I mentioned the problems that had been described during the intake interview.

I had to adapt to the uniqueness of each individual patient in order to establish a therapeutic alliance with her, a task that was especially difficult to achieve at the beginning of treatment. This process was complicated by the parents' lack of involvement, by their emotional unavailability to their children, and by their not understanding the significance of therapy. I felt alone, without a team. Parents play a crucial role in the progress of their children's functioning. One of the girls, Laura, brought to the surface the difficulties of establishing a therapeutic alliance when a parent is absent.

Laura, a Latina, was 15 years old when she joined the group. She was a short girl who dressed provocatively and wore heavy makeup. Her mood during sessions generally was depressed. She did show affect appropriate to content, which covered a full range of emotion from humor to tears and depression.

Laura's father was dying from AIDS and was in a drug rehabilitation program in prison. Laura lived with her mother, Ms. R., and an older sister. A half-brother was a drug user and dealer and the father of two children. Ms. R. expressed concern about Laura's school performance: "We've tried to get her to do homework, but she doesn't, and she's all strange in school." She also resented her daughter's popularity with boys. Ms. R. also said that Laura was troubled by her father's situation; she loved her father dearly. Ms. R. mentioned that her own younger brother, the wife of her older brother, and a nephew had all died of AIDS and that this circumstance had been very depressing to her and Laura.

Laura's mother had used drugs and alcohol while pregnant with all three children. Although her first two children were planned, Laura was not. Ms. R. recalled, "I just didn't want to have another kid with that drug addict: her father used to shoot dope, be gone for days, beat my face. And I had two other kids already." Laura had been a fussy baby, rarely sleeping through the night, and was the object of her sister's resentment. The mother recalled that Laura had had recurring ear infections. Laura was allergic and asthmatic.

Her parents broke up when she was two-and-a-half-years old. When asked about significant events in Laura's childhood, Ms. R. told of Laura's sadness at age four upon being sent to day care while Ms. R. attended a job-training program; and four-and-a-half-year old Laura's finding her mother having intercourse with one of "many boyfriends." Ms. R. noted that "my kids all hated my boyfriends." Her narrative suggested that her kids hated being neglected and left with their maternal grandmother for weeks at a time while their mother partied.

Ms. R. mentioned Laura in an off-hand comment: "Teachers always liked her and she's smart, but she was always running her mouth. They complained about that." In junior high school, Laura suddenly became more rebellious. She was involved in fights with girls and cut classes. Laura was described by her mother as having been popular all her life. On entering high school, Laura joined the "negative crowd." She glowingly claimed to be a member of the Latin Heavens, who would "hang tough." In her narrative, Laura claimed that she felt secure knowing that "someone is watching my back." At the same time, she said, "When I'm in school, I feel really scared, like someone's out to get me." At home the mother would hit Laura and curse her. Then, to "cool out," Laura went to live with her brother.

At the time of intake the mother had been married for two years. Her husband was alcoholic and more or less out of touch with the family. I know little about Laura's father, her childhood, or her family of origin. Ms. R. reported Laura's father had been using heroin since she met him; he had stolen her money, beat her, and disappeared for long periods of time. When asked to describe her childhood, Ms. R. said, "My mother was a bitch. She'd smack you first and ask questions later." Ms. R. described herself as a child as always fighting because other kids picked on her. She recalled running away from home when she was 15 years old. She dropped out of school after she became pregnant.

Laura's difficulties parallel her mother's at the same age. During Laura's childhood, her mother struggled with her own depression and was not available. To maintain the connection with her mother and to avoid rejection, Laura erected defenses against her own depression and emptiness; she caused trouble by cutting classes, running away, and lying. The sense of abandonment that Laura had already experienced as an infant and child were compounded by the news that her father was dying from AIDS.

It should be noted that adolescents are rarely self-motivated for treatment. Their parents, teachers, or other adults who are always engaged in struggles with them are the very ones who refer them. Laura, for example, was referred by the school counselor after she cut classes, chronically came late to school, and was disruptive in class. She did not show up for the first session. In a telephone conversation she explained that, even though her mother knew about her session, she had asked Laura to supervise her nephew. I asked her if she was interested in my calling her mother to explain the significance of Laura's being in treatment. Laura agreed, but all my attempts to reach the mother during the first few weeks of treatment failed. She answered my message a month later.

While generally we attempt to establish solid relationships with the parents of our adolescent patients, in part because they are the ones who will decide whether or not to continue their children's therapy, such was not the case with these girls. The parents of the traumatized adolescents described here were absent, unavailable, uninvolved in their children's lives. Laura's interactions at home were chaotic, disorganizing, abandoning, abusive, and humiliating. Coming from such a home, she did not have the developmental prerequisites for experiencing the therapeutic alliance on her own. There was not much for me to build on to make her feel the possibilities of making an alliance. I learned that traumatized adolescents are likely to be unable to form therapeutic alliances early in treatment or, indeed, for long periods of time. Moreover, this alliance, once formed, is easy to break down.

To overcome her initial resistance and to establish even a tentative alliance with Laura during the beginning phase, I had to be fairly active, outgoing, directive, and open. I encouraged her to discuss her anger and ambivalent feelings about being referred for treatment and her reluctance to reveal her true feelings and concerns to a stranger. It took me a long time to realize that, in the light of Laura's and the other girls' deprived and traumatic lives, it was only natural that these patients should wish to have fun and good times in the sessions, rather than always feeling that they had to deal with their pain. In the beginning, we did not have a mutual agreement about the therapeutic work to be done, and we did not work together toward a common goal. I wanted to work through the girls' anticipatory grief, vis-à-vis their impending losses, but they came to the group to socialize.

From Laura's point of view, my role as a therapist was to make her happy and not to upset her by discussing her grief or her father's AIDS. There were a few sessions that Laura spent entirely in playing basketball and board games. There were times that the girls performed as if they were on stage, singing together. While they performed, they would laugh and make jokes. When Laura asked Nataline why she had stayed so long in the group, Nataline repeatedly responded, "I stayed so long in the group because it is fun." The girls were not motivated to form a treatment contract with me and stick with it. They were motivated by other things, and I learned to follow them rather than to lead. I needed to feel some sense of alliance around treatment goals if I were to have the conviction that the treatment was moving forward.

After a few months of reluctantly following Laura's request just to have fun, I was struck to hear her say, "I can feel upset because I'm having fun here." I learned from her to value the shared experience of "having fun" as a path to experiencing other feelings. I could develop this environment only by joining the girls in having fun. Gradually, we established working alliances around reciprocal understanding and mutual empathy and respect. Laughing together, making jokes, and enjoying playing set the groundwork for feeling safer to dive into the deep pain, shame, or humiliation associated with their traumas.

The middle phase was marked by Laura's increased interest in working through her worries and her fears of losing her father.

Adolescents rarely give direct, verbal indications that the process is working. They seldom say things like, "You are helping me." Therefore, I had to look for indirect or nonverbal indications. The most striking indication that something important might be going on was the girls' persistence in attending despite their protests. There were some indirect indications that the girls were indeed beginning to be involved in a therapeutic process and that an alliance was beginning to form.

Since Carmen lived farthest from the clinic, she asked to have the sessions begin earlier so she would get home earlier. Even though Nataline had to rush from school in order to make the session on time, she asked the girls to accommodate Carmen. At one session the sisters, Dee and Lisa, announced that they would have to leave early but refused to explain why. They became so involved in the group discussion, however, that they stayed until the end of the session.

In another session, Laura did not show up, and in accord with our routine—phoning the absent girl during the session—Nataline called her. Laura was crying, and Nataline asked me to talk with her to calm her down. Laura was upset because she did not have anyone to accompany her to see her dying father in prison, and the girls wanted to hear me say that I would accompany her, which I later did.

When Carmen and Nataline called their mothers in my presence to let them know that they had arrived safely at the clinic, they talked with their mothers about their problems at school or with friends. After each of them hung up, the other girls asked questions about what they had overheard and a serious discussion followed. Carmen suggested that her mother be referred to therapy because she needed help. Michelle was conflicted about returning home and expressed her need to discuss this issue at length with me. Nataline suggested that I also meet Michelle's mother, and Carmen asked me to get Michelle's mother to promise that she would never hit Michelle. Michelle herself asked me to see her mother individually, and I did see her for a few sessions individually.

One summer when I was on a two-week vacation, the girls exchanged phone numbers as a substitute and arranged to meet on their own.

In another session the girls brought in their favorite cassettes. Because I did not know the words of the songs, they wrote out the lyrics so that I would be able to join them in their singing. Nataline and Carmen tested my memory of the melodies, and Michelle and Lisa enjoyed explaining to me the meaning of lyrics I did not understand.

Another instance of a growing therapeutic alliance occurred when Michelle's younger sister ran away. Michelle felt guilty that her sister had imitated her. She was worried that the family would fall apart, her mother would be blamed for dysfunctioning, and she would be placed with a foster family. She asked me to write a letter asking her caseworker not to make any decisions without consulting with me first. I wrote this letter, which she carried with her. She asked me to call her during the weekend to make sure that she was all right, which I did.

Nataline called before a session and asked my permission to bring her best friend for only one session so that her friend could get help as well. I suggested that we first discuss the matter with the girls in the group and also that the girl's parents call to give me permission to see her friend. I also reminded Nataline that this group was a special one that her friend did not fit into but that I would be happy to help her anyway. The friend's mother called and asked me to see her daughter, who was depressed.

During the session, while the friend waited in the waiting room, Nataline asked the girls if they were willing to help her best friend. She did not give any information about her friend, even though the girls in the group questioned her. Nataline said, if they wanted to know anything, they should ask her friend directly. (I had said the same thing to them earlier in the group sessions before a new group member joined the group.) Nataline told the girls that with this friend she cried and shared her feelings toward her mother. All the girls asked to let the friend join the group, and I let her join us for the last 20 minutes.

The friend said that she had asked to join our group because she had heard good things about it. She added that she had troubles with her 25-year-old boyfriend, and was worried that she was pregnant. The group moved to a discussion of the meaning of relationships with older men and to their conflicts about pregnancy and abortion. I referred the friend to another therapist.

During the termination phase, when Dee and Lisa wanted to leave the group, Nataline said that for her it was fun to be in the group and that, if the sisters did not believe that, they had problems. She said that they needed help and would leave sooner or later anyway. Nataline added that we could not force the sisters to come to therapy, that they had to come of their own free will. This was one of the first direct illustrations of the existence of a therapeutic alliance.

Michelle disclosed in the group that she felt embarrassed that she still sucked her thumb and that she needed help to stop it because she could not control herself. In another session, Michelle told us she had received an award for writing the "best poem," and her school did a book of her poems. She was proud to tell us that she had been accepted to a regular school. She mentioned that the group had brought good luck to her life. She brought Furman's (1974) book, *A Child's Parent Dies,* to another session. She asked my opinion about the book and mentioned that she hoped to be a journalist, because she liked to write—or else maybe a social worker.

Consciously, or at least preconsciously, adolescents are fearful of becoming embroiled in yet another dependency relationship; whereas unconsciously they hope, yet fear, to find in the therapist the gratification of various irrational and childish wishes. Although this struggle manifests at all ages, during adolescence it is most intense and conflicted. Because of these emotional currents, adolescents typically utilize various techniques to avoid establishing a therapeutic alliance.

For my traumatized patients, the alliance was so fragile that a slight action on my part, such as being five minutes late, was experienced as a lack of caring and could elicit a very strong reaction. Such moments revealed how very fragile the level of trust and felt safety was for these traumatized adolescents. These girls opened the door to levels of dread, anger, panic, humiliation that were always close by, waiting to be tapped. They were ready to react in an emergency mode (e.g., suddenly distancing, responding with anger, seeing confrontation or abandonment threatening) when it was not called for. These patients were so vulnerable as a result of molestation, betrayals, lack of parental responsiveness, and the general harshness of the interaction with their parents that had occurred in their early life, that it sometimes seemed as if the damage was beyond repair. Any disappointment they felt about my reaction to them would be experienced with an intensity that reflected their traumatized parts.

To establish a working alliance with these girls, I had to proceed cautiously and expect repeated "testing" behaviors, such as their use of obscene or provocative language, coming late to sessions, unresponsiveness, and hostile and rebellious behavior. These behaviors gradually diminished during the middle phase as the girls and I became more comfortable relating to each other.

I usually had to be "satisfied" with indirect indications of the appearance of a therapeutic alliance. Such indications were evident when Laura asked to have longer sessions so she would have more time to talk; when Carmen wrote down the words of songs so that I could join her in singing; when Michelle announced that she had come to the session even though she was sick, and when Nataline brought her best girlfriend to get help from me.

Speaking for one school of thought, Meissner (1996) believes that, more often than not, distortions in the alliance reflect underlying transference issues, so that interpretation of these transference distortions is necessary to increase collaboration. With my adolescent patients, however, any attempt to interpret the transference only jeopardized the therapeutic alliance. These multiply traumatized adolescent patients experienced my transference interpretations as controlling, intrusive, hurtful, humiliating, or potentially retraumatizing them.

I realized that, to establish a therapeutic alliance, I had to shift to a holding approach (Winnicott, 1960), expressing empathy and acceptance that would allow safety and security to evolve. Nonverbally I had to create a safe environment that would allow the girls to experience the possibility of shared experience. As a holding object, I did not hesitate to make use of such transitional objects as sending postcards during my vacations, giving my patients gifts on their birthdays, and phoning when they missed sessions.

There has been an ongoing controversy concerning whether or not the therapeutic alliance is a useful concept. Most authors take the position that a therapeutic alliance is based on the patient's conscious and rational wish to be rid of suffering and is thus wholly unobjectionable and, indeed, necessary (e.g., Sandler, Dare, and Holder, 1975; Gutheil and Havens, 1979; Rangell, 1992). Greenson (1967) specifies further that the core of the working alliance is the "real relationship" between analyst and patient. Yet he postulates that a "real relationship" implies that the analyst can be perceived as and can react as a "real person," free of transference contaminations. From this point of view, the therapeutic alliance is not transference and should be distinguished from it (Gill, 1982), though it may be conceded, transference can aid as well as interfere with the therapeutic alliance. But where, then, to draw the line?

Novick (1992) argues that the therapeutic alliance is "motivated by rational and irrational forces including the transference to treatment of adaptive and maladaptive earlier psychic organization" (p.92). Yet, when one considers patients such as I am describing in this book, it is not easy to see how the available "irrational" forces reflecting a "maladaptive" pattern offer the therapeutic alliance anything beyond basic hopes for rescue and perhaps sustenance. On different grounds, Hoffer (2000) rejects the usefulness of the concept of a therapeutic alliance. He argues that acting deliberately to create an alliance contradicts maximal autonomy for self-examination. This prospect, however, leaves hanging what one does when the capacity for self-examination is profoundly constricted by the threat of retraumatization.

In sharp contrast to Hoffer, Shane (2000) believes that the new object experience that is created through the establishment of a therapeutic alliance carries developmental potential. I concur, but then there is the ongoing problem that the new object relationship will again be contaminated by the old. Where does the therapist find the needed room to maneuver to challenge projections if he is consumed with the need to maintain a developmentally nutritive newness? Finally, Meissner (1996), who has attempted to synthesize definitions of therapeutic alliance from different orientations, discusses the therapeutic alliance from a "mutual interaction" point of view. I find his emphasis on negotiation very much to the point:

According to this view, the interacting personalities of analyst and analysand contribute essentially to the alliance. In this sense the therapeutic alliance resembles contemporary intersubjective models, according to which the therapeutic alliance is inseparable from the relational matrix. . . . Negotiation is a core component of this process . . . , allowing for meaningful contributions by both participants toward establishing a shared consensual reality [p. 6].

Obviously, an effective therapeutic relationship or working alliance ought to entail such things as mutual and reciprocal affirmation, understanding, empathy, and respect. But, if one thinks of a negotiation as the basis for all these, then perhaps the best place to begin is with respect. Many of the rules pertaining to what went on between my adolescent patients and me were negotiable. But some were not open to question. In any negotiation, each party gains something and gives up something, and that was so between my patients and me. My adolescent patients had to give up their rebellion and engage with me if they were to have a corrective emotional experience. I had to give up the safety and the distance of the traditional theoretical stance, and be open and willing to collaborate with the girls, in order to sustain the connection.

Safety Phase
Mutual Tenderness

Best Friend Betrayed

You were my best friend
I told you secrets that no one else knew.
Why did you do what you did?
My heart hurts,
But I never want to talk to you again.
I trusted you,
You lied, you betrayed me,
I don't understand,
So good-bye.
How do I say good-bye to what we had?
How do I say good-bye to yesterday?
How do I say good-bye when it is all gone?
How do I say good-bye when I know?
So much that I know I will miss.

Many authors have emphasized the complexity of the treatment relationship with adolescent patients (A. Freud, 1958; Blos, 1962; Giovacchini, 1974; Tylim, 1978; Gartner, 1985; Mishne, 1986; Bernstein and Glenn, 1988; Amodeo and Drouilher, 1992; Brandell, 1992; Anastasopoulos and Tsiantis, 1996). When adolescents have experienced severe trauma along with their developmental struggles, the analyst's emotional responsiveness to them becomes crucial—particularly the analyst's expression of tenderness. The therapeutic atmosphere of tenderness is, in the first instance, what will enable these patients to share their traumas. Historically, the early psychoanalytic literature about love focused on erotic love. In that literature, the analyst's "love" was more a love of truth than love for the patient. Ferenczi (1932), who treated traumatized patients, first recognized the significance of creating "maternal friendliness," love in the treatment context, and later used the word tenderness. He described tenderness as the preoedipal register of experience and explained the importance of this kind of response in the therapeutic setting.

> Patients cannot believe that an event really took place, or cannot fully believe it, if the analyst, as the sole witness of the events, persists in his cool, unemotional, and, as patients are fond of stating, purely intellectual attitude, while the events are of a kind that must evoke, in anyone present, emotions of revulsion, anxiety, terror, vengeance, grief and the urge to render immediate help; to remove or destroy the cause or the person responsible; and since it is usually a child, an injured child, who is involved (but even leaving that aside), feelings of wanting to comfort it with love [p. 24].

I concur. Traumatized patients need something other than intellectual understanding. Nurturance and love are the core of what will heal them. In my experience with the girls, after a period of intense resistance, a mutual tenderness was created by all of us toward each other. This atmosphere, once it was developed, led to the girls' sharing their traumatic experiences of losing their parents to AIDS and of being sexually abused. The further evolution of the transference–countertransference matrices between the girls and me are related to what Ferenczi (1933) described as the "confusion of tongues," traumatic experience in which passion is confused with tenderness.

In the psychoanalytic canon, the confusion of tongues theory reestablished sexual traumas (as opposed to fantasy) as a cause of psychological disorder, although Ferenczi also included emotional trauma as an essential pathogenic agent. The theory developed a line of thought that is present in a series of Ferenczi's papers starting around 1929 with "The Unwelcome Child and His Death Instinct." In this paper Ferenczi introduced the concept of the importance of parental love and tenderness in the development of a child's "life force." Ferenczi believed that, in the absence of love and tenderness, the destructive instincts would begin to stir immediately in a child's psyche. These children, he added, develop an "aversion to life." Ferenczi emphasized that those who do not experience tenderness with their parents do not get a supply of "positive life-impulses" and develop psychopathology. Ferenczi further related these patients' self-destructive attitudes and behavior to the early incidence of trauma in their lives above and beyond the absence of tenderness.

Ferenczi's (1933) final formulation of his trauma model introduced what we would now call a relational view of trauma. In his theory, the child first is traumatized by sexual seduction. The child continues to have connection with the abuser but seeks *tenderness* not sexual passion. The adult fails to show tenderness to the child and continues to violate the child, who cannot refuse the sexual advances of the adult because the child feels helpless and paralyzed by fear. My girls had been sexually abused by their mothers' boyfriends and by relatives; the experience left them starved for tenderness. Those who abused them sexually had betrayed their trust. To get to their injured selves, I had to gain the trust that they had lost in other people.

In meeting the girls' needs I had to survive their destructiveness. I felt pulled into repeating the girls' childhood trauma. They put me in the role of the "bad parent." When their destructiveness disabled me from feeling tenderness toward them, the girls felt overanxious. Sullivan (1953) described conspicuous elements of the "malevolent" transformation; in one, children, wishing for tenderness, evoke anxiety in their caregivers, who then induce fears and anxiety in the children. My letting the girls express their rage might have moved them toward an object-used state (Winnicott, 1969). The object, if it is to be used, "implies that [he or she] is part of external reality" (p. 113). This struggle for survival became "the unconscious backcloth for love of a real object; that is, an object outside the area of the subject's omnipotent control" (p. 111). This movement toward love of a real object (teachers, friends) was evident in the girls' lives during the middle phase of treatment, when they started to express tenderness toward people in their lives, including other girls in the group and me.

When Nataline was about to lose her mother, she developed a very close relationship with her teacher, a symbolic substitute. But Nataline also faced a loss with her teacher because she had to move to high school. Nataline purchased two identical pendants, each half of a golden heart. She wore one half, and the teacher wore the other. Following Michelle's invitation to bring her family album to a session, Nataline brought her school album. She described students and teachers whom she was going to miss and said that she cried when she thought of not attending this school any more.

By this middle phase, the girls had become accustomed to the group process and felt safe enough with each other to explore their vulnerabilities. Lisa initiated playing "Monopoly." Negotiating purchases brought up the issue of money and their experiences of feeling deprived. Nataline said she wished to have a big house (she did not have her own room; she slept in the living room). Carmen wished for enough money to be able to leave home and live by herself (at times when her mother was hospitalized, she stayed with neighbors, who did not welcome her). Laura talked about her need for more clothes, and Michelle spoke of her desire to study and be able to support herself financially. This sharing was a way of getting closer to each other.

In that atmosphere of mutual tenderness, the girls began to share their deep pain and their longing for love. They discussed the meaning of love and tenderness in relation to boys and how they would know whether or not the girls' feelings about the boys were true. Nataline stated that she knew her boyfriend loved her by his facial expressions when he said that he loved her. Laura said that the measure of love was "what the boyfriend is willing to do for you." She was proud that her ex-boyfriend had been ready to fight physically to protect her. Carmen announced that all boys "fool around with other girls" and suggested that the girls be suspicious about their boyfriends' real feelings.

Michelle, who was upset that her boyfriend had left New York, initiated a discussion in the group about conflicts in expressing her feelings. She cried as she told us that her boyfriend would return next summer instead of next month as he had promised. She brought his letter to the group. Nataline and Lisa suggested she tell him that she was upset instead of saying that she was "okay," as she had planned to do. Carmen suggested that Michelle curse him.

Michelle called him during the session and received a lot of support from the other girls afterward. Lisa said she sounded strong, and Nataline affirmed that Michelle would make him sorry about leaving her. Michelle generally had difficulty expressing her feelings spontaneously. She expressed herself through her writing. At the next session she read two poems about her feelings of love and hurt in connection with her boyfriend.

> 1.
> *Please don't go*
> *You don't know how I feel for you.*
> *I can't show you but I do care*
> *I know I went back with him.*
> *But I don't know.*
> *Please tell me you still want to be friends.*
> *I guess I heard a lot and really did*
> *Not know what to believe.*
> *So, I went back.*
> *Please never go too far.*

2.
Did I break his heart first?
We live so far apart and I would wonder
what he was doing in B. and think
He did not really care for me.
That I was his M. girl and now I can't forget him.
If this is love, why it hurt so much?

From speaking about people in their lives, the girls moved to talking about their parents, whom the girls were going to lose to AIDS. If at the beginning of treatment they had expressed anger toward their sick parents for becoming infected with the HIV virus, now they shifted to expressing tenderness toward them. This tenderness was especially expressed by Michelle.

Michelle was a Latina, 15 years old at the time of intake. She had run away from her mother's home and was referred by a social worker in a homeless shelter, where she reported that she had been physically abused by her mother. In addition, she reported that she had been raped twice by her mother's boyfriend a year before. A rumor that the perpetrator had come back to New York after fleeing aroused fear and anxiety in Michelle.

Michelle lived with her aunt and two cousins. Her aunt obtained custody of Michelle after she ran away from her mother's home. Michelle reported difficulty sleeping and had occasional nightmares when she lived with her mother. She said she had not been eating well. In addition, she described delusions of seeing her attacker on the street, and panic attacks at the thought of his reappearance. Michelle's constricted affect during the intake interview while she related the details of her rape implied some degree of dissociation from the traumatic events. Michelle agreed that she needed to come for therapy because she was "all confused."

Michelle was born two months prematurely. During the pregnancy her mother experienced frequent asthma attacks. According to Michelle's aunts, the mother abused neither alcohol nor drugs during the pregnancy. Michelle's twin sister died at birth. The mother described Michelle as an abnormal child, who at birth "did not have nails or eyebrows." Owing to her poor condition, Michelle stayed in the hospital for three months after birth.

As an infant, Michelle was hospitalized twice for pneumonia. For unknown reasons, she was not returned to her mother after hospitalization, but at three months went to live with her Aunt S. Michelle lived with

S. from three months to eleven months and then was returned to her mother for a trial period. When Michelle was two years old, her father began to visit her. Because he was often drunk, Michelle was afraid of him and used to hide when he came to see her.

Michelle lived with another aunt, D., from the time she was two and a half years old until she was 12. Michelle's mother saw her infrequently and made no effort to have her daughter returned to her. D. could not report any desire expressed by Michelle to be reunited with her mother but said that she always asked a lot of questions about her father. D. stated that Michelle had led a sheltered life at her home and was not allowed to go outside alone until she was 12. When Michelle was 12, D. remarried, and her husband felt that it was time for Michelle to live with her own mother. Michelle was forced to leave her aunt's home and reunite with a mother she had never really known. In a group session, Michelle shared entries from her diary about her life; they summarized her feelings about having to move from relative to relative and maintain a façade that hers was a "regular, happy family."

Michelle always had trouble getting to and attending school. She was attending an alternative school at the time of the intake, was truant from school for a good part of the time she lived at her mother's home, and had particular trouble with math and reading.

Michelle's mother had six children but had never married. It was unclear who the father of each child was. According to Michelle's aunts, her mother had a new boyfriend "every six months." Apparently, one of her mother's relationships had been with a man who physically and verbally abused her and raped two of her daughters (Michelle and her younger sister, who subsequently had an abortion). Michelle's father was a neighbor of her mother's. He was married with six children and had many affairs with women besides Michelle's mother.

According to the background information reported, Michelle was born addicted to cocaine, had significantly delayed developmental milestones, and was in special education classes. She needed to work on accepting her disability, as well as on her ability to deal with her emotions. She worried about being abandoned by those she cared for and tended to become overly involved in the problems of her peers as well as her family.

During intake she expressed her desperate wish to find her father, whom she had not seen since childhood. She had been told that he was dying of AIDS and hoped that the therapist would help her to find him. Michelle wrote a touching letter to her father, which she read during a group session.

When I was growing up I always wanted to have a dad like my friends. I remember in 1st grade my teacher said, "Make a father's day card." I started crying and said, "I don't have a dad" I lost contact with him. I wish I could see him again. I wish I could say, "I love you daddy" some day and tell him everything and let him know how I really feel and hear about him. I hope I find him. And for all the people who know their dad, be happy you know him and can spend time with him before he dies.

I was witness to many painful moments in the girls' lives. They used the phone in my office, for example, when they needed support for making a call, support that they could not get at home. Our agreement about using the phone was that they had to share with us first why they needed to use the phone.

In one session, Michelle told the girls in the group that her social worker had located her father. She asked if she might call her father's wife during the session, since the wife was the one who could tell her about her father. Although I asked Michelle to explore her feelings before making the phone call, she refused; I let her make the phone call anyway. Michelle was excited to learn that her stepmother had remembered her birthday. Her stepmother told her that her father was very sick; in fact, he was unconscious. Michelle refused to talk further about her father.

In the next session she told the girls that the previous weekend her aunt had told her that her father had died. She cried for two days, went to pray for him, only to learn that she had been misinformed and that her father was still alive, though hospitalized. As best we could we prepare Michelle to see her father. She arranged to go with her half-sister. She arrived at the next session laughing hysterically—she told us that her father had died before she was due to visit him at the hospital.

A few sessions after Michelle's father died, she came to the group and read from her diary. She shared her writings and poems about discovering her father, losing him, and going to see him too late. She recalled how she had heard from her sister that her father had contracted AIDS from working in a men's toilet filled with needles. She told of his deterioration, how skinny he had become, his failing memory, and how quickly he had aged by the time he died. She pretended not to care. Michelle wrote:

To My Father

Why did you have to die?
I can't believe I feel such pain
I hardly knew you.

I always cared.
Why didn't you live just one more day
And let me see you one last time?

Father

Do I know my father?
I wish I did.
We met just once or twice.
Now it's late, too late.
He's gone today, gone tomorrow
Gone like dinosaurs.

Michelle's theme of having gone "too late" to see her father before his death was very much present in Nataline's experience of losing her mother.

When Michelle was preparing to see her father, Nataline said, "I cannot handle this. You are stronger than me." She did not accept my offer to accompany her on a visit to her mother in the hospital. Nataline mentioned that she was crying too much and without any reason. Only two months later, Nataline's mother was dying. Like Michelle, Nataline had to decide if she wanted to see her mother in the hospital. After her mother had been hospitalized for a month, Nataline decided to see her, and, in an uncanny repetition of Michelle's experience, she also arrived 30 minutes too late. Her mother had died before she got there.

On getting a phone call that Nataline's mother had died, I asked Nataline if she wanted me to come to the funeral. Nataline said, "Don't bother to come because I am not going to enter the cemetery." She turned down my offer to stay with her outside the cemetery. I sent her a sympathy card. She came a week later to session and thanked me for sending the card. "It was nice of you," she said.

Nataline did not want to discuss her feelings about losing her mother. "It is done. I will talk about my mother only when I have my own kids," she said and almost cried. Thankfully she did not keep her word. A few sessions later she proudly brought a picture of her mother at the age of 14, Nataline's own age, showing us how much alike they looked.

While Nataline, Michelle, and I were looking at these pictures together I asked Nataline to tell us about her mother. I knew that, looking at the pictures, she would have greater access to those memories. I also said that I would like to know any dreams she has had about her mother. She told us a dream about herself and her mother: In the dream, Nataline saw her mother, who was healthy, standing at the top of a flight of stairs and offering Nataline her hands. Nataline, at the bottom of the stairs, tried to reach her mother, climbed the stairs, but could not reach her mother's hands.

After a few moments of silence, I said, "You miss your mother. You would like to have a chance to hold her hands and to bring her back to your life." Nataline responded tearfully that she was sorry she had not kissed her mother; instead she had cried hysterically when she saw her mother lying dead on the hospital bed. I tried to explore her feelings further, but she shouted at me to keep my mouth shut. She said that she did not want to talk about this any more.

In another session, Laura told the girls that her father, who had AIDS, was receiving treatment in prison and that she was scared by how her father looked. She cried while Carmen hugged her. A few sessions later, Laura was visibly upset. The girls, who had become quite sensitive to each other, asked Laura if she had met with her father. She and her brother had, in fact, visited him in the hospital. During one hour-long visit, their father had slept. She described him as very thin and connected to many machines. She added that she did not know if she could visit him again.

Nataline apologized for not accompanying her because she felt unable to watch a person dying from AIDS. Laura corrected Nataline to say that her father was not dying, but a few weeks later her father lost consciousness. Laura was sobbing and Michelle suggested she visit her father in case he returned to consciousness. At the end of the sessions during this period, the girls helped me to put things away, which was quite exceptional.

Not only were the girls willing to accept my tenderness during the middle phase, I was also able to acknowledge my need for tenderness from them. I found myself responding with a great deal more tenderness and empathy than before. At first I could not understand why I now felt a sense of identification with the girls that I had not felt earlier.

Reflecting on my own reactions, I thought of my encounter with Nataline's mother during the previous phase. That had been my first experience of dealing with a patient who was dying of AIDS. The mother smelled of alcohol, was painfully thin, and was toothless. Her image had stayed with me for days. This image, I realized many months later, had been painful for me in part because it reminded me of my own father's appearance at the time of his death.

It is required in Jewish tradition that someone identity the dead person, and I was the one chosen. It became clear to me that the girls' expressions of anger had touched on my own anger relating to my father's death. A few years earlier I had watched him die. I had been especially angry at his failure to take good care of himself and guilty that I had not paid enough attention to his deterioration. My father was inaccessible and refused to talk about his illness. Only after his death did we learn that he had lost consciousness a few times at his job. We watched him struggle to breathe and begged him to see a more experienced cardiologist than the one he had been seeing for years. During his last year alive he was hospitalized several times.

At one point my father asked to come home, and we suspected he knew he had only a few days to live. He wanted us to move on with our lives and chose not to share with us this devastating news. He knew how much my mother and I and my three sisters loved him. He probably could not tolerate watching us grieving for him.

Unlike the girls in the group, I did not arrive "too late" to know my father. During his last year of life we became especially close. I was curious to know more about my childhood, and he was willing to help in my exploration. He treated me like a friend with whom he could share his experience as a father.

The girls and I shared the experience of losing a parent. Their negative transference was shifted to a positive one. In indirect indication of that shift, Nataline shared with the group her plans to form and lead a group of young girls in their neighborhood. She said that those girls always asked her for advice, and she believed that it would be very helpful for them to be together in a group. Michelle asked to be her co-leader.

On another occasion the girls asked to have a longer session, but I could not stay longer because I had a session immediately after this group session. After the girls brought up the possibility of longer sessions, I realized that it was important to leave some free time after each group session so I could add time as needed. I rearranged my schedule so that I had a 15-minute break after the group session. Thus, the girls had a chance to separate from me and from each other gradually, which was more comfortable for them.

During this middle phase, Michelle started to come earlier in the hope of seeing me individually. I kept my door open when I was not seeing patients. Michelle would come directly to my office and ask if she could talk with me for a few minutes. She, however, refused my suggestion that we schedule individual sessions. So I tried to be as flexible and available as possible. I tried to allow some time before the group sessions and kept my door open so that the girls could see me individually if they wished. I told the girls about this option, but only Michelle took advantage of this opportunity. After a while Michelle asked to celebrate her birthday in the group. I was very moved. The group had a discussion about how the girls celebrated their birthdays. It was heartbreaking to hear their stories.

Carmen: Can you believe that my parents never celebrated my birthday?

Nataline: Mine also, and I know why.

Etty: It is upsetting.

Laura: I know what Nataline is talking about. My mother always told me that I was a burden from the day I was born. She always was angry with me, so each year she punished me at my birthday by not buying me a gift.

Etty: Nataline, is that why you never celebrated your birthday? Can you tell us? [Nataline remains silent.]

Lisa: Let's celebrate our birthdays including yours [she faces me], but you have to bring a cake for yourself.

Michelle: I suggest that we copy our cassette and give it to Etty as a gift for her birthday.

Etty: That's a great idea. It will be a pleasure for me to celebrate all our birthdays here, together.

By now it was a few months into the course of treatment, and we had missed celebrating only Nataline's birthday. Michelle asked me to buy her a roll of film; she said that she would like to have memories of her family. Nataline mentioned that she would like to take pictures of her mother because she did not have any pictures of her as an adult. It was very clear to me that having pictures of their loved ones spoke to the girls' fear of losing them. I bought Michelle a roll of film. I also gave a roll of film to Nataline, whose birthday had passed uncelebrated. I said, "I'm sorry that I did not bring a gift on your birthday. I didn't know you well enough then to realize that, even though you did not ask, you really would have liked a present from me." Touched, she responded, "How sweet."

I believe that sharing my feelings of tenderness toward Nataline enabled her to discover her own tender feelings, which she had always resisted. Nataline and the other girls, who had been so deprived emotionally and traumatized in so many ways were starving for tenderness. They had never experienced their parents or others significant in their lives as tender toward them, so they were, to say the least, cautious about expressing tenderness toward others.

It was very interesting to listen to what the girls asked for their birthdays.

Carmen asked for chocolate cake, Coke, and French fries. After she blew out the candles, she cried while silently making her wish. The girls were quiet, communicating only by glancing at each other. They seemed very sad.

The sisters, Lisa and Dee, wanted to celebrate their birthdays together. They both asked for "glitter colors" to make pictures by sprinkling colored glitter over glue. When the time came for the birthday celebration, they were excited that I had not only remembered to buy exactly what they had asked for but that I had given them even more colors than they expected. But they were concerned that I was spending too much money.

Clearly, the transition from negative to positive transference was heightened. Further solidifying this shift, Lisa and Dee offered to share their glitter colors with the group so that the girls could use them not only during the birthday celebration, but during subsequent sessions. While the girls were working on their glitter projects, however, I had to be silent. I must say, though, that my being silent and the girls' making colorful pictures provided a few sessions of joy-permeated relaxation.

The girls looked as though they were in a hypnotic state as they concentrated on putting the glitter colors on the glue at the right places.

At the end of one session, the sisters gave me their gifts for my birthday, two paintings with the glitter colors. I was moved. Dee's painting was two eyes with arrows pointing toward them; one eye was tearful. She explained that people looked at her as weird and that she cried too much. Lisa wrote on her painting the words "love" and "peace." She explained that, even though she wished to have peace with her mother, it wasn't going to happen. Her mother had disappointed her too many times. But, she added, she loved her mother.

Laura asked me to buy her a blank cassette so she could record the girls' favorite songs. Over several sessions each girl brought her favorite tape and asked to record a specific song. Laura suggested that the girls record for my birthday a song "Here and Now" by the singer Luther Vandross, which they often sang during sessions. The song was about loving, caring, happiness, and touching.

Music was always in the background during sessions. They played the cassette they had created of their favorite songs. Some of the girls performed while singing together as if they were on stage. While they performed, they laughed and made jokes. "Here And Now" was their favorite, and the girls would often sing it. We discussed the questions of love, caring, and touching.

For her next birthday Nataline asked me to buy her a cheesecake. (This time she was willing to ask for tenderness.) When she blew out the candles, she said that she was sure the girls could guess what she wished for. She told us that she had written a paper for school on AIDS. For the first time the girls were open about how their parents had acquired the HIV virus. Discussing their mothers' drug use and promiscuity led Laura to state she had been raped. Nataline tried to encourage Carmen to "tell them." Carmen explained that she was not going to share her "very upset story" during Nataline's birthday. She promised to tell us at the next session, but she did not keep her promise.

Michelle asked us to surprise her for her next birthday. She had always dreamed that her family or friends would throw a surprise party. In response to my attempt to understand her wish, she said that it was nice to see that people thought about her. The sisters gave Michelle one of their glitter color pictures. Carmen gave a picture of herself so that Michelle would have a memory of her. Laura brought a cassette. Nataline brought a collage poster and emphasized the long time she had spent preparing her gift. I bought Michelle a notebook diary.

Later in treatment Michelle shared with us parts of her diary. Reading to us from her own life story, she described how painful it had been to move from one family to another during the first 12 years of her life. Her return to live with her stranger/mother at age 12 was traumatic. She was physically abused by her mother. "We were having things that were not supposed to happen to us [siblings]," she wrote. Her mother repeatedly threatened that one day Michelle and her siblings would wake up and not find her anymore. "I am young but, with the stuff I have been through, I am older," she had written in her diary. Michelle had a formula for survival: "You don't let bad things that happened to you to strike your life. You have to survive, you have to go on, you have to recover."

The girls, who were at that point regressed children in their most needy and vulnerable state of losing their parents to AIDS, were searching for parental love from their friends as well as from me. The girls needed me to create a nonjudgmental, sincere, caring, warm, maternal atmosphere. Lacking this atmosphere, the girls would continue to feel lonely and abandoned, the same unbearable experience that filled their lives.

Such a maternal atmosphere evokes what Balint (1952) called "primary love." The girls wanted my tenderness without having to give anything in return—an unconditional love none of them had ever experienced. These deprived girls were so angry that their own tenderness had become difficult for them to feel. They fought against love and drove it away. Berman (1986) has observed that patients who have suffered severe narcissistic injury during childhood characteristically withdraw part of their capacity to love and keep it locked up within the self. At the beginning of treatment, there was within the group a repeated cycle of disruption and repair (Benjamin, 1992).[1] After I had survived a few rounds of the girls' attacking me without my retaliating, a heightened relatedness and tenderness evolved among all of us.

During one session, Michelle described having physical fights with her mother when she came home late. Her mother would hit her and call her names. On occasion, Michelle had hit her mother back. She wondered where she might go if she again ran away from her mother. She asked for my suggestions. She smiled but did not respond to me when I asked if she had some idea in mind.

Then Nataline described her conflicts with her uncle, who repeatedly accused her of stealing money from her grandmother. She believed that he was the one who stole the money. She ran away from home but returned after a few hours because she did not have any place to go. Nataline said, with a smile, that maybe both of them would be able to go to "someone." And they both looked at me.

When I coughed during one session, Dee suggested that I looked sick and should stay home. Lisa added that, when she met her mother, she was coughing all the time. We discussed their fears of getting AIDS. Nataline asked me if I used drugs and if I practiced safe sex. I returned these questions to them. Laura was the only one who admitted that she used drugs, and the other girls just looked at each other. Nataline said, her voice becoming louder, that she would never use drugs because that was what killed her mother. "I am not going to do it to my kids," she said sadly.

---

[1] See Winnicott's (1971) discussion on destruction and survival and Pizer's (1992) discussion on negotiation of ruthlessness and concern and ongoing creation and destruction of intersubjectivity.

Erotic Phase
Confusion Between Tenderness and Passion

Her feelings were confused.
She is confused because she gets mixed messages.
I say, "I don't want you for sex."
My mother says, "He is only with you for sex."

In the third phase, which overlapped the termination phase, the traumatic experience not only was discussed but was enacted in the therapeutic relation. The feelings of safety that had been established in the previous phase allowed the girls to begin to talk about the sexual traumas they had suffered. Talking, in turn, led to their enacting different aspects of these traumas. The residue of these traumatic experiences created a confusion between the safety and tenderness of the previous phase and the unsettling and disturbing feelings of passion. We engaged in a dance in which the girls demonstrated their confusion verbally and nonverbally. The girls essentially were saying, "We are confused by you— do we feel tenderness or passion?" and I questioned myself about my feelings toward the girls: "I am confused by you—is my tenderness passionate?"

As discussed earlier, Ferenczi felt that a crucial aspect of trauma came at the point when a child's play was misconstrued by an abusive adult as sexual seductiveness. It is this "confusion" that for Ferenczi can make it impossible for a patient to find a way of expressing what had happened. Beyond the confusion of playfulness and tenderness as sexually seductive, the girls of the group were "double tongue-tied." First, they were confused by the secrecy relating to their childhood experiences (parents' drug use, physical and sexual abuse). Later, they also had to keep another secret because their parents were dying from a stigmatized disease. The girls needed their parents' help to understand and verbalize what had happened, and the dying parents were unable to provide this help. Although the girls were tongue-tied, a part of themselves wished to be helped to speak about the trauma so that they could feel less alone, less confused, and less dysfunctional.

These girls came to deal with issues of sexuality relatively late in the group therapy. They were young, sexually mature, alive girls, but for most of the first year of treatment they kept at bay issues of desire because of their more immediate issues of trauma over death.

Dee cried and covered her face with her hands while describing how her mother's boyfriend and her cousin had molested her at night when she was 13 years old. As noted in chapter 2, they threatened to harm her mother if she told anyone about the abuse, so a year passed before she told her mother. Dee felt ashamed that her sister, Lisa, who shared the bedroom with her, might have watched the abuse but protected her by never mentioning it.

Since the time of the abuse, she had not been able to sleep at night. She was having flashbacks of the rape. She also had nightmares but refused to share them with me. Dee never brought the sexual abuse into the group.

Laura reported experiencing intrusive memories of having been molested. These memories emerged two years before she started therapy when a friend was raped by an uncle, who was then arrested and jailed. Laura's difficulties in school, and her sense that she "can't remember what really happened," have intensified. Exploring her sexual molestation, Laura said, "This real bad thing happened to me when I was very young [she was six years old]. You know, 'cause I was like molested real young by this guy, and I keep thinking about this."

She shifted in her chair, tearful, momentarily avoiding direct eye contact. The perpetrator was her brother's best friend. "I remember he always used to touch me, and he kept putting his fingers where he shouldn't," she said. I asked if she was referring to her vagina, and she nodded yes. She continued, saying tearfully that she wanted to kill him— "he did not have to do that." After we had discussed the importance of her sharing these experiences with her mother and the family social worker, she agreed to disclose the abuse. She refused, however, to come to any more individual sessions and asked to be treated only in group.

Carmen's cousin had attempted to rape her, but she succeeded in escaping. Her mother did not press charges against the cousin because she thought that there was not enough proof. Having herself been raped as a teenager, she felt that prosecution would be too difficult to deal with. After Carmen left treatment, Nataline hinted that Carmen had given birth to a child, a son living in the South. But this speculation was never confirmed.

Although Nataline did not confirm my suspicions, I had reason to believe that she too had been sexually abused, probably raped. Her mother and grandmother both complained that Nataline had spread a rumor that she had had an abortion. The girls wrote a "motherhood" play, in which Nataline played the role of a young woman who got pregnant by her mother's boyfriend and was forced by her mother to get an abortion.

Michelle was detached emotionally as she described her sexual abuse with few details. It sounded as though she were telling a story about another girl. She related how her mother's boyfriend had raped her twice, the first time a year before treatment began and the second time six months later. She said her mother's boyfriend who committed the first rape had been drunk. He had locked up her mother, her younger sister, and her and threatened to harm them with a knife if they did not obey him. Since her sister had her period, he raped Michelle twice (one time for her sister), once while her mother and sister watched. And the second time when her mother was absent.

Michelle did not know how many times he had raped her sister. She only knew that her sister became pregnant and had to have an abortion. Michelle added that, since her mother and maternal grandmother had also been raped, she did not ever want to give birth because a girl would be raped. She wanted only boys.

She described, in addition to sexual abuse, emotional abuse by her mother. For example, if she did not clean the house on time, her mother would punish her by demanding that she stay alone naked in the bathroom for hours. When her punishment was over, she had to leave the bathroom naked to get her clothes. It was on one of these occasions that her mother's boyfriend first saw her naked.

Not only were they sexually abused, the girls grew up in sexually overstimulating homes. It was striking to learn how the girls' lives in some ways paralleled their mothers'. During parent guidance sessions (without the presence of Carmen) Carmen's mother disclosed that she had been raped three times before the age of 19. Dee's mother was raped once when she was homeless. During parent guidance sessions (without the presence of the sisters), she disclosed to me that she herself had been sexually molested by her brother at the age of six. A few years later she was raped by six men. The three girls—Michelle, Carmen, and Dee—knew about their mothers' sexual abuse, but did not know the details. Each of the mothers believed that by telling the girls now they would prevent their daughters from suffering as they had—even though the girls had already been sexually abused.

Michelle, Laura, and Carmen knew about their mothers' promiscuous relationships and were themselves acting out sexually. They saw their mothers go out with different men who came and went. So, naturally, Laura would not accept her mother's demand that she come home early while her mother returned home from parties in the morning hours or invited men to stay overnight with her.

Toward the end of the middle phase the girls started to explore their sexuality. Michelle and Laura described their relationships with boys in detail, but Carmen was more secretive. Michelle and Laura discussed their wish to get pregnant so that they could force their boyfriends to stay with them, maybe even marry them.

The sisters were not involved in such high-risk behaviors. Lisa and Dee avoided any relationships with boys. All the girls, even those who were not sexually active, agreed that there was no sense using condoms because "all condoms have holes." Nataline was the first to bring up the subject, and the other girls joined her with this rationale for not practicing safe sex. All my attempts to provide some sex education were unsuccessful.

When I suggested that we discuss different ways to practice safe sex, Nataline asked if I practiced safe sex. Michelle commented that I probably practiced safe sex but then asked me what prophylactic I used. Laura was mostly interested at what age I had first had intercourse with a boy. Carmen asked Laura why she assumed that I was straight; maybe I was a lesbian. I tried to explore the meanings of the girls' different questions instead of simply answering them. But the girls refused to continue to discuss this subject with me. They announced that they would discuss practicing safe sex only if I answered their questions. Looking back at this dialogue with the girls I realize that I failed to discuss with them the importance of having these questions answered specifically by me.

Laura brought up the issue of her sexuality when she told the girls about the two abortions she had undergone and the pregnancy she was planning. When I asked her to share her thoughts and feelings about abortion and about her wish to be pregnant, Nataline shouted at me that it was none of my business and stopped the discussion. The other girls did not disclose their feelings about this issue and remained quiet, listening to Laura and Nataline.

Later in session, in relation to Nataline's AIDS project in school that she had brought in to read in the group, most of the girls did discuss safe sex. Dee and Lisa did not participate in this discussion. Michelle talked about the risk of hurting one's body when having an abortion. Laura mentioned that she had been sexually abused, and Nataline cryptically asked Carmen to tell the group something known only to the two of them, but Carmen refused.

Michelle, who had disclosed to her mother that she was sexually active, went with her mother to a gynecologist, who recommended birth control pills. Michelle shared her feelings about this experience with the girls. Five girls discussed their experiences with gynecologists, and all of them focused on the pain they had felt during the physician's finger and speculum penetration.

Lisa, the only one who had not met with a gynecologist, wondered about the gender of their gynecologists. All the girls had gone to female gynecologists. Lisa stated that she was planning to go only to a male gynecologist, but she refused to elaborate. Michelle suggested, laughing, that if the doctor was handsome and young she might not feel the pain. After a few sessions Michelle shared with the girls the side effects she was experiencing from the birth control pills. Nataline brought to the next session an article from a teen magazine that debated the use of birth control pills. The girls tried to convince Michelle to stop using the pills. Nataline said, "It's better to give birth than to hurt your body." I learned that education about sex, whether good advice or not, would have to come from the girls themselves.

Michelle first met her new boyfriend when he also was a patient in the clinic. She was unhappy because he did not express any tender feelings toward her and became more anxious when he told her that he was not ready to have sexual intercourse with her. At each session the girls were very interested in hearing about Michelle's relationship, especially because they knew the boy. During one session, as Michelle danced seductively while listening to the radio, the girls expressed their concern that she might be using drugs. Michelle denied that she was and said she was only disappointed that she had not yet had sex with her new boyfriend, and she thought her mother had a crush on him. In another session, Michelle related that she had discovered that her boyfriend had dated another girl. She wrote this poem about her feelings.

Is It Love?

I have a feeling it's weird
I never felt it before,
but it's here when I'm around you.
My heart beats faster.
I start sweating, my knees feel weak
No one knows what is going on.

But, I wish someone knew.
I wonder if it's love . . .

During this phase Michelle initiated discussions about abortion, and the girls explored their conflicts on this issue. Nataline had also started to date and was proud to tell the girls that he had a lot of money and a car and had bought her many expensive presents. But her boyfriend had recently broken up with her to date one of her best girlfriends. She regretted that she had practiced safe sex because she believed that if she had gotten pregnant he would not have left her.

Michelle wrote a summary essay about our discussions on sexuality:

> My opinion is you had the pleasure of the penis inside so take the responsibility with it.
>
> The reasons I am against abortion is because if you're out there having sex then you know what can happen while sex is happening. You know that babies come from having sex. You're not stupid.
>
> In some cases I agree with abortion. If you were raped, then how are you supposed to raise a child that you did not really want [her younger sister who was raped had an abortion]. Then again, there is adoption. But, why do you have to go through the pain of child birth? Another reason I agree with it is, if you do not have the money and cannot give that baby what it deserves, then, have the abortion.

During the erotic phase, which proved to be the termination phase, all the girls manifested tender and passionate transference. Discussing sexuality shifted to enacting their sexuality.

Michelle usually dressed in unisex clothing but she occasionally danced a pretend strip tease. Some of the other girls dressed provocatively and flirted with me; others did so openly, while seemingly totally unaware of their impact on others. Carmen, Laura, Lisa, and Michelle wore "low riders," exposing their belly buttons. Laura regularly appeared for sessions dressed in a skin-tight miniskirt and a halter top. As she sat provocatively draped in the chair and gazed invitingly at me, she frequently railed against boys who made passes at her.

I felt an aggressiveness in response to the girls' seductive behavior, which I experienced as coercive. I felt frozen. Concerned that things might get out of control, I pulled back to a more parental role. I wanted to convey to the girls that sexual feelings and seductive behavior are a normal part of their sexual development, but I felt that I had failed on a few occasions to maintain the appropriate therapeutic boundaries by putting limits on the girls' seductive behavior during sessions. Since the girls resisted my attempts to interpret their behavior, I asked myself whether their oversexualized demeanor during the sessions ought to be restrained. Their parents had not provided adequate limits, nor had they had been able to serve as models for appropriate demeanor. As a result, the girls were not able to control their drives. They did not know where the boundaries were.

On the other hand, should I try to create an environment in which they could reenact their sexual traumas? Within the seductive transference to me, the girls' flirtations were now more clearly sexually tinged than ever before. Laura, Michelle, and Dee sometimes seductively draped themselves on the armchair, exposing more of their legs than usual. The girls compared their hairstyles and makeup and devalued me as just not quite fashionably "with it." I found myself wondering if, in fact, it was not time for a new hairstyle.

Nataline and Michelle talked about their fantasies of being lesbians. Nataline suggested that she would be the male figure. Michelle later said that she would like Nataline to be her sister. They talked about lesbians who made love only by touching, without penetrating. They could be more comfortable with one another than they could ever be with boys, they said. They talked about their confusion with their boyfriends: did their boyfriends really love them or were the boys nice to them only to get them to agree to "have sex"?

Sometimes Nataline, Carmen, and Michelle would pull up their T-shirts to show off their bellies. They talked about their physical changes. At other times Michelle and Laura would show each other a new bra or underwear. I asked how they felt about exposing their bodies or watching other girls.

Michelle said that it reminded her of stripping at parties in the past. Nataline said that she was very happy that she had lost weight, and Carmen said that she did not care about her weight because the boys did not care. Laura had terminated already by the time of this discussion, and Lisa stayed quiet. Dee was restless and left, for the first time, to go to the restroom and was out of the room for almost 10 minutes; the girls did not usually leave during the sessions.

It was after the work on Michelle's and Nataline's losses that Michelle began presenting fragments of her memories of being raped. Exploring her memories about her sexual abuse precipitated a kind of confusion of tongues (Ferenczi, 1933) that brought her needs for tenderness and her experiences of disturbing passionate encounters into conflict. Her mother's boyfriend, from whom she had sought tenderness, had reciprocated with violent passion. Nataline tried to shift our discussion to another subject, but Michelle insisted that we talk about these traumas. Nataline felt threatened by Michelle's story of being raped and increased her resistance. Nataline blamed me for forcing Michelle to talk about the rapes. She cursed at me—"Fuck, bitch, asshole."

Nataline felt that I had failed her just as her mother had. She was looking for something special in a mother figure. But, if I had been responsive to Nataline's need to defend against working through her traumatic experiences, I would not have been able to respond to Michelle's need to uncover her sexual trauma. By identifying with Michelle, Nataline created a situation where I had to choose between them, and, regardless of the choice I made, I would lose. I admitted to the girls that I was conflicted about whether to follow Michelle's wish to explore her trauma or to delay this exploration because Nataline was not ready for this type of work. I also expressed to the group my struggle about giving advice because of my worry that giving advice might be perceived by Nataline as controlling and intrusive. The girls did not respond to my confession.

When I suggested to Nataline that she might feel toward me feelings of disappointment similar to those she felt toward her mother, she said that I could not be her mother because, "You don't give advice. You're only here one hour a week. You don't help. I still have my problems." In what was perhaps another empathic failure, I did not respond to this expression of her need for an available mother. I said, "You want more from me. You want my advice, and you want me to be more present physically in your life." Nataline was so angry (and underneath so hurt and rejected) that she said that she could not tolerate being in the same room with me, much less continuing a relationship with me.

Every move I made with these girls had the potential of being perceived as abusive. After Carmen, Dee, and Lisa had terminated therapy during a session for which Nataline did not show up, Michelle gave me her camera and asked me to take pictures of her in seductive poses. I asked Michelle for her thoughts and feelings about asking me to take those pictures. She told me to keep quiet and to take the pictures.

While I was silently taking those pictures, she started to describe in detail her rape experiences. This was the first time that Michelle had described the rape in detail accompanied by the full range of emotions: anger, sadness, guilt, shame, and excitement. While she was describing the second rape, she stopped posing. She trembled, wept, held me physically, put her head on my lap while I caressed her head. I did not explore with

Michelle our mutual touching. It was a painful moment that we shared, and we both spontaneously needed this human touching. Exploring its meanings at the time would have felt like detachment rather than the contact she needed. At the end of this session, she finally expressed relief.

The girls' erotic transferences stirred up in me an anxiety that kept me from intervening. The girls reacted unconsciously, increasing their sexual behavior during sessions in order to bring my attention to this important issue in their life. Moreover, their longing for tenderness, which they presented as homoerotic feelings, had less access to my consciousness. Therefore I had a difficult time interpreting their interactions with me as well with the other girls. I believe that, in working with patients who were sexually abused as children and who felt at that time confused between their abusers' tenderness and the abusers' passion, we therapists reenact the scenario. At the same time, I felt tremendous tenderness toward the girls who were losing their parents to AIDS. But this tenderness, I believe, evoked their erotic transference.

It is inevitable that therapists who treat traumatized patients, and especially adolescents, will at times experience sexual feelings that may be dissociated. Unfamiliar homosexual and bisexual feelings may emerge, as well as identifications with sexual aggresssors and voyeuristic fantasies (Pearlman and Saakvitne, 1995). Homosexual transferences are more frequent when both patient and analyst are females (Lester, 1985).

Male psychoanalysts (Freud, 1915; Blum, 1973) have long reported female patients' developing strong erotic transferences to them. The defensive nature of this reaction, the disturbance in reality testing, and the connection to resistance have long been recognized. An analyst's distaste for exploring a patient's erotic transference may, however, be an indicator of countertransference resistance (Gorkin, 1985). Gorkin notes that, when analysts avoid discussing sexual issues, patients may unconsciously understand that their sexuality threatens their analysts. Gorkin believed that sexual countertransference emerging in his awareness helped him to understand his patients.

Fionna Gardner (1999) argues that exploring these feelings, of both the patient and the analyst, can provide a medium of transformation whereby what felt abusive can turn into something creative in the course of the healing process. Gardner believes that erotic aspects of the transference are always present in sexually abused patients. She adds that the erotic countertransference and transference feelings of those patients emerge within their psyches, within the analyst's psyches, and in the space between them.

In my countertransference feelings with the girls, I despaired of ever being able to reach them. At the same time, however, I was determined to try to understand their dynamics. They resisted my tenderness because it felt like the intimacy that had been forced on them by their abusers. In addition, the betrayal by their parents, who had not protected them, led to similar expectations of their transference feelings toward me. I felt that I was being tested all over again, and the slightest slip, such as being five minutes late, would be construed as an enormous betrayal.

Their feeling of powerlessness took its opposite form in therapy in this, the termination phase. They were trying very hard to present themselves as powerful (a reaction formation) so as to defend against humiliation. What had been passive—their being the victims—became active—their becoming the abusers in an identification with the aggressor, so to speak (A. Freud, 1936).

The girls were expressing their object hunger by their seductive behavior. I shifted between facilitating the expression of their sexual feelings and inhibiting their sexual seductiveness toward me. I found myself mostly deemphasizing sexual issues, and I became immersed in the girls' transferences. Being aware of this interaction led to my struggle to find my way out by raising the girls' awareness of our transference–countertransference enactments. I tried to point out to them that, because they were growing up in a sexually overstimulating environment, the only way they felt they could communicate their yearning for contact with me and other was through their seductive behavior. They remained quiet and made no response.

In our group, the confusion between tenderness and passion brought up a few questions: Did my patients perceive my tenderness as passion, sexual expression? Did my tenderness function as a defense against my erotic, voyeuristic, and sexual feelings? What were the meanings of my choices in interpreting and acknowledging our mutual erotic feelings? Did I feel comfortable with my own sexual feelings? Did I convey to my patients an openness to our sexual feelings? What concerns did I have about the generation boundaries, the sexual provocations, and the tension in the room? What was the meaning of my decision not to comment on the girls' provocative physical appearance? Should I make a judgment about the girls' sexual behavior during sessions? Did their sexual behaviors signify that a developmental breakdown had taken place?

These traumatized girls were not ready to deal with their sexuality. For doing so would bring up their traumatic memories of being raped. They were at a developmental stage that led to the search for their identity and body image. They experienced their bodies as damaged. Exploring their sexual abuse was unbearable, as was connecting to their experience of losing their parents, who were unavailable and did not protect them. As much as losing their parents to AIDS was traumatic, they were able to work through this traumatic experience. But, for adolescents struggling to find a mature way to interact sexually with others, being sexually abused led to more confusion. Working through their sexual traumas would evoke such feelings as humiliation, shame, guilt, anger, and disgust. These feelings would touch their deepest, most vulnerable soul. They were not ready for this work at this traumatic period of their lives.

Erotic feelings also emerged in my work with some of my male patients. David, a 13-year-old Hispanic boy who looked his age, was court-referred to the clinic for leaving home for hours at a time and sometimes overnight. David stole money from his mother and ran away. He had been diagnosed with ADHD and had been on Ritalin for a few years.

David reported feeling angry at his mother. He blamed her for his not having friends, since she did not let him go out. So he ran away. He stole money to have fun with his friends. He also blamed his mother for placing him in a special education class. David reported watching his father beating his mother. He used to hide under his bed at those times.

The mother, Ms. L., was born and raised in New York City. She is the only sister among five brothers. When Ms. L. was 10 years old, her father died. Her mother, who was overwhelmed by raising six children, asked her parents to raise Ms. L, who was only 17 years old when she lost her grandparents. David was born five years prior to his parents' marriage. The parents were divorced three years later, and the father was never involved in his son's life.

David was an unplanned child. At the time of pregnancy Ms. L. was homeless and lived in a shelter until she gave birth in normal delivery. Ms. L. described her son as an active boy, who was never full when fed. Ms. L. emphasized that David had always had behavior problems, and that was why he was in special education classes. He had attended four schools during the last two years beforee his treatment with me.

David's acting-out behavior seemed to be in response to his struggle to negotiate the adolescent stage of separation-individuation. On one hand, David wanted to go out and to do things on his own or with friends. On the other hand, David had poor judgment and showed poor impulse control.

During sessions David presented a picture of enormous isolation. Because his mother did not let him leave home on weekends, he was left to play computer games for hours. His mother did not wish to engage with him and made no efforts to involve him in the family activities. He had a certain way of drifting off in school, and he did not know what had actually been said in class. David interacted with me in a listless fashion. He used a minimum number of words. We were connected by nonthreatening boredom. Soon, however, he began to lose control. He became physically aggressive; he enjoyed spilling his soda on my bag or my appointment books. I, in turn, became at times verbally judgmental. But reminding myself of his terrible story of his childhood brought back empathic feelings toward him.

Two years into treatment, David began to share with me his vulnerability and pain at having witnessed his father abuse his mother physically. David elicited strong compassionate feelings in me. I found myself wanting somehow to compensate for the horror in his life. I extended the sessions and tried to plan my vacation so that he would miss the fewest sessions.

When David was 15 years old, a dramatic change occurred. David initiated "Spit," a high-contact card game. In "Spit," both players try to smack their hands down on the winning pile of cards. Playing the game, though, David left his hands on mine and refused to take them off. Although I tried to keep within the boundaries drawn by a rule against touching, he had succeeded in breaking that therapeutic rule by arguing that touching is inevitable in the game.

I felt uncomfortable; I was concerned that he would experience my tenderness as a sexual overture. I asked myself why I felt this way specifically with David, and not with other traumatized male adolescents I had treated. I could not find words for creating interpretations and exploring the therapeutic interactions. At that time I did not want to believe that I might have felt attracted to this bright, handsome boy. Only after termination was I able to recognize my erotic feelings toward him.

For a long time I engaged with David in a kind of dance when his play manifested erotic transference. Without being fully aware, I kept the secret of the forbidden and avoided an exploration of his feelings toward me. By not discussing David's sexual feelings, by viewing the countertransference as only an asexual, maternal one, I colluded with him. The intensity of treatment (twice a week for three years) might have enhanced the development of an erotic transference in David as he struggled to consolidate his sense of sexual and personal identity.

David's school performance improved dramatically. Comparing the teachers' comments from his school report in the beginning of treatment with the comments made two years later, I could see a shift as the teachers moved from dislike to admiration. To some extent I echoed this shift.

When he was 16 years old, David moved with his mother to another state to live closer to her family. Though he quickly adjusted to his new school and established close relationships with teachers and friends, David was upset and angry at being forced to move again. "My mother again messed up my life," he said. We did not have much time to work through a termination process because of the abruptness of the move.

I feel much affection for David and had an investment in his future. I hope that David will carry his academic and social achievements with him. One session before the last, David asked me to buy him a "goodbye" gift, cards that would be from me. We explored the significance of the cards in our relationship. I bought him what he had requested, and, surprisingly, he brought me a gift, a gift certificate to a movie theater. He explained that he wanted me to have fun with my husband. I thought to myself that he wished he could be the one who would join me. I was moved by his effort to make an intimate connection with me and by his effort to make himself face reality.

The treatment resolution of the erotic transference may be critical to an adolescent's developing a resolute sense of his own identity (Atkinson and Gabbard, 1995). In my countertransferential feelings with David, my stance guarded against psychic violation of incest taboos involving transferential parent/analyst seduction of the adolescent patient. Moreover, since his father had physically abused David, I was extremely cautious not to intrude.

Lester (1985), a female analyst, has noted the absence of reports in the literature about male patients developing erotic transference to their female analysts:

> It is hypothesized that the expression of strong erotic urges to the female analyst by the male patient is somewhat inhibited by the fantasy of the overwhelming pre-oedipal mother. In contrast, such erotic feelings are freely expressed by the female patient [p. 292].

Lester's hypothesis is just one of the explanations in the literature for the absence of clinical reports on erotic transference of male adolescents with female analysts. Atkinson and Gabbard (1995) discuss analysts' concerns in exploring adolescents' erotic transferences: fear of parental retaliation if they learn about this line of exploration; the possibility of allegations of sexual misconduct; and worries that they may have manipulated the adolescent patients into having such thoughts. Gabbard (1994) believes, therefore, that, as a defensive reaction, the analyst's countertransference takes the shape of being an all-giving, benign, omnipotent, and asexual parental figure.

III

FINDING A TREATMENT PLAN

Gender in the Dyad

Lay your head on my pillow
Show me what you said is true
Let's talk
Tell me how you really feel
Just relax
I have to think
Tell me
Maybe our love
Can be saved
Just let me think.

What is the meaning of gender? Freud and other classical analysts derived their ideas about gender from their views on the anatomical difference between the sexes. Derrida (1976, 1978) argued that Western thought in general wishes to avoid uncertainty and to claim universal truth for the prevailing cultural categories of masculine and feminine. Thus, psychological rigidity is the norm vis-à-vis the category of gender. Derrida believed that masculinity and femininity are not opposites but actually coconstruct each other and have meaning only in their relation to each other.

Like Derrida, many contemporary gender-identity theorists view development as a relational process of integrating identifications and separation issues (e.g., Chodorow, 1978; Fast, 1984; Benjamin, 1991). These theorists move the struggle with gender difference from the oedipal to the preoedipal period of separation-individuation, the rapprochement phase (Mahler, Pine, and Bergman, 1975). During this period, girls identity with their fathers in a relationship embracing mutual recognition of each other. Benjamin (1988) holds that, because of gender inequality, the dialectic of assertiveness and recognition breaks down in that phase.

For some youngsters, like Yael, whom we met in chapter 1, gender contradictions are experienced as traumatizing and therefore lead to splits in the self.

Yael was 15 years old when she was hospitalized in a psychiatric inpatient unit, a hospitalization that lasted for more than a year. She initiated her hospitalization after she had lost weight, presented amenorrhea, and was suicidal.

Yael's mother went back to work a month after she gave birth. During Yael's first year, a few babysitters took care of her, and then she was enrolled in a nursery school. She was sleep deprived and was on medication to calm her down.

Yael has one brother, a year older than she. Her mother was preoccupied with her son and did not pay much attention to Yael when Yael was born. As she got older, Yael would pretend to be sick in order to get her mother's attention. Her father, retired from the police department, worked as a stockbroker. Her mother was a school nurse. The parental relationship was in turmoil, and the children witnessed the parents' throwing dishes at each other, yelling, and cursing each other. At these moments Yael, afraid that her parents would become aggressive toward her, would lock herself in the bathroom.

Although Yael's mother was unavailable emotionally, her father was, as Yael said, "the love of my life" during her early years. When she was a child her father liked to hug and kiss her on her lips, and she liked to sit on his lap until she fell asleep. She often slept with him in her parents' bed while the mother slept in Yael's bed.

Yael began menstruating and started to develop secondary sex characteristics when she was 13 years old. She became depressed, lost weight, suffered from sleep disturbances, and would stay in her room for days without taking a shower. Then, because she felt dirty, she would sleep on the floor rather than in her bed. Her academic performance deteriorated dramatically. For two months she refused to go to school. Her relations with others were schizoid in nature; her primary relational conflict was her ambivalence about attachment to others. She craved closeness and yet distanced herself from others.

When describing this breakdown to me, she drew a wall, which was both metaphorical and real for her. She went to the trouble of bringing watercolors and paper to the session. She painted a wall that was constructed of stones stacked horizontally on the page, not unlike the Western Wall next to the temple mount in Jerusalem. In the middle of the wall she drew two eyes with blue color (she herself had strikingly black eyes), a nose on the right side of the wall, and, on the left side of the wall, an angry mouth.

Yael felt that the wall had been built all at once during her breakdown, not gradually, stone by stone. Behind the wall was the "real Yael." On the other side of the wall were all the people who could not see the "real Yael."

Her parents described Yael as always liking to eat. She was a chubby child. Her parents used to put the food in the middle of the table, and Yael "ate it all." During her latency period, Yael was overweight and complained that her father would comment on her appearance and her eating habits. Her father, who had been her admirer, now became her enemy. He gave her a hostile look when he believed that she had eaten too much.

When she was 14 years old she went on a strict diet and lost weight, and her father's attitude shifted once again from being hostile to being affectionate. He forced her to eat and threatened to hit her if she did not eat what was expected of her. Although he never did hit her, she always had the feeling that he was going to. What frightened Yael the most was that her father liked her only as an attractive girl with a perfect figure.

Bulimic attacks followed a few months of losing weight. Vomiting followed binges. After vomiting, she felt that she had to change her clothes and clean her room. During this period she developed obsessive–compulsive behaviors. She was obsessed with eating in small bites and as slowly as she could. She could take as long as an hour to eat an apple. She washed her hands as many as 30 times a day. She was careful not to touch her face or her hair, for they were oily and she was worried that by touching herself she would end up with oil in her mouth.

She explained that she experienced food as unclean. It dirtied her body, and it was a risk for others who touched her. During sessions she described the binge experience as a sinking into a vat of tar. She said that it was a false enticement—she expected to find a treasure in the hole but instead she was dirty with tar, unable to clean herself, even after many showers. Only petroleum jelly could clean her, but then she was smelly. She believed that I noticed her dirt. Generally, when people touched her, she felt she needed to wash herself. Since her father did not touch her, she believed that he was clean. When she described these idiosyncratic thoughts, she could not sit still and walked restlessly back and forth.

Yael characterized herself as a tomboy who liked to play sports with boys. She felt comfortable with them but did not feel any sexual excitement. She was aggressive toward girls. She had refused to wear skirts since her childhood; she believed that she was too hairy and always wore shirts with long sleeves. She announced to her parents that she did not want to have children.

Yael acknowledged that getting her period had been traumatic for her. She remembered this moment exactly but refused to talk about it. She became confused about her sexual identity. She felt that having a period was like being a baby who uses diapers. She used only pads and refused to use tampons but could not explain why. Wishing to stop her bodily development, she slept on her stomach in the belief that she would be able to stop the development of her breasts. She wished to be asexual, without breasts or genitals. She shared her feeling that the subject of her femininity would not bother her anymore because she had learned that losing weight could stop her period.

There was a clear relationship between Yael's eating disorder and her sexual development, which, in turn, was experienced through the lens of gender identity. Through her eating disorder Yael controlled and reduced the feminine aspects of herself. The eating disorder, moreover, became a means of gaining entrance into the masculine world and thus seemed to free her of anxiety or guilt. To become an adult female was frightening, a fear that was allayed by her identifying with male figures, her father and older brother, whom she perceived as free from such tumultuous feelings.

Yael's breakdown and her suicide attempts might be considered an expression of her intolerable struggles over the integration of her gender, body ego, and sexuality. Her first attempt, swallowing pills, occurred when she was 14 years old, just after her parents had forced her to eat and gain weight. To encourage her, her father commented about how much more feminine she had become, which was a big blow, for she desperately wished to look masculine. For three years, starting at age 14, Yael lost her period as a result of her eating disorder. When her period returned, she made another suicide try by attempting to hang herself.

By virtue of the rigid construction of gender, as it had been transmitted to her through the family milieu, Yael was not allowed to identify with the father's autonomy. Boys are expected to achieve independence and to deny dependence. Masculinity means assertiveness, omnipotence, and individuality, whereas femininity means submission. Nonetheless, her father was the subject of her identification. He was seductive and intrusive and spent many years alternately treating her as his perfect feminine object and as a damaged feminine object. Yael chose masculine identity to regain attention from her masculine mother and to save herself from an oedipal father. Yael struggled with the complexity of her gender identification (see Harris, 1991). Yael's memories of the emotionally absent mother of her early childhood were horrifying: she was an angry, unhappy woman, furious in the face of any expression of her daughter's needs and dependency. Even though Yael's father nurtured her emotionally when he was present, he was often absent physically because of his work as a police officer. Then, when Yael reached puberty, he became controlling, and her world crumpled.

Deprived of a stable and permanent caretaker, Yael experienced the emotional abandonment as traumatic. That kind of emotional abandonment can be the worst form of trauma (Ferenczi, 1931b, p. 138; 1933, pp. 163–164). Yael's difficulties sleeping and her general restlessness attest to renewed separation anxiety and depressive states.

Her gender dysphoria erupted as she sought emotional refuge by renewing her latent cross-gender identification. She had been aware early on of her anatomical differences from boys. Her mother recalled that when Yael was three years old she told a boy, "I know that I will have a peepee [penis] like yours." The mother, who was more proud of her son than of her daughter, revealed some of her own gender-identity issues during family sessions. The mother did not feel good about herself as a woman and was not pleased to have a daughter. Yael felt that, if she were a boy, she would gain her mother's affection. She maintained the "boyness" (Harris, 1991) position to avoid uncovering the female vulnerability that evoked despair and loss.

She chose a female therapist because of the defeat, disappointment, and longing she felt with respect to the longing for her mother—arguably, Yael was seeking to work out the basic issues of abandonment and gender in displacement. She could not, of course, explain her request to have a female therapist when she was first hospitalized. She teased me about putting on makeup and lipstick. "You look like you're in costume," she said. She also commented that pants fit me better than skirts or dresses. Yael wanted me to be a woman who looked like a man. She did not like my colorful clothes. She wore black pants and T-shirts, as her mother did. She was envious that I looked thinner than she and said she wished I were fatter.

I saw Yael three times a week. In addition, since I worked in the hospital emergency unit three other days, I visited her frequently to see how she was doing. There were extra sessions and scheduled phone contacts to create a holding environment for her. I saw the family once a week. During the first few months of treatment with me, Yael was quiet and passive. She expected me to "feed" her, which is what I mostly did. I asked her about her feelings and her interactions with others and kept quiet when she did not respond. I wondered if she might perceive my being active and directive with her as intrusive and controlling, as she experienced her parents. Later, as I got to know Yael better, I learned that she needed me to be active; she could then see me as involved and caring. Nonetheless, metaphorically, any attempt to "feed" her ended up with her "vomiting," saying that nothing could help her, or with her "starving herself" by becoming silent and passive. Her metaphor for her experience at that time was that she wanted to be in the sea and let the waves work for her.

Her suicidal ideation put me in a chronically hyperalert state. There were moments when I felt frustrated, impotent, and depressed as I watched her suffer but was unable to get through to her. I never gave up, though, for I felt that Yael needed to see me fighting for her life. I was tormented about having to forbid Yael to leave the unit during weekends, which would provoke her tearful rage toward me.

After a few months of resisting awareness (Gill, 1982) of her feelings toward me, Yael started to describe her therapeutic experience with me in metaphors. It was important for her to stay with the image of the wall that she had built when she got her period. She believed that she and I walked on two parallel paths toward the wall. The goal was not to reach the wall, she believed, but to smash only one stone in the wall, so that the wall would have a window.

She was afraid that someone would smash the wall and see the real Yael. She wanted to see herself first, but she was frightened of discovering who she really was. She was the most fearful that the whole wall would be smashed in a moment, as quickly as it had been built up.

Yael found it was very painful to explore her possible sexual orientation in relation to the nurses, other female patients, and me. She became close only to female figures. Although the eating binges stopped while she was in the unit, they continued at home. Her explanation was that in the unit she did not feel alone; at home she felt invisible. As family therapy progressed, however, her binges also stopped at home.

Preparing to leave the inpatient unit to go to a group residential care facility, she asked me to make sure that she would have a female therapist. When I asked why, she said, "I understand that I am struggling with my sexual identity. I need to feel warmth from a therapist, something that only a woman can provide." Although she found it difficult to be more specific and direct toward me, she had learned to appreciate my deep investment in her psychic and relational life. She did not report any sexual feelings; it seemed that she was not ready at that point to work through this anxiety-provoking issue. She began, through, to be able to tolerate her feminine self and to begin a process of integrating her gender multiplicity. She gained weight, her period returned, she did not have binges, and her spirit became hopeful.

In retrospect, the relational approach to gender opened things up for me. As I looked back on Yael's case, obviously Yael's issues with gender were prominent in the history of her difficulties. Yet in her social milieu, whose tacit understanding of gender as "fixed" I largely shared, there was little room for articulating the various subplots contained in her conflicted gender and cross-gender identifications. Gender was, at the conscious level, an all-or-nothing affair; Yael either accepted her identity as an adult woman coming into being—or she didn't. Her "wall," though clearly informed by other meanings as well, was indeed an appropriate metaphor for the choice that seemed to face her vis-à-vis gender: was she on this side or that side, male or female?

In contrast to the traditional point of view of gender, for relational analysts gender is multiple and fluid (e.g., Harris, 1991). They also share the same ground focus on different aspects. Dimen (1995) points out that, even though "different feminism" talks about women's difference from men, "any given woman might, on any given day or in a lifetime, be and feel more the way men do or are said to, than the way women do or are said to" (p. 308). She proposes to incorporate a postmodernist perspective in which gender is perceived as multiple, shifting, ambiguous, overdetermined, and conflicted. Dimen adds that women and men alike struggle to incorporate this multiplicity. Thus, we have to question, rather than assume, the gender aspect of our patients' experience since gender identity is always in process and is always emerging.

Goldner (1991) argues from a constructivist point of view that for neither men nor women is an internally consistent gender identity desirable or even possible because of its artificiality. She advocates that therapists allow their patients to tolerate ambiguity and instability in gender in order to develop a more flexible and less pathological sense of self.

Mitchell (1997) clarified the distinctions of thought about gender between Freud and contemporary psychoanalysts. Other contemporary analysts discuss the desirability and power of femininity, which becomes an object of envy as well as of dread. Fast (1984) points out men's envy of women's capacity to give birth. Here femininity, not only masculinity, is envied.

Benjamin (1996) calls for an awareness of cross-gender identifications in normal development. She bases her arguments for bisexuality on Fast's (1984) differentiation model, in which boys and girls prior to age three believe that everyone is the same and all possibilities are open to them.

As they learn, between the ages of three to four, that there are differences between boys and girls, the girls realize they will never have a penis and boys realize that they will never give birth. Benjamin emphasizes that the bisexuality of the preoedipal period is never completely relinquished later in life. On the other hand, Layton (1998) holds that Benjamin's work on gender ambiguity in early cross-gender identifications, which suggests that children do not feel the effects of culture until a later age, is implausible.

Gender identity during adolescence might be constructed as a formation secondary to the development of gender identity during childhood (Cohen, 1991). In adolescence, gender identity intensifies mainly because of rapid physiological changes and sexual maturation. Generally, theorists of adolescent development have failed to elaborate the evolution of gender during adolescence, even though they acknowledge the importance of bodily changes and new opportunities and expectations for sexual identity.

Sexual abuse may very well affect adolescent gender identity development and sexual behaviors. For girls, sexual overstimulation, violating penetration and the terror instilled by these experiences affect their relationship to their bodies and to others. For example, Michelle and Laura, who started promiscuous relationships early in adolescence, had mothers who engaged in sexual behavior with various men they brought home while the girls were at home. Their constructions of what it meant to be a female were based on gender-role stereotypes: being passive, masochistic, and hyperfeminine. Carmen, who was longing to reconnect with her father, dated older men. And Dee, who had been repeatedly raped by her relatives, avoided being around boys. To protect herself from the external threat of abuse and the internal threat of shame, she strived to become asexual. For Dee, being female meant being abused, betrayed, violated, exploitated, and humiliated.

During our sessions, gender issues were particularly conflictual and emotional. Some of the girls' "seductive" behaviors during the erotic phase (described in the previous chapter) can be seen as the girls' attempt to consolidate and project a rudimentary adult gender identity following severe traumatization. I believe that such traumatization tends to glue the individual to the interactive scenario in a way that makes it almost impossible to play with and explore gender. These girls, like Yael, had their own "walls." But they mostly experienced themselves as being on only one side of the wall—boys being wholly on the other side. In the face of trauma, gender becomes more rigid. Thus, gender and gender identity issues were less accessible as overt topics in the girls' group than they are in untraumatized girls.

The psychoanalytic literature of the last decade (Gilgun, 1990; Aiosa-Karpas et al., 1991; Green, 1994; Pearlman and Saakvitne, 1995) indicates that pathological sexual behavior and confusion about sexual identity may be products of traumatic sexualization occurring before the completion and consolidation of gender identity and sexual orientation in childhood and adolescence. Aiosa-Karpas and colleagues (1991) write about how the trauma of sexual abuse fragments female adolescents' gender identity and sexuality. They found that adolescents who experience identity in a fragmented way are more aware than are other youngsters of the variety of sex roles in their external environments such as home and school. Moreover, these researchers argue, the confused identities serve to maintain the secrets of the adolescents' victimization.

When we are dealing with a patient's experience of childhood sexual abuse, gender factors are intensified in the transference and counter-transference reactions. Thus, gender in the dyad becomes a prominent issue.

The question of gender fit between analyst and patient was a source of concern of psychoanalysis from the beginning of the last century. Freud (1917) argued that for male patients there is greater negative transference than for females because males resist submitting to another male. Since that time, various classical authors have approached gender combination in analysis in terms of oedipal constellations. Blos (1979), however, adds a new and valuable dimension to this way of thinking by considering matters from the standpoint of the developmental challenges of adolescence. Those challenges include, notably, adolescents' reality-based need to separate from parental figures in the face of a revived Oedipus within. Transference engagements, both oedipal and preoedipal, thus have a regressive pull for adolescents that may be more than they can handle.

In this general context, Blos further proposes that the gender of an adolescent patient affects the analyst's countertransference, especially when issues of preoedipal manifestations with young girls revive with a female analyst. He added that preoedipal ambivalent struggles with the mother can be among the most difficult developmental conflicts for young girls, who must struggle against the revival of these conflicts.

As I have already discussed, I believe that the traumatized girls' reliving past experiences and our engagement in mutual enactments were nonverbal ways to communicate and were crucial to my understanding of the girls' deep inner struggles. For example, Nataline's disappointment and anger with her dying mother for abandoning her and not being able to care for her were transferred to me. She was extremely bossy and demanding. Her sadomasochistic relations with me and others, and the persistent hostile transference, were her way to preserve her self-determination. Her reaction to me might be connected with my gender, but I believe that many other factors enabled Nataline to participate in treatment the way she did. Among those factors might have been that, because of my work with very young children, who are generally more fluid in their tendency to regress in treatment, I have learned to feel comfortable in tolerating regressive reactions.

Analysts who treat sexually traumatized patients have very different opinions about analysand–analyst fit. Although gender may be critical to fit within the therapeutic dyad, I disagree with those therapists who focus only on gender as the main factor in a good fit. For example, Pearlman and Saakvitne (1995) and Briere (1996) discuss different counter-transference patterns within particular therapist–patient gender pairs in therapy with traumatized patients. Such pairs include female therapist with female patient, female therapist with male patient, male therapist with female patient, and male therapist with male patient.

Other therapists (Bolton, Morris, and MacEachron, 1989; Hunter, 1990) also focus on therapist–patient gender. They argue specifically for same-sex analyst and patient. Their rationales for same-sex analysand-and analyst are that only a male therapist can help to develop in a male a healthy sense of masculinity; that a sexually abused man may feel freer to explore sexual issues in treatment with a man; the abuser/father, being of the same sex as his son, even though he is the object of terror, may be the more nurturing parent, and therefore a male therapist is called for.

Some analysts recommend a specific analyst gender in treating sexually abused patients. Davies (1997) points out that male incest survivors contend with intense rage toward women, particularly women in power, and that these reactions often emerge in highly eroticized transference reactions. Thus the relationship between a male incest survivor and a female analyst may be a particularly difficult one. Gartner (1999) concurs, arguing that men who were abused by women (often their mothers) are more vulnerable to abuse by female therapists. He adds that female therapists of these patients report erotic maternal preoedipal and oedipal countertransferences. On the other hand, from her experience working with adult males who were sexually abused as adolescents, Shapiro (cited in Gartner, 1999) points out that these patients asked to be seen by female therapists because they felt uncomfortable exploring their sexual orientation or gender with male therapists.

Still other therapists focus on factors other than gender in determining analyst–analysand fit in treating sexually abused patients. Evans (1990), writing about sexually abused men as well as male Vietnam veterans, believes that "gender stereotyping" and "gender attitudes" of patients, as well as therapists, are factors that affect the analytic dyad more than does gender of the therapist. Evans calls for therapist flexibility regarding gender roles. Crowder (1995) believes that it is crucial that sexually abused patients work through embracing both genders. He adds, however, that it is important to respect a patient's request to work with a therapist with whom he or she feels safe, whether or not the request is gender based. Courtois (1988) adds that careful analysis of the reasons for a patient's choice is necessary. Although she believes that female therapists have greater ability to understand sexually abused female patients without excusing or rationalizing the abuse, some male therapists can productively treat these patients. Courtois argues: "Even more important than therapist gender is therapist sensitivity and knowledge about incest and its therapeutic management, as well as awareness of potential problems due to gender issues" (p. 239).

Bigras (1990), an analyst treating traumatized female adolescents, believed that those patients who chose to see him as another male figure felt compelled to go through the same sadomasochistic pattern, the compulsion to "incestuous repetition," that they had experienced before. Bigras emphasized the importance of analysts' changing their attitude and manner of working so as to accept the importance of the real, as well as the transferential, relationship with these patients. Bigras held that traumatized adolescents face a serious countertransferential problem that is linked to their profound oral deprivation. Therefore, the great needs of these patients place many burdens on their therapists. Tremendous work is required within analysts' own (self-)analyses, and within their supervision, to find ways to be kind without being overprotective, to be present without being intrusive, to be available without being aloof. From his own experience and that of analysts under his supervision, Bigras found that male and female analysts had different, but equally severe, difficulties in working through traumas.

Bigras's wise perspectives on gender are helpful in treating traumatized adolescents. From my clinical experience, including work supervising male therapists, I have found that the same issues come up with male therapists and survivors as with females. Treating trauma, it seems, is less a matter of the patient's or therapist's gender than of the particular personality and cultural fit between the partners of the therapeutic dyad.

Although trauma affects men and women in some of the same ways, there appear to be divergent pathways in the pathological development of gender identity and sexual object choice in girls and in boys (Green, 1994). Thus, it is crucial to evaluate a patient's sexual development throughout his or her life cycle from early childhood onward. I believe that raising awareness of gender dynamics in therapy with sexually traumatized adolescents is essential and opens multiple avenues for working through these issues.

The issue of gender also affects my choices in my countertransference disclosure. I establish different boundaries with female than with male adolescent patients. With female adolescents, I find myself feeling more comfortable disclosing my emotions. David, for instance, was interested in knowing whether I was married or had a serious boyfriend. The same question held many different meanings for my female adolescent patients, gender identity and sexuality during adolescence being a core issue of this development period. David's question, on the other hand, revealed erotic transference. When I asked him about his fantasies, he confidently stated that he knew that I was married because I had money. He could not, or did not want to, explain himself. Thinking that I was married helped him to deal with his erotic transference by creating these boundaries.

The same question from, Michelle, however, revealed a search for connection and identification. Also assuming that I was married, she wanted to know if I was afraid that my husband would leave me as she felt her boyfriend might leave her. She also asked how I could know that he was faithful and for how long we had loved each other. She was mostly interested in knowing if I asserted myself in expressing what I wanted from him. I found myself having an easier time exploring Michelle's fantasies toward me than David's. After David could not explore his fantasies about me as a married woman, I did not pursue it further. I did ask, however, if our relationship would be different if I were married, and he answered that it did not matter.

Gender-related transference and countertransference reactions are inevitable in any therapeutic connection. Treatment with traumatized adolescent patients is no exception. Clinical work with sexually abused adolescents is especially intensely gender related. Optimally, therapy offers an invaluable opportunity for traumatized patients to consolidate their identity as women or men.

9

Treatment Planning
Is it Possible?

Three Months Old

I want to know why my mother did not have me?
I have heard many different things.
I want to know the truth the whole truth.
My aunt told me "My Mother did not want Me because
she thought I was retarded."
My other aunt said "someone abuse my brother and I
but they did not know who."
One day My mother went to an apartment from a high
risk clinic.
And friend next door said
your children been crying all day.
When she went inside we had bruises.

To formulate an appropriate treatment plan for an adolescent, a therapist should consider different treatment modalities and their contradictions. I believe that fragile and vulnerable adolescents who lack reliable emotional attachment with their parents need mostly one-to-one interaction if their therapists are to provide them a holding environment. With the safety of individual therapy, there is hope of working through past trauma. Combined individual therapy and group or family therapies can be useful in some cases.

Group Therapy

The literature on group therapy tends to focus on whether or not individual therapy is the treatment of choice for adolescents. Both Singer (1974) and Brandes (1977) have cautioned that group therapy may not be indicated for all adolescents, for example, when they are developmentally immature or when the diagnosis is too severe. Josselyn (1972) suggests that, when the presenting complaint of an adolescent results from *ego depletion* with panic and disorganization barely contained, the adolescent is not a candidate for outpatient group therapy, at least not before a period of individual therapy.

Meeks and Bernet (1990) describe another category of adolescents who cannot benefit from group therapy, namely, those who are fixated at a level of development at which they require a nurturing, infantile feeding relationship with adults and do not value the opinion of peers.

Similar failures, more dangerous to the group than to the patient, may occur with antisocial, acting-out adolescents. From the point of view of ego psychology, Buchholz and Mishne (1994) describe the contraindications for group therapy for those adolescents. Those authors point out that adolescents with minimal self-control or tolerance for frustration tend to spread their disruptive behavior to the group, making therapy impossible. Buchholz and Mishne also suggest diagnostic contraindications for group therapy for adolescents who present narcissistic personality disorder. They point out that, since these adolescents are unable to empathize with their peers or tolerate public self-exposure, individual supportive treatment is more appropriate for them.

Before I took over the girls' group, I tried to have individual sessions with all of them so that I could gain a fuller understanding of their struggles and begin to establish a therapeutic alliance with each of them. The girls, however, had their own agendas, and I had to accommodate myself to their needs and their manifest scorn and distrust. The girls, who had come from homes characterized by abuse and neglect, were hostile and suspicious of me as an authority figure and hence were difficult to engage in individual psychotherapy.

During the beginning phase, the *girls struggled against becoming attached to me.* They needed to preserve their readiness for yet another disaster—my abandoning them. Not all the girls were ready to explore their traumas (Nataline, Carmen, Laura); and those who started this work during individual sessions (Dee and Michelle) insisted on joining the group just at the point when they were becoming more emotionally invested. It might be that this was not the right time for them to deal with the issue of abuse; the potential loss of their parents might have been a more urgent issue. Or perhaps exploring the sexual abuse was too humiliating for them to share in the group. I respected their objections to dealing with their traumas and welcomed the request of Dee and Michelle to join the group. The abuse of the girls represented an aspect of their selves that they had shut down in order to sustain their severe dissociative self-states at this difficult point in their lives. One-to-one interaction might have revived the intimacy they wished to experience with their parents. Thus, the group became a safer place for them to get therapeutic help on their terms.

I respected Nataline's request not to see me individually before joining the group. Nevertheless, there were those times in the beginning phase when only she and Carmen were in the group or when she was alone with me because Carmen had not arrived. At those times she had to admit that she needed all the attention from me and that she enjoyed the closeness. Recall that she gave me her artwork and asked me to play board games with her.

Lisa agreed to only one individual session with me but did not talk much; she spoke only when giving information. Although Carmen and Laura agreed to see me once individually before they joined the group, they were much more revealing of their pain and grief in this session than they had been during the intake interview. During the phone discussion before our meeting, I confirmed that they would join the group after one individual session as they had requested. I emphasized that I would leave open the option for them to see me more often in individual sessions. In this session, both of them discussed their sexual abuse with more emotional involvement and in greater detail than either had previously. In addition, they expressed a wide range of feelings toward their AIDS-stricken parents.

Realizing that Dee and Michelle felt too threatened to explore their sexual trauma, I offered them time-limited individual sessions, thus respecting their need for control. Dee and Michelle agreed to six individual sessions, even though they both later tried to break our contract. Michelle, who suffered from a lack of boundaries, had disclosed to others (teachers, neighbors, friends) the details of her sexual abuse. She disclosed to me for the first time, however, her physical abuse by her mother. Later, during the termination phase, Michelle continued to work on her trauma. Dee disclosed to the intake interviewer the realities of her sexual abuse. During individual sessions with me she started to work through her traumatic experience but never again brought up this issue in the group.

Adolescents in general are drawn to participation in groups. Group formation is an essential part of adolescence: adolescents need to leave their parents' milieu to establish psychological autonomy. Sullivan (1940) proposed that peer relationships in adolescence allow the affirmation of self-worth necessary to break the ties of dependence on parents. For a child entering adolescence, peer bonding becomes increasingly important as the child deals with fearsome emotions and events. Adolescence has been described as "the great second chance" (Blos, 1979), providing for some a sense of belonging and acceptance that is no longer possible in the family of origin.

The use of groups for psychoanalytic work with adolescents was pioneered by Aichhorn (1935, 1964) and Slavson (1943). Aichhorn, who tried to treat adolescents' antisocial behavior, used group therapy with institutionalized delinquents. His group was called "aggressive" because he insisted that the boys be allowed the freedom to work out their anger and frustrations. He used groups that were homogeneous according to sex as well as to diagnosis (based on behavioral symptoms). Aichhorn (1935) emphasized the importance of grouping children "in such a way that group life will favorably influence the behavioral difficulties" (p. 144).

Gabriel (1939, 1944), a psychiatric social worker, was another clinician working with groups of adolescent girls. Gabriel began an adolescent girls' group, ages 15 to 17, for which she used both activity and verbal discussions. The goals of these groups were to change attitudes and resolve personality conflicts by talking out and reliving the situations in which their conflicts had arisen.

There is a growing literature on both the theoretical and the practical aspects of group therapy with adolescents (Berkovitz, 1972; Brandes, 1973; Sugar, 1975; Azima and Richmond, 1991; MacLennay and Dies, 1992; Buchholz and Mishne, 1994; Rachman, 1995; Kymissis and Halperin, 1996). In addition to discussing the general principles of group therapy with adolescents, some of these authors (e.g., Berkovitz, 1972; Azima and Richmond, 1991; and Buchholz and Mishne, 1994) have addressed group therapy issues for specific populations, including minority teenagers, depressed girls in foster care, delinquents, and alcohol- and drug-addicted youngsters.

During the past decade, a great variety of preventive and reparative group modalities for adolescents has been employed in inpatient and outpatient settings, in schools, and in publicly run youth organizations (MacLennan and Dies, 1992). Short-term psychoeducational or focus groups in schools have also expanded rapidly. Topics covered by these groups range from substance abuse, AIDS, and suicide prevention to social skills training, relaxation techniques, and anger control.

Scheidlinger (1994) differentiates between younger and older adolescents. He points out that younger teenagers respond better than older adolescents to same-gender groups employing activities and games, since denial and externalization are characteristic of this age group. Older adolescents, by contrast, do well in coeducational talking groups. Once trust is established, they are often able to share thoughts on such subjects as family, school, and the human condition.

Meeks and Bernet (1990) also make this distinction between adolescent stages and describe different functions of group therapy in various developmental tasks. Early adolescence, the authors note, is a time when youngsters turn to peers as a way of emancipating themselves from the family. As the youngsters grow older, the peer group serves the functions of modifying the superego, loosening the constraints of the latency conscience, and providing an alternative, reality-based system of controls. In light of these considerations, I chose to restrict the girls' group to a single age stage (adolescence proper) and gender.

Minority groups are severly underrepresented in the literature. Stebbins (1972), working with African American adolescents, found that outreach work was important in creating trust while also providing crisis services. He used an experiential approach to building trust.

> It is not advisable to encourage ventilation and insight production as the sole purpose for group activity. It is more rewarding for both adolescent and therapist to place primary emphasis on action resulting from an intrapsychic focus where there can also be some experiential, recreational, social, and informational values to groups for teen-agers [p. 133].

Reiser and Kushner-Goodman (1972) describe the characteristics of a "drop in" therapy group, which may be a helpful structure for minority adolescents. The drop-in group evolved gradually from a crisis-oriented group treatment modality into a multipurpose group that "tended to become more stable and ongoing by providing to these very deprived youngsters acceptance, affiliation and security which were not available to them in other social group contexts" (p. 151)

I believe that, in treating groups of impoverished minority adolescents, it is crucial for the group leader to develop skills dictated by the emotional needs of individual patients: flexibility with therapeutic techniques, emotional involvement by the therapist, action-oriented techniques, and acknowledgment and appreciation of cultural factors in treating minorities.

The literature on treating traumatized patients debates the appropriate modality for this population. Some writers argue that most trauma victims benefit initially from individual therapy. Individual therapy allows disclosure of the trauma, the safe expression of related feelings, and the reestablishing of a trusting relationship with at least one other person. Van der Kolk (1987) states that "individual therapy allows for a detailed examination of a patient's mental processes and memories that cannot be replicated in a group therapy setting" (p. 163). However, van der Kolk adds that individual therapy with traumatized patients tends to reinforce dependency on the therapist and may decrease the subjective sense of mastery, whereas group psychotherapy is less likely to foster dependency.

> It [group therapy] allows for more flexible roles, with mutual support and alternating positions of passivity and activity. In a group patients can start reexperiencing themselves as being useful to other people. Ventilation and sharing of feelings and experiences in groups of people who have gone through similar experiences promotes the experience of being both victim and helper. . . . In a group the therapist can facilitate reempowerment by encouraging mutual support and by exploring the patient's resistances to taking an active role [p. 163].

Courtois (1998), who writes on incest survivors, believes that combined individual and group therapy provides the most effective treatment. In her recommendation for group therapy as a treatment of choice for these patients she says:

> Group allows for the breaking of the secrecy, isolation, and stigma resulting from the abuse and fosters exploration and resolution of the trauma and its aftermath. The sharing and empathy derived from common experiences and reactions, as well as the analysis of the interaction between members, are of great therapeutic value [p. 244].

Children and adolescents who, like the subjects of this book, come from abusive or neglectful homes are almost always hostile to, or suspicious of, authority figures; hence they are often difficult to engage in individual psychotherapy. This reluctance to depend on adults, coupled with their natural inclination toward peer-group formation, is another reason why group psychotherapy is often the treatment of choice for people with a history of childhood or adolescent trauma (Scheidlinger, 1982). Herman and Shatzow (1984), writing about sexually abused women, state that "in individual therapy it is difficult to come to a full resolution of the issues of secrecy, shame, and stigma" (p. 608). Group members are able to use each other as mirrors to reflect traumatic memories and feelings, which allows a shared reliving of the trauma.

It is therapeutic for traumatized patients to learn to use words to gain a sense of mastery over their emotions. By hearing others express their emotions verbally, and by learning how others manage to deal with trauma through reflection rather than action, many patients become capable of using similar maneuvers to deal with their own helplessness and pain. The main task of the group is to explore its own interpersonal processes (Pines, 1985). Envy, competition, assertiveness, sharing, and intimacy are more readily evoked, discussed, and confronted in group therapy than in one-to-one therapy (A. Freud, 1974). I found that in individual therapy confrontation is easily seen as rejection rather than as help; in a group, confrontation by one person can be balanced by the support and empathic identification of other group members. Many patients find it difficult to discharge and express hateful or merely negative feelings in one-to-one relationships because they fear that the relationship will be jeopardized. In a group, the sharing of both confrontation and support often makes the examination of the negative transference easier.

The task of the group leader is primarily to promote group members' relations, rather than to provide psychotherapeutic attention to individuals. The leader must create an environment in which members can explore their relationships with each other and with the leader. Anna Freud (1974) emphasized that interpretation alone cannot undo the damage caused by traumatic experiences, even though it may clarify the past and help the patient to deal with the consequences of the trauma. Group psychotherapy provides the traumatized patient with relational experiences in addition to interpretations. In a group, therefore, sharing and reliving past relations takes place, thus facilitating entrance into a world of adult relationships where others can be regarded as both subjects and objects (van der Kolk, 1987). By experiencing the effect of others on themselves and vice versa, patients can learn to modulate their responses to others.

While in principle groups for traumatized patients have many advantages, the destructive potential of groups is equal to their therapeutic promise.

> Conflicts that erupt among group members can all too easily re-create the dynamics of the traumatic event, with group members assuming the roles of perpetrator, accomplice, bystander, victim, and rescuer. Such conflicts can be hurtful to individual participants and can lead to the group's demise. In order to be successful, a group must have a clear and focused

understanding of its therapeutic task and a structure that protects all participants adequately against the dangers of traumatic reenactment. Though groups may vary widely in composition and structure, these basic conditions must be fulfilled without exception [Lewis, 1992, p. 58].

It is essential that the therapist at all times be aware of this negative potential and be able to respond accordingly.

Family Therapy

Another useful modality to explore is family therapy. Over the past three decades, a number of approaches to family therapy have been developed. Structural family therapy, as developed by Minuchin (1974), is a short-term approach. This approach bases its family diagnosis on the family members' interactional flexibility and limits. The therapist employs tasks and directness in order to restructure the family to handle the presenting problem. Strategic and systems approaches have been developed by the Mental Health Research Institute group in Palo Alto and the Milan group (Selvini et al., 1980). The therapeutic task of the strategic groups is to interrupt ways of handling the problem that do not work, that is, patterns that are dysfunctional. In the problem-solving approach, represented by Haley (1976), the goal of therapy is limited to solving the particular problem that is presented. The therapist's task is to formulate the problem in behavioral terms and to design a treatment plan to change the family dysfunction.

Other psychodynamically oriented approaches of family therapy present different treatment goals. Ackerman (1958), who represents the intergenerational approach, argues for an assessment and treatment that explores the complexity of multigenerational family patterns and their connection to current dysfunction. The aim of therapy is for family members to confront and deal with one another directly so as to work through unresolved conflicts. Bowen (1978), another intergenerational family therapist, believes that the goal of therapy is to assist adults to modify troubled relationships with their families of origin and to achieve a higher level of differentiation and reduced anxiety in direct contact. In all these family approaches, the therapist is the authority who provides knowledge, and the family members have to fulfill specific tasks or follow the therapist's lead.

Yael in Family Therapy

When I began treating Yael and her family, I experienced a tension between the therapist the family would have liked me to be and the therapist I would have liked to be.

I treated Yael and her family for a year in an Israeli inpatient unit. Treating Yael led to my acknowledging the usefulness of family therapy. I saw Yael and her parents separately before putting them together in the same room. In the beginning, I met weekly with the parents and three to five times a week with Yael. I respected Yael's refusal to participate in family meetings. I addressed her discomfort and resistance with an assurance that there would be some protection from their attack. As treatment proceeded and the therapeutic alliance was established, she expressed her need to involve her family in her treatment since that would be the only time she would have a serious discussion with them. A flexible frame was necessary. I did not have an agenda, and I tried to plan the treatment with Yael as we went along. At those times when Yael's eating binges increased, she asked me to see her and her parents separately. She said that she did not have the energy to deal with them. I worked with the whole family and concurrently met only with Yael and her brother. Yael felt close to her brother but had difficulty expressing her feelings. She felt that her brother was angry with her, and she wished to know more about his anger.

I followed Masterson's (1972) recommendation on the preferred conditions in family therapy. Masterson, who treats borderline adolescents, recommends the use of conjoint family sessions only after a therapeutic alliance has been established with the adolescent and a "latent observing ego" has been reached. He believes that, because of the symbiotic relationship within the family, a therapeutic alliance can be established with the adolescent only when the family is excluded from contact. Conjoint family sessions reduce the pathological bonds between adolescents and their parents by allowing the youngsters to verbalize their anger about their abandonment by their parents.

Regardless of individual diagnosis, a treatment plan that is preferred by the adolescents should be offered (Offer and Vanderstoep, 1975). I respected Yael's request to see her and her parents separately as she started therapy. Yael, who was enraged with her parents, had to work through her feelings first so that the family therapy experience could be constructive. Offer and Vanderstoep base their argument on the idea that some adolescents prefer to meet the therapist only privately and will refuse to meet conjointly with their parents. Other adolescents will consider treatment only if the entire family participates. These preferences can function as their defense or their willingness to work through their problems.

The Scharffs (1987), taking an object relations approach, suggest that adolescents' defensiveness and lack of motivation are an indication for family therapy instead of individual work. Since in these cases the parents are the ones who are motivated, it is more effective to treat the adolescent when the parent is in the room.

Obviously, matters are turned on their head when one is dealing with a hospitalized adolescent or with an adolescent who has been mandated to be in treatment by the courts or by the school or a foster care agency. Then the Scharff's rule of thumb no longer applies. Rather, it falls to the therapist to secure an alliance despite treatment's being more or less compulsory. Securing that alliance may require working individually with the adolescent and excluding the family, whose premature presence might only make worse the adolescent's expectable resistance against being coerced.

Recall that as Yael's binges became more frequent at the beginning of treatment, she asked to see me only individually. I colluded (Frankel, 1993) with her in a mutual withdrawal from her family. Yael and I tried to escape from her parents' demands to get better or to do better. Doing so gave both of us the illusion of control, although we were unconscious of this collusion. At this point, Yael got some control over the treatment. As I became aware of the transference–countertransference experience, I consciously allowed Yael to be in charge, raising a discussion of what she was escaping from. Yael explored her traumatic experiences when her parents tried to control her weight. They had used every means: yelling, denigrating her, forcing her to eat when she lost weight, or teasing her and forbidding her to eat when she gained weight. After our therapeutic work, and knowing that I was aware of the family dynamics and would protect her, she was ready to meet with her family.

During the first few family sessions I saw only Yael and her parents. The parents argued that their son, Avi, who had been close to Yael even though he was the mother's favorite, had "had enough" and they did not want to expose him to "Yael's poison." I thought that they were worried about disrupting the family alliances that had become totally entrenched in the wake of Yael's illness. The parents did not want her to break down the natural idealization that had developed between them and their son. During this time I felt bullied by the mother, who blamed me for being too soft on Yael. However, when the father expressed his regret for being too tough on Yael, I felt more empathic toward him because I knew how difficult it was for him to let his guard down.

Yael's family interaction was characterized by indirectness, a suspicious, detached stance on her part, and a profound sense of helplessness and incompetence on the part of the parents. They wished that I would take over and tell them both what to do to change the situation. Despite active attempts at interpretation and clarification, I had great difficulty both interpreting adequately and helping the family members talk directly to one another.

The father was guilt ridden and ineffectual; mother, insensitive and blaming. Yael remained aloof, detached, unrelated, and sullen. The parents, perceiving her as fragile and unpredictable, responded to Yael with hesitation. The mother was the spokesperson and monopolized the conversation. When I asked Yael to express her feelings and thoughts, her mother interrupted before Yael could speak. "I'll tell you what she thinks," she would snap and then proceeded to answer for her. The father passively watched the family interaction without responding. When questioned about his role in the family, he admitted that he had given up trying to get a word in. Interactions were based primarily on criticism and accusations, with both parents and Yael denying fault.

At the beginning of therapy Yael kept "the wall" up between herself and her parents. She stated that she could not forget or forgive the way they had treated her as a child. Her brother, Avi, was angry with her and at the same time loved her. But Yael felt that there was a high wall between them. A few months into treatment Yael asked my help in creating openings in the wall between herself and her brother. She felt that Avi really did care for her. She told of an incident at home when her brother brought her a glass of soda. She felt that he might be trying to manipulate her by putting something in the drink. She told him of her concerns, and he brought her a closed can of soda. She was grateful that her brother did not resent her not trusting him, that he did not take it personally. Yael suggested I have a session with both of them so she could have a discussion with him. She was concerned that he was angry at her, and I believed that she could handle such an open discussion.

> *Etty:* We scheduled this session at Yael's request so that you can both work through the feelings between each of you.
>
> *Avi:* Yes, I have a lot on my mind, and I am not sure that Yael wants to hear.

Yael: Yes, I want to hear. I don't want to hear things many years from now that I did not know about.

Avi: I am so angry at you. I may feel this way all my life. [silence]

Avi: Mom and dad did everything for you, and you never appreciated them.

Yael: Maybe you don't want to see how badly they treated me.

Avi: What are you talking about?

Yael: You are so angry that I feel you cannot listen to me now.

Etty: Tell us [Avi], what are you angry about?

Avi: I tried so many times. I felt things getting better with Yael, and then another crisis came up. The whole family was in turmoil because of you [Yael].

Yael: I think you don't understand the meaning of my bulimia. Things got out of my control.

Avi: Let me remind you, at the most intense point of your crisis, I was in high school. My grades dropped. It affected me.

Etty: It affected you because of your concern for Yael. I am wondering if underneath the anger you feel upset and frustrated because you cannot help Yael.

Avi: Yes, I thought I had an effect on her. She always listened to me. But not anymore.

Etty: You're saying that you feel hurt, that Yael does not care about you.

Avi: Yes.

Etty: What do you think about what Avi says?

Yael: [sobbing] You always have been important in my life. I cannot control myself. I want to get normal.

The session with Avi brought up guilt in Yael. After that session, in family therapy Yael told her parents how guilty she felt about giving them a hard time. I asked the parents to share their feelings toward Yael. The mother expressed her guilt for not having spent enough time with Yael when she was a child, and the father expressed his guilt for being too tough on Yael. I asked Yael what she felt about what her parents had just said. She was astonished, especially about her father's statement. She believed that her father had been too tough on her, but she did not realize how bad he felt about his behavior toward her.

Although family therapy can be useful in treating adolescents, there are patients for whom this treatment modality is not feasible. The girls in my group came from broken homes. Their mothers or other caretakers could not make a commitment to attend therapy sessions. At best, some parents were able to attend sporadically for parental guidance.

Yael's family, difficult as it was, was tame as compared with some of the inner-city families I worked with. As hard as it was for Yael to invite her family into her psychological space, it was impossible for Carmen. For long periods of time, when Carmen's mother was hospitalized, Carmen and her sister were separated from each other, each were being cared for by relatives or friends in different states.

It may be impossible even to bring some adolescents and their families into the same room. During one group session, Michelle described how chaotic it was to live with her mother and siblings. Hitting was so normative in her family that the children hit their own mother, who, in turn, physically abused them. Putting all of them in the same room would be potentially destructive.

These kinds of traumatizing homes are fraught with alliances, secrets, and hatreds. For example, both Laura and her brother were deep into drug use. Their mother, busy partying, was not remotely aware of their drug habit. Returning from her parties in the wee hours of the morning, she could not possibly know how late her children had come home. All the members of this family led separate lives and ignored repeated invitations to meet together as a family.

The severe trauma that affects individual family members also affects the family unit, often shattering it. This discombobulation, in turn, reverberates back to the individual. For instance, Nataline's mother, Ms. B., continued her drug use even though she was dying from AIDS. The family was in turmoil, each blaming the other for Ms. B's illness. She, often hospitalized or bedridden, was unavailable, and the other family members refused to get help as a family since they would have to deal with their intense guilt and shame.

No ordinary kind of treatment planning can apply to the families of multiply traumatized adolescents. Treatment "planning" with this population is difficult at best and is usually catch-as-catch-can. The one abiding rule is to keep the adolescent's needs and wishes at the forefront.

10

Contact with Parents

My Mother

My mother is sweet
My mother is kind
Yeah she corrects us
You may say
"oh no, she is mean."
But, it is only because she loves us.
All of us.

Within the literature there is a controversy regarding how much, if any, parent–therapist contact should take place in the course of treating an adolescent. Parent–therapist contact is thought to interfere with the adolescent's development of a therapeutic alliance, as well as with confidentiality and autonomy. I believe that, when one is working with a disturbed adolescent who presents high-risk behavior, such as extensive substance abuse or unsafe sex, some parent–therapist contact becomes necessary. Some case material illustrates this proposition.

I met the girls with their parents before they joined the group. In these initial sessions I emphasized that what the girls shared in therapy would be kept private. I made clear to the parents, however, that whatever they told me during appointments or by phone would be shared with the girls. I suggested, therefore, that the parents or caretakers inform the girls and obtain their permission before arranging a contact with me. Although I expected to have minimal contact with the parents, I was surprised that the girls asked me, directly or indirectly, to meet their parents. As these girls themselves had to assume the role of parent, they welcomed the opportunity to share the burden of taking care of their ill parents. They not only gave me permission but actually encouraged me to meet their parents more often than I intended to. For each girl I took a different approach for responding to her individual way of coping with her healthy or sick parent or caretaker. Michelle and Laura preferred to participate in the sessions with their mothers, who were healthy. Nataline and Carmen asked me to meet separately with their mothers, who were dying from AIDS. Dee's foster mother was not involved and the sisters wished to keep it that way.

Most of the adolescent patients I treated when I worked in a public clinic were inner-city, impoverished youngsters. Many factors in their lives interfered with their development. They had witnessed and experienced their parents' violent ways of handling frustration, as well as violence in their neighborhood. The high incidence of alcoholism and drug use contributed to the atmosphere of potential and unpredictable explosiveness. In crowded apartments children were inadequately protected from sexual stimulation. Sleeping in the same room, or often the same bed, with siblings or seeing or hearing parental intercourse could produce feelings of overwhelming confusion and anxiety.

Inner-city life typically entails complications in the development of ethnic identity. Splits within families often occur when adolescents assimilate to the outside culture in a way that disturbs parents who are more rooted in their original culture. Altman (1995) has noted:

> Adolescent assimilation may reflect a wish to differentiate from parents that itself is culturally specific to the United States and that may be interpreted by parents only as unwanted defiance. The form of American culture into which inner-city adolescents may wish to assimilate is "street culture," which is especially disturbing to parents worried about drugs and crime [p. 2].

The girls of my group had been raised in unstable environments, in families that harbored secrets of sexual and physical abuse. Sexual abuse was but one part of the girls' traumatic experience. They had suffered deprivation and rejection; a few had been removed from their families and lived in foster homes.

The pioneers of work with parents were Winnicott, Fraiberg and her collaborators, and Furman. Winnicott (1971), throughout his writings, demonstrated how consultations to parents can be useful. Fraiberg, Adelson, and Shapiro (1987) and Furman (1957), who worked with parents of infants and toddlers, believed that the interactions of the parents could have an effect on the children's inner world. Furman reasoned that it is essential for therapists to find out whether or not the parents are ready to *be* parents, that they are mature and responsible enough.

Following Furman, Daniel Stern (1995) also views motherhood in developmental terms, but he believes that motherhood can be activated at any point in a woman's life. Interventions are therefore useful from birth through the life cycle of the child. Green (2000) encourages parents to work with the positive transference, since it creates a sense of safety within the parents. This safe atmosphere will lead the parents to identify with and internalize the therapist as a "reactivated or new developmental object" (p. 31), and, through this process, the parents will be able to reflect on their child. In working with dysfunctional parents, Green asks, "How much pathology do you take up in parent work?" She answers:

> Where the ghosts in the parents' own pathology came to haunt their relationships with their daughter, the therapist gave room for the "historical" link but repeatedly brought this back to the present situation. I do not wish to suggest that parent work takes place only in the present in relation to the child, nor to counterpose this to adult psychotherapy as the place where further exploration of the past would be invited. Rather I wish simply to throw open for consideration whether there are stages in work with parents where one might focus more on the present than the past or, indeed, vice versa [p. 35].

Meeks and Bernet (1990) focus on the significance of work with adolescents' parents.

> In many respects, the management of the complex relationships between the youngster and his parents and between the parents and the youngster's therapist is the most important and delicate task of psychotherapy during adolescence. The therapist must obtain and keep the trust and cooperation of the parents without compromising the adolescent's movement toward independence from the family [p. 267].

I did not have the luxury of regular sessions with the girls' parents. They were uninvolved, often abusive mothers. Likewise, I did not have a chance to meet the fathers, who were absent or whose whereabouts were unknown. I learned that my work with the mothers was severely limited to what they could manage. I felt frustrated by not being able to help them to improve their mothering or to start a positive parenting process to improve the girls' situation. Since the girls' mothers or caretakers did not come regularly to parent guidance sessions, the telephone became the only way to stay in contact with them. They were told that they should tell the girls when they called and the general topic of the conversation. Involving these mothers or caretakers was difficult, at times impossible.

The difficulties of maintaining contact with the mothers or caretakers exacerbated the many crises with which I had to contend during my work with the girls. Michelle ran away; Laura revealed her heavy drug use; and Carmen, who did not practice safe sex, was concerned about being pregnant. I felt I was walking a thin line between overinvolvement and failing to assume appropriate and helpful responsibility. The girls' mothers or caretakers manipulated me to take sides and to take all responsibility in resolving the crises. And I had to overcome my anger and support the mothers emotionally in order to help them handle their daughters' problems. While these mothers or caretakers requested advice on how to discipline the girls, I explored in parent guidance sessions the goals of parental discipline, leaving the methods completely up to the parents.

Sadly, in these girls' families sexual abuse had occurred across generations. Their mothers had histories of sexual abuse, unresolved loss, neglect, and physical and emotional abuse. Their experiences had left them with little sense of self-worth, and they reenacted their past traumatic relations by having relationships with abusive men. These women, who knew or even watched the abuse of their daughters, reexperienced their own abuse and were too overwhelmed to think about their daughters'. For these families, abuse seemed an ongoing and predictable pattern of life. The mothers could not establish a reliable attachment. These mothers were unable to provide their daughters with a secure base in their lives (Bowlby, 1988).

Many abusive parents have a history of early disturbance of attachment to their own parents, which influences the bonding process to their children (Ainsworth, 1980). These mothers, like their daughters, had experienced physical, sexual, and emotional neglect. They had never received help to process this neglect. Instead of confidence, shame permeated the mother–daughter relationship. To deny the shameful situation, the mothers tried to avoid interacting with me. They expressed their guilt toward their daughters through aggression and accusation. As Steele (1980) puts it: "It is likely that in many instances the parents' early abuse affected their personality development, limited their empathic abilities with their own children, and set the stage for a replay of the abusive environment" (p. 52).

During the beginning phase of the girls' group, the parents were more involved in their children's therapy than they later proved to be. As they realized that the girls were committed to the therapy, they took less responsibility. My impression was that the parents believed my job was to "fix" their children without their involvement. The parents failed to follow through on my requests for some ongoing parental guidance, despite their complaints, voiced during phone calls, that they were emotionally exhausted and frightened by the girls' self-destructive behavior. My repeated emphasis on the need for more cooperative parenting fell on deaf ears. The parents remained absent and unreachable, repeatedly failing to show up to parent guidance sessions and not leaving messages. My concern about the girls only made the mothers angrier. When they did attend parent guidance sessions, they withheld information. My knowledge of the parents' background and my own struggle in treating the girls, however, helped me to empathize with the parents. There were times when I identified with them; they were exhausted from trying to manage the girls' acting-out behavior. So was I. Three girls, Nataline, Carmen, and Lisa, would calm down only after they had provoked me. I became judgmental and controlling in my interpretations or so distant and withdrawn that I could not be appropriately active in therapy.

Michelle

I was concerned for Michelle's safety. Her mother had abused her physically and emotionally. She had even threatened to murder Michelle with a knife at night while she was sleeping. Michelle had nightmares that disappeared after she moved to live with her aunt. These nightmares reappeared one night after she unexpectedly saw her mother in the subway.

A few months into treatment, Michelle's aunt asked to see me with Michelle. Michelle expressed her wish to have this session because of her plan to move back to live with her mother. Michelle explained that her mother had a new boyfriend and that they were planning to move to another state. Her aunt did not know about this. Michelle was afraid of losing her mother and her siblings, just as she had lost her father. She asked me to keep this information confidential, since her mother would be in trouble if the caseworker knew about it.

Aunt: Why didn't you tell me that you are going to see your mother?
Michelle: She is my mother and I am allowed to see her.
Aunt: How could you see your mother after all she did to you?

Michelle: She told me that she was sorry.

Aunt: I have custody of you, and I have to know everything that is going on in your life.

Michelle: I am not a child.

Etty: Michelle, tell us, why did you want to meet your mother?

Michelle: I miss my siblings. I have not seen them for many months. All of them live at home and I want to be with them.

Aunt: Are you saying that you want to move back to live with your mother?

Michelle: Yes [looks down].

Etty: It seems that you have a difficult time looking at your aunt.

Aunt: Of course. She betrayed me and she feels ashamed. By the way, we have to talk with her caseworker to have another court meeting.
[silence]

Etty: [to Michelle] How do you think you will feel if you leave your aunt?

Michelle: [to aunt] You have too many rules. I have a boyfriend, and you never want him to come to visit me. What do you think we are doing?

Aunt: Now I understand why you want to return home [sarcastically].

Etty: Michelle is saying that she is upset that you don't trust her.

Aunt: I want the best for her. I care for her.

Michelle: You may care about me, but you don't care about my mother. You are always angry at my mother. Maybe you need to meet each other with Etty. But I don't want to be at this meeting.

Etty: I believe that there is a tension between both of you since Michelle wishes to have more freedom and you [to aunt] wish to have more discipline. As you care for Michelle, I believe that Michelle cares for you.

Michelle: I am in the middle, and this is difficult for me.

Etty: It seems that, whatever you [Michelle] choose, you will hurt someone.

Aunt: I agree with Michelle. It will be helpful if I meet my sister here since we are so angry at each other.

The mother and her sister had not seen each other for a year. When at last they met in the session, they cried and hugged. The mother did not tell her sister about her plan to move with her new boyfriend. She did say that she wanted to move because she was afraid that her ex-boyfriend (who had raped Michelle) would kill her. Sadly, she expressed her wish that Michelle would stay with her aunt during the week and visit her during the weekends. I was glad that Michelle had chosen not to be at this session. She was so starved for her mother's love but now, again, was being rejected. I assumed that Michelle had tried to protect herself by refusing to come to this session.

After a court hearing, Michelle returned home under the condition that she stay in the same school and continue group therapy with me. The mother was required to be in therapy as well. Meanwhile her mother's boyfriend broke up with her. I saw the aunt one other time before Michelle moved to live with her mother. I tried to help the aunt understand Michelle's wish to reconnect with her family. Michelle's mother rejected my attempts to meet her for a parental guidance session, and Michelle was hurt further by the knowledge that her mother did not find time to meet with me.

Nataline

Nataline refused to participate in a session with her mother but asked me to see her mother, who she believed needed help. In the first parent guidance session, her mother complained that Nataline had stopped visiting her during the weekends. She was aware that her physical appearance had deteriorated, and she believed that Nataline found it difficult to see her dying. Sobbing, she asked me, "Please let me see my daughter happy before I die." I could not hold back my tears. I did not have the chance to see Nataline's mother again. I did, however, have a few phone conversations with her before she died. She called me several times from the hospital to ask me to persuade her daughter to visit her. She missed her terribly, she said. She expressed her envy of Nataline's grandfather, because, when he was dying, Nataline had been at his beside his bed until the end. I suggested that she call Nataline and tell her of her feelings and her wish that Nataline visit her.

Nataline was being cared for by her grandmother. After my repeated efforts, the grandmother came to one parent guidance session. Nataline did not want to participate; she said she was tired of hearing her grandmother's complaints. I asked Nataline if there was anything she wanted me to ask the grandmother. Nataline said she wanted her grandmother to let Nataline's mother live with them. The grandmother refused, claiming that she could not watch her daughter using drugs while she was dying. The grandmother described her worries about Nataline, who was isolated socially.

After Nataline's mother passed away, the grandmother called to let me know of her death. She described Nataline's reaction to her mother's death. Nataline was upset and crying. She expressed her anger toward her mother's boyfriend, who she believed was to blame for her mother's death. Nataline believed that he brought drugs to her mother. He also had AIDS. The contacts with the grandmother were always extremely useful since she provided me with information about Nataline's emotional states, which did not come up in the sessions. In the group Nataline could not expose her vulnerability, which would damage her image as a tough girl.

Carmen

Carmen refused to participate in a session with her mother. She asked me to fill her mother's role, for example, to call her teacher and ask how she was doing. Carmen claimed that she wanted "a real mother." She was angry toward her mother, who stayed in bed most of the day and did not have the energy to cook or clean the house. Carmen could not bring friends home because her apartment looked like a "pigsty." Her mother came to only two parent guidance sessions. She was often hospitalized for long periods, and Carmen stayed with different people while her mother was in the hospital. Carmen, feeling abandoned, acted out when the mother returned home. I tried unsuccessfully to convince the mother to have a permanent plan for Carmen when she could not take care of her. She insisted that she did not have anyone she could rely on and resisted trying to think through her other options. In addition to feeling abandoned by her mother, Carmen was envious of her younger half-sister, who stayed with her paternal grandparents while she stayed at times with strangers.

Parental Self-Revelation

The girls in my group knew about their parents' HIV/AIDS, but they were not told about the seriousness of their parents' health status. They expected more from their parents, who repeatedly let them down.

Telling youngsters that their parents have HIV/AIDS is never easy. When I was a coordinator of AIDS Support Services in a children and adolescents' clinic, I treated children and adolescents whose HIV/AIDS-infected parents had been facing the painful and conflictual issue of disclosing their HIV/AIDS infection to their children. There is no right way to deal with this disclosure. A few questions must be considered: Should the child/adolescent be told? If so, when should he or she be told? Who is the best person to talk to the child/adolescent? How much should he or she know? What if questions about death arise? Who can help the child/adolescent with his or her feelings?

Information needs to be presented in a way that is appropriate for the child's developmental stage. The truth about this diagnosis can elicit terror, rage, shame, or guilt. Parents who are HIV-positive or have AIDS often try to shield their children from the diagnosis out of sense of guilt, shame, or the desire to avoid hurting their children or because they fear rejection by their children. Parents may become too permissive in their efforts to compensate for what they perceive as their failure to care for their children. Parents may fear that the children will be unable to keep their parents' diagnosis secret from those not in the family. In my experience, however, I have found that children tend to remain loyal, in part because AIDS carries a stigma that children feel reflects on them as well as on their parents. Consequently, children defend their parents and guard the secret. In the absence of information, children devise their own complicated, often incorrect, and self-punitive explanations. Whatever the family decides, it is important for the parent to assure the child that he or she will be safe and secure. For children, the biggest fear is that they will be left alone. When there is only one parent, who is sick and who is the only one who cares for them, this fear intensifies.

Even when parents have tried to hide the secret of HIV/AIDS from their teenage children, usually the youngsters have known all along and were keeping the secret to protect the parents. This secrecy is maintained especially when the parent has been battling HIV-related illness requiring lengthy hospitalizations and frequent clinic visits. Having to keep the secret deprives the adolescent of the opportunity to discuss the situation with the parent and to prepare for future bouts of illness.

Adolescents often know a lot about medicine and disease but are careless about prevention and engage in high-risk behavior. It is difficult for their parents to reach them and persuade them to change their thinking, attitudes, and behaviors. Adolescents, for their part, ask their parents private and intrusive questions. Before the diagnosis is disclosed, it is important to explore adolescents' knowledge of HIV/AIDS by asking them how much they already know about HIV infection, AIDS, and related subjects, such as sex and drug use. Where did they get the information? From friends? School? Media? Is it accurate?

From my clinical experience, I was able to identify the needs of parents around the subject of disclosure. The AIDS organization, Body Positive, and my clinic organized a workshop, "How Do I Tell My Kids?" A diverse panel of parents who had made different decisions about when, whether, and how to talk to their children about their HIV gave advice and told their stories. I presented different perspectives on HIV disclosure to children by parents, grandparents, and other family members. I discussed the reactions that parents could expect from children of different ages.

We offered parent groups following these workshops. Believing that this kind of disclosure required a long-term working-through process. At first I did not limit the number of sessions. No one responded. After I limited this group to 12 sessions, I was amazed to find a large response. I learned later that the parents wanted to believe that their struggle could be resolved in a short time.

Several groups were established. One consisted of four single mothers with HIV/AIDS who were struggling with disclosure to their teenage children. At the time of my working with these mothers the AIDS "cocktail" was not yet available, and their death was a real threat. I interviewed each mother for one session before she joined the group. The session focused on their relationships with their teenagers, relationships that were mostly in turmoil.

Kelly was a 31-year-old, African American mother of an only child, Keisha (mentioned in chapter 1), who was then 14 years old. Kelly was on public assistance. She went to school full time. As a teenager she had used drugs and turned to prostitution to support her habit. Both she and her daughter had been raised by her aunt and uncle.

Kelly's mother was 17 when she gave birth to her. She felt unable to care for her baby, but Kelly's father, who was white, did not want anything to do with her. Her aunt, who was unable to conceive, was happy to take Kelly in. Until Kelly was nine she thought her aunt was her mother. An active drug user and prostitute, Kelly left her daughter with friends or later with her aunt and uncle. During Keisha's childhood, Kelly was in and out of detox programs and was on and off methadone. She had been raped and had her picture in the local newspaper when it did a story on prostitution. She was diagnosed with full-blown AIDS but decided not to tell her daughter. Keisha encouraged me to see her mother in the group of other mothers who were struggling in their relationships with their children. I felt uneasy, however, knowing that Keisha was unaware of what the group was really about.

Roberta, a 39-year-old Hispanic woman, had three youngsters, ages 12, 16, and 18. Each of the children had a different father, none of whom was involved in his child's life. Roberta learned about her HIV-positive status two years before she joined the group. She was worried about who would take care of her children when she was too sick. Roberta's father had left when she was three years old. She had been an obedient child. She had not been allowed to bring friends home and therefore felt isolated socially. She had been sexually abused by her two older brothers and as a result made several suicide attempts. While she was growing up she was frequently in the cojmpany of drug-addicted men; three of them were the fathers of her three children. She contracted HIV from a man who later died from AIDS. She lost her two older brothers to AIDS. She married a man who was drug addicted. Suspecting that she cheated on him, he physically abused her. Her children did not get along with him.

Nancy, a 42-year-old Hispanic single mother of a teenage son and a nine-year-old daughter, discovered that she was HIV positive four years before she joined the group. She had contracted HIV from a boyfriend who died from AIDS a few months before she joined the group. Her father had disappeared from her life when she was seven years old. This had been a traumatic loss for her. The only girl in a family of four children, Nancy had been her father's favorite child. He was the nurturing and protective parent, and his abrupt disappearance from her life had a great effect on her.

Nancy described her mother as an intelligent, strong, but cold woman. Nancy's mother was often absent, and relatives took care of the children. Nancy was not close to her brothers, who lived in other states. She described her childhood as traumatic. She had been physically abused by nuns because of her behavior problems. She had been teased by her peers about being overweight. She was in individual therapy for five years because of abusive relations with men to whom she was drawn. At the time Nancy was in the group, she was married to a man who was serving a life sentence for murder. Nancy expressed her concerns about her son, who was following a bad crowd. She rationalized her conflict about disclosing her worries to her son on the grounds that he might act out risky behavior, such as using drugs.

Rosa, a 34-year-old African American woman, joined the group because she was struggling with whether or not to disclose her AIDS to her mother, twin brother, and 16-year-old son. Her son acted out in school, used drugs, and was sexually active. She suspected that he had had a baby by his last girlfriend. She described him as a very angry boy. Rosa took care of her aunt, who lived with her. This was a big burden for her, especially as her health deteriorated. Rosa's parents each had been divorced several times. Her father was a gambler and had affairs with many women. She had seen her father abusing her mother.

Rosa had mixed feelings toward her son, an unplanned child. His father had demanded that she have an abortion, but she refused. When her son was two years old, she discovered that his father was married. As he distanced himself from them, Rosa started her individual therapy. After Rosa found out that she had AIDS, she tried to find her son's father to make sure that he would take care of their son when she became too sick. The father refused, and she lost a court fight to force him to assume custody.

This group of mothers raised children without consistent help from father figures. Because the women were sick, they could not work and were on public assistance. They faced the complex responsibilities of parenting alone. They were from backgrounds lacking in healthy attachment to their own parents. The families of these mothers could not provide the support they needed. And yet, these mothers found the strength to struggle against great odds as they sought to provide adequate care for their children.

Psychoanalysis has long discussed the destructive effects on child development when the father is absent (Loewald, 1951; Neubauer, 1960). In the absence of the father, there is a "lack of oedipal stimulation, normally found in the continuous day-to-day interplay between the child and each parent, and especially as evidenced by the relationship of the parents to each other" (Neubauer, 1960, p.305).

Loewald (1951) believed that the function of the father was to protect against the threat of maternal engulfment. Siegler (1983) described some findings from her clinical work with families in which the father was absent.

> We repeatedly have found that the effects of the father's absence on the child's development are determined by the ways in which the mother experiences and defines this event for the child. Mothers have countless

ways of keeping the image of the father alive, or, conversely, destroying his image, if that is their wish. While there is no question that it makes a difference when a child is raised in the absence of a father, the more interesting question focuses on what sort of a difference it makes. The meaning of the loss of the father in both the life of the mother and that of the child depends on whether the loss was incurred through death, illness, separation, divorce, or abandonment [p. 97].

Using process notes and direct observation, Herzog (2001) shows how "father hunger" impinges on boys' ability to manage their aggression. He explains:

Without a father to help him integrate and moderate it, a boy's aggression typically appeared as a foreign force in his dreams and fantasies. I came to postulate that the father's careful use of his own aggression as a part of his parental functioning constituted an opportunity for the consolidation of the boy's masculine sense of self and beginning basis for his own management of drive and fantasy [p. 22].

We live in times when children, especially in the inner city, grow up without fathers. Many of the mothers I worked with in the clinic had been abandoned by the biological fathers of their children. Their very lives embodied the difficulties of being a single parent. The hunger to have a father, Herzog says, is an "affective state experienced when the father is felt to be absent" (p. 51). Herzog focuses on boys' emotional experience when father is absent.

More work is done with mothers in groups than with fathers (see, e.g., Weisberger, 1983). Siegler (1983) described group work with single mothers of children three to six years old. In this group she used interventions based on ego psychology. Her aims with this model were to understand the function of the family, mother–child interactions in the absence of the father, and the special task of single mothers during oedipal development.

The single mothers in my group were a subset of the larger category of families with absent fathers; these mothers struggled with ways of disclosing their HIV/AIDS status. Since this group was a short-term one, the therapeutic work could not include deep understanding of such issues as the mothers' relationship with their teenaged children, their own emotional struggles with terminal illness, and their relationships with abusive and dysfunctional men.

The Mothers' Group

The account that follows is based on the 12 sessions I had with the mothers.

Session #1

Four of the mothers attended. I began with a restatement of the group contract. Even before the group members introduced themselves, Rosa started sobbing as she described her relationship with her son, her older brother, and her mother and her inability to tell them about her illness. She worried about feeling rejected and being blamed.

Kelly shared similar feelings but emphasized that she felt relief that she had disclosed to her aunt and uncle. Rosa was interested in knowing more. Kelly described her despair when she realized that her uncle had begun urinating in the bathroom sink after he learned about her HIV. He thought he might otherwise catch AIDS from the toilet. Kelly was worried that, if she disclosed to her daughter, her daughter would refuse to drink from the same cup, as she used to do.

Roberta stated that her three teenaged children were overly concerned about her physical appearance, and she was afraid of how they would react when her health deteriorated. Nancy described her last hospitalization and how she had managed to hide from her children the reason for the hospitalization. Kelly asked the other women how they had been infected with the HIV virus. I was amazed that these four women, who were strangers to each other, could share their most intimate experiences. I did not say much during this session but tried to make empathic statements.

Session #2

Roberta did not show up for this session. She left a message that one of her teenaged daughters was sick. The others turned to their relationships with their children. They noted that some of their children acted out, came home late, cut classes, and did not practice safe sex. I asked what had triggered their children's acting-out behaviors. I suggested that the mothers encourage their children to express their feelings and worries.

It was painful for the mothers to talk about their guilt about getting sick. As a substitute, ironically, they talked about their attitudes about death. Rosa stated that she would like to end her life since everything was too difficult to bear. She believed that she would have a more peaceful time after her death. Kelly described her prayers each evening for her daughter and herself. She believed that, because of her prostitution and drug use, God had punished her. She also believed that after her death she would have a better life. Nancy announced that she could not believe in God any more. I reflected on Kelly's and Rosa's expressions of guilt, regret, and self-blame while Nancy expressed her anger at others. I suggested that they all share these feelings. I asked Kelly and Rosa if they felt that others were to blame for their suffering. Each described at length her traumatic childhood. They later shared their rage toward the men who were the cause of their getting HIV/AIDS.

Session #3

All the members attended. It was a very emotional session for all of us.

Rosa: I thought about last session and what I said about my wish to die. I think it is really giving up my son.

Kelly: Sometimes I feel like giving up my daughter. Can you believe that my daughter complained to the school nurse about my tough attitude toward her and expressed her wish to be with her father, who never took care of her?

Etty: You would like your daughter to be more direct with you. It is important to initiate conversation with her.

Kelly: She always has complaints.

Nancy: My kids also always have complaints. I am struggling for my life and they are concerned about having another pair of sneakers.

Etty: [to Roberta] You are quiet today. You look upset to me.

Roberta: I am upset because it is too difficult for me to take care of my three kids without getting any help.

Etty: You all made a choice not to disclose your illness to your children. But what you are all saying is that as time passes it becomes more difficult. I believe that you would like to get help from your children, to know that they feel compassion toward you, but the unknown consequences of the disclosure really scare you.

Roberta: Sometimes I wonder if they do know something. My younger son told me about his dream. In it he came home from school and my mother informed him that I had passed away. He said that if something happened to me he would run in the street without stopping.

Etty: What do you think he wanted to tell you?

Roberta: He told me that he would commit suicide or he would get in a deep depression if something happened to me. With my older son I am concerned that he will get into drugs and alcohol. I need to tell them about my condition, because I am worried that I will collapse at some point. I already have some liver complications.

Etty: Roberta, you brought up a very important issue about this difficult disclosure. It is very important to disclose when you are doing well. But it is also very important that you all work through your feelings before disclosure. You first have to take care of yourselves.

Nancy: I don't believe that I can do it.

Etty: You may not be ready now, but I believe that your children need to see you as strong enough to discuss this privately with them. You have to take the time you need to understand your feelings about your battle with your illness.

Kelly: I will be devastated if my daughter asks to live with her aunt instead of with me.

Rosa: I know that my son likes to drink. I am worried that he will become an alcoholic if I disclose my illness to him.

Etty: Perhaps some of your children need to get into psychotherapy to deal with your illness, but let's discuss first what you believe causes their "acting-out" behaviors.

Kelly: There is no one in my family who can take care of my daughter when I get sick.

Nancy: Don't talk like you are going to die.

Roberta: But I know that I will die, and it really scares me.

Kelly: Everyone will die. I am too tired now. How much time is left?

Session #4

Kelly did not make the session since she was in bed and felt weak. Nancy also cancelled because her son refused to babysit his younger sister. Rosa initiated a discussion of her feelings about telling her mother and brother of her illness before she talked with her son. It was clear that she would like to disclose at least to them before she had to be hospitalized. After Rosa talked about the issue, she decided to disclose to them together. She believed that her brother would soften her mother's inevitable blame. Roberta asked where and when Rosa would like to disclose. Rosa decided to visit her mother and ask her brother to join them. "What will you say is the reason for this meeting?" Nancy asked. Roberta said that she would tell them that there was something personal that she wanted to talk with both of them about.

I remarked that it would be important to decide before the meeting whom would she like to care for her son in case she needed more help. Nancy expressed her envy of Roberta's having a family to rely on, while she (Nancy) had no one. She was concerned about one of her teenaged children who used drugs. I suggested she consider referring him to a clinic near their home that worked with teenagers. She decided to disclose to her three teenaged children together instead of separately. I agreed that, since all three were at the same developmental stage, it would be appropriate to disclose to them together; they would then be able to support each other.

Session #5

Rosa did not show up but left a message that her son was sick and that she had to stay at home with him. Kelly asked us to fill her in, and Roberta summarized our last session. Kelly expressed her belief that because her daughter was acting out and their relationship was in turmoil, it was not the best time to disclose. Nancy responded that, if she waited until the relationship with her son improved, she might never disclose. The discussion in this session centered mainly on who would take care of their children in case they needed help. It was very sad to realize that these three mothers had such a difficult time thinking of someone they could rely on to take care of their children. I told them of the importance of listening to their teenaged children about what they thought about their mothers' decision about who would take care of them at difficult times.

Session #6

All the group members were present. Nancy, who did not have any symptoms, asked if it was beneficial for her two children to know about her illness at this point. The four mothers were in different stages of their illnesses, an important variable in disclosure. Nancy was HIV-positive, was perfectly able to protect and care for her family, and may live without medical complications for many years. A valid decision for her might be to allow the child a normal life for as long as possible. Kelly, Roberta, and Rosa all had such symptoms as tiredness, weakness, fever, and different kinds of pain. These three women had been hospitalized already. I felt it was important that they make their decisions regarding disclosure while they were healthy.

Session #7

In this session Kelly initiated a discussion about her daughter's father. She told us how she had met him and described their relationship until she gave birth. He had never been involved in her daughter's life and was in and out of jail. Rosa described her son's father. She loved him and was deeply hurt when he rejected custody. Roberta said that she was not sure who her children's fathers were. And Nancy announced that she had never been in love and that Kelly and Rosa were lucky to have had this experience. Kelly jumped in and reminded Nancy that, for her, love was a one-way street and she wished she had never met her daughter's father. Hoping they would ask to extend the number of sessions, I reminded the group that we had five more sessions. They did not respond.

Session #8

Rosa started the session by saying that she was going to have lunch with her mother and brother the next day. She felt ready to disclose to them and decided to ask her brother to take care of her son in case she died. She was reluctant to disclose to her son.

> *Rosa:* I am going to feel so sad and will cry. My son hates to see me cry.
> *Kelly:* I am worried that my daughter will say, "I knew it" and will blame me for lying. I feel so guilty.
> *Etty:* Talking about your HIV infection and AIDS is extremely complex. If you feel guilty, sad, nervous, or embarrassed, don't be afraid to say so. Bringing your feelings into the open can

help break the tension. Besides, your children will sense your uneasiness, even if you don't mention it.

Roberta: I have three teenagers at home, not one. They won't listen to me.

Etty: If your first conversation is cut short for any reason, don't give up. It is important to try again. This disclosure is a process, not a one-time event. It is important to have an ongoing process. Your children will need your help in discussing their fears and worries.

Roberta: My older son is in therapy now, and I hope that his therapist will help him with this.

Etty: It is great that he is in therapy. It is very difficult to raise three teenagers by yourself. It does seem, Roberta, that your younger son is depressed. He may also need to see a therapist. I am concerned about him.

Roberta: But he is doing very well in school.

Etty: He is a good kid, but he probably has some worries that he does not want to burden you with. A therapist might be able to help.

Nancy: You are all talking about teenagers, but my daughter is nine years old. I don't know if she even knows what HIV is.

I recommended that Nancy tell her children separately about her illness when the time comes. Since her two children are at different developmental stages, each needs an approach that is appropriate for his or her cognitive and emotional level. For example, her daughter probably would be aware of the negative connotations surrounding AIDS and was likely to feel shame about her mother's HIV diagnosis. I suggested she tell her daughter that HIV is a virus that causes damage to the body's immune system and that it can take a long time to start working. I also suggested she discuss HIV transmission in general terms to her latency-age daughter. If her daughter were a teenager, it would be a very different kind of disclosure. Her teenage son, on the other hand, would be able to understand the illness in greater detail. Knowing that HIV is transmitted through sexual intercourse and drug use, however, he might see his mother in a bad light. I emphasized that, even though I was discussing disclosure to children in terms of their biological developmental stage, it was crucial to consider their emotional development as well.

Session #9

Kelly did not show up because her daughter had gotten an award for her achievement in school. Rosa, smiling, said, "I did it" and described in detail her disclosure to her mother and twin brother. She was surprised at their reactions. They were compassionate and immediately decided to find another solution for her aunt, who lived with Rosa. Roberta and Nancy asked for more specific information, such as had her mother and brother asked how she had become infected, how long had she been infected, and who knew about her illness? Kelly answered in tears. She asked her brother to take care of her son if she needed his help, and he agreed. Her mother also offered her help as would be needed.

Session #10

Crying, Kelly started the session with the news that her uncle had passed away. She blamed God and questioned her religious beliefs. She felt guilty for not visiting her uncle frequently enough and not telling him all that she felt toward him. I asked her to say everything she would have liked to say to him. She said that she had never expressed her appreciation and gratitude toward him for raising her and her daughter. Other group members cried. Kelly revealed her fears about death. The discussion shifted immediately when Rosa told Kelly how she had disclosed to her mother and brother. Her brother then secured a job for her son so that he would be busy in the summer and earn some money, thus lifting some pressure from his mother. Her mother bought Rosa vitamins and promised to continue to do so.

Session #11

Kelly shared with us her feelings about her uncle's funeral. She related memories of her uncle and brought pictures of the two of them together. Kelly expressed her relief at having her daughter in therapy with me so that there was someone to share responsibilities with her. Rosa described a bond that had begun to develop between her son and her brother.

The group had another discussion about who might be able to take care of their children.

I reminded them that the last session would be the next week and asked for their thoughts and feelings. All of them wanted to terminate as we had planned. Kelly and Rosa, who were in individual therapy, suggested that they continue to work with their therapists on their struggles with their illness. They asked me to call their therapists and fill them in about the group sessions. In addition, Kelly also had parent guidance with me regarding her daughter, Keisha, so we would continue our work together on disclosure. Roberta said that she did not have time to commit to therapy and would call me if circumstances were to change. Nancy asked me to continue to see her individually, to which I agreed.

Session #12: Final Session

I was moved to find that the four mothers had brought to the last session drinks and food they had cooked. They had decided after the previous session to have some fun. Kelly shared with us that she had asked a couple who were close friends of hers to take care of her daughter if she became ill. She knew that her daughter liked them and would agree to this arrangement. She was happy to tell us that her relationship with her daughter had improved dramatically. Roberta and Nancy mentioned their continued hesitation to disclose to their children, and I emphasized again that they needed first to work through their own feelings. Rosa said that her family's support had given her the strength to consider disclosing to her son. Each of the group members described how the group had been helpful, and I focused on the importance of continuing the work we had started. I also expressed my appreciation to all of them for their courage in discussing a very painful issue. The mothers asked if we could add some time, and I extended the session by 15 extra minutes.

Nancy continued therapy with me for two years. Her son was referred to another therapist in the clinic. Nancy never disclosed her condition to her son as long as I knew her. In other areas she was doing well. She got a job as a receptionist and broke up with her husband, who was jailed.

Kelly disclosed to Keisha, who already knew, as Kelly had suspected. The first time they discussed the illness, Keisha overwhelmed her mother with many intrusive questions. Later, in her individual therapy, she talked with me about her feelings. She told me that she had known all along that something was wrong with her mother's health. Searching in her mother's bags and dresser drawers, she found pills and asked the school nurse what they were for. She kept this secret to herself and was relieved to be speaking to me about it. She was pleased with her mother's decision to have her mother's friends take care of her. She had tears in her eyes when she mentioned that. Following my repeated encouragements, Kelly initiated more discussions with Keisha. These encounters became increasingly intimate and heartfelt.

Parent groups offer a relatively unthreatening milieu in which information can be exchanged, discussed, and explored. Information to parents about their children's developmental tasks can eliminate distress both in children and parents.

These mothers attended meetings voluntarily. This parent group was partly supportive, partly insight oriented, and partly didactic. Continual self-examination was facilitated. Although interpersonal dynamics among the group's members is usually analyzed in a psychotherapy group, in this parent group I avoided exploration of these dynamics. I believed that emphasizing relationships among group members would undermine the goals of the group. I may have been wrong. My agenda was to have the mothers disclose their HIV/AIDS to their children, but the mothers were overwhelmed by their own intense feelings in connection with their illness. Work in the group enabled them to begin exploring feelings that led to some emotional relief. I feel now that that was what they needed from me.

The group provided a holding environment through ongoing support. In the group setting, the mothers supported each other and addressed common issues such as dealing with their traumatic past, battling with HIV/AIDS, struggling to raise their children, and disclosing to their families. Since this group met for only 12 sessions of 90 minutes each, it was difficult to stay focused on the topic of HIV/AIDS disclosure. I also realized that these mothers did not want to focus on their illness. Unfortunately they resisted engaging with me more intimately in therapy. In part, this resistance might have resulted from the knowledge that the group was to be of short duration (even though they had requested a circumscribed time frame). When dependency needs were strong, as they were with these four mothers, and long-term gratification of those needs were ruled out, as it had to be in such a short-term group, deeper commitment was withheld. The only two members who were in individual therapy, Kelly and Rosa, had formed a personal friendship.

At times parents do have to deal with issues that they keep secret to protect their children from the pain of any kind of revelation. Secrets may concern divorce, serious illness, sexual orientation, and financial difficulties. The issues I have explored in this chapter are relevant for dealing with all kinds of secrets in family lives. The secret that the mothers in this group faced, however, was the most painful one: the fear of leaving their children orphans.

This group had a strong impact on me. The mothers' stories of their traumatic childhoods broke my heart. Learning about their HIV infection and their subsequent struggles to battle with this disease evoked in me feelings of unresolved grief at the loss of a friend of mine to AIDS. We had worked together after I arrived in the United States. He died only a few months after that. He never told me about his battle with AIDS; I heard only from mutual friends. Like the children of the mothers in my group, I felt that something was wrong with him but did not ask. I did feel hurt at being excluded. But as time passed I respected his choice to keep his privacy. He disclosed only to his best friends, and I was not one of them. After he died I regretted not expressing my feelings. At his memorial I had a chance to share with his family and friends how significant a friend he had become to me in such a short period of time. Like the mothers in my group, I experienced the inner tension of encouraging them to disclose to their children about their HIV/AIDS versus respecting their own choices about their readiness. Their disclosure to their children was inevitable, but I had to work through my wish to impose my expectations on them to disclose at a time when they were not ready. I kept reminding myself of the emotional process I had gone through with my friend, and I was able to feel empathic and responsive to them.

11

Termination—Traumatic for Whom?

Goodbye

How do I say Goodbye to what we had?
How do I say Goodbye to yesterday?
How do I say Goodbye when it is all gone?
How do I say Goodbye when I know there is
so much that I know I will miss?

Termination—a phase, a state, a special treatment goal—is especially significant for adolescent patients who need to separate emotionally from preoedipal and postoedipal parental objects. From a relational point of view, however, the treatment goal in working with traumatized adolescents is to focus primarily not on separating from primary objects but on nurturing and enabling the adolescent to develop new and more nuanced relationships with significant others. The aim is to foster a mutuality between parents and adolescents that allows increased autonomy alongside dependency as well to enhance many kinds of relationships. Since repetition of old relational patterns is inevitable, relational analysts (Gordon et al., 1998), following Pizer (1992, 1996), believe that therapeutic progression depends on the analyst and the patient being able to "find new and more flexible ways to move beyond these repetitions, to free up their relationship, and to construct and negotiate new ways of being with each other" (Gordon et al., 1998, p. 51).

Few analyses of children and adolescents are terminated according to plan. Many are interrupted by external circumstances, such as the patient's or the therapist's moving away or a change of school. Some terminations result from resistance that is rationalized by the patient or the parent for "valid" external reasons. An important technical consideration is whether termination comes suddenly or whether there is some preparation for it. I have experienced both kinds of termination. Sudden termination was typical among the deprived, high-risk girls in my group. More conventional termination is illustrated by the case of Yael, the Israeli adolescent whom we first met in chapter 1.

As a mental health officer in the Israeli army, I had been assigned to work in an inpatient unit in Israel for one year. I divided my time between outpatient and inpatient units. In the latter, using behavioral, cognitive, and mostly psychoanalytic approaches, I treated children and adolescents who suffered from severe disorders. I specialized in working with patients who suffered from eating disorders. In this ward patients were hospitalized for a few days to more than a year.

Yael was transferred to my care after a few months of therapy with a social work intern. I saw her at least three times weekly. I was uncertain about whether or not to discuss with her from the very beginning the inevitable termination of our work, for I feared that such knowledge would prevent the establishment of a therapeutic alliance. Nevertheless, I decided to share with Yael that our time together would be limited. She understood. Anyway, she said, she hoped to be discharged from the hospital before I left.

For the first six months on the ward Yael lost weight, did not have her period, binged, reported suicidal ideation, and as a result was often locked up. As I got to know Yael and observed her participation within and outside treatment, I realized that she needed me to be available to her at critical moments. Once, after a family visit, she felt the urge to binge and asked me to join her at a delicatessen. Hesitantly, I accompanied her and watched her eat without being able to stop herself. I was appalled at how much she ate, but I felt her deep pain. My presence was clearly significant for her. This was a session without words but with intense emotional participation by both of us.

In our next session she explained that she did not want to be alone during those horrifying moments of bingeing, even though she was embarrassed. She explained what had precipitated the recent binge: her family had visited and upset her by putting pressure on her to call a friend.

After this and other, similar experiences, I gradually came to understand what prompted Yael to binge. When I first met her, I did not know how to be her therapist. Only after our struggles through the transference–countertransference interactions was I able to discover *how* she needed me to be as her therapist. I learned from her how to be a "usable" object (Winnicott, 1969).

In many sessions Yael kept her silence; in others, she shouted at me for recommending that she remain in the ward on a weekend instead of going home. During those weekends I always called her, and we talked for a few minutes. I believe that my phone calls stemmed as much from my own guilt as from my sincere concerns about Yael. After six months,

Yael's situation began to improve. We began to discuss the option of transferring her to a group residential unit for adolescents as a transition prior to returning home. Yael liked this plan; and, knowing that there was a waiting list to get into this well-known residential group, we started the process of admission to the group home. Yael explored her feelings toward the staff and me.

It was a few days before Rosh Hashanah, and we exchanged wishes for the New Year. To my surprise, she wished that I would "keep being as you are now." I asked her what she meant, and she explained that she saw me as serious and as a listener. She added that she appreciated that I saw her every day during the week, even for a few minutes, and that I never looked at the clock, something she had noticed with previous therapists. She also mentioned that I was reliable, that I kept all my promises. I always started sessions on time, and I maintained their frequency. She told me that, after each family session, her parents told her how lucky she was that I was her therapist. I was stunned to learn of her positive transference.

I suspected that knowing we were going to be separated made her feel safer in getting close to me. I commented on the importance of her expressing positive feelings, which had been difficult for her. Yael responded that, by my serious behavior, I had opened a "hole in her wall." Her relationships with her family improved and significant peer relationships started to evolve, and I believe that what she called opening the "hole in the wall" represented a creation of new relationships with others alongside the old ones.

Yael needed to experience concretely my presence, which provided her with a holding function. Winnicott (1947) noted that some patients need literally to be held during certain stages of the treatment. As was discussed in previous chapters, Yael's parents were unavailable and did not provide the nurturing environment she needed. Her father was sexually stimulating and at the same time was emotionally abusive; her mother was preoccupied with the care of Yael's brother. During her first years of life, she was cared for mostly by a series of babysitters. Analyzing this dynamic, Yael said that only her illness had "woken up" her parents. Initially, she had believed that she had to shake me up in similar ways to get my attention.

About eight months into treatment, Yael started to conform to the ward's requirements, and she maintained a stable weight. She was concerned, however, that the staff was not interested in her any more, since she was doing much better. Regrettably, that realization led to a relapse. She was locked up after she reported some suicidal ideation. Patients who were locked in the hospital were required to remain in pajamas to discourage them from trying to escape. Their attire also helps the staff identify those who are at risk. Yael felt humiliated to be in pajamas. She asked the staff to let her wear her clothes and promised not to leave the ward. They trusted her and agreed. She told me how much it mattered to know that the staff really cared and respected her. She never betrayed their trust. She said she would visit the staff after her discharge from the hospital. She explained, "They are often good to me." I asked her to be more specific, and she mentioned three staff members whom she would find it difficult to leave. When I asked what she would take with her from each of them, she said:

> From the chief nurse, I take integrity and honesty, something I never had with my family and others in my life. I also take her humor. From the nurse Shoshana, I take stubbornness in dealing with my binges. She was the one who directed me and showed me how strong she was in facing my binges and always being there for me. From the occupational therapist I take consistency. She insisted that I work with wood because she saw my talent. She did not let me give up, even though I frustrated her. About you I can say only that I hope that in the group home I will have a therapist like you. I would like to have only a female therapist. I need to have a warm therapist, and only women can give that.

Yael repeatedly voiced her concerns about her future therapist. She was worried that a new therapist would be passive and inattentive. If that happened, she would feel frozen and silent. She felt a great relief that I was more active than other therapists she had seen.

In our discussions of her mourning process about leaving the ward, she acknowledged the safety that the staff provided. She, however, resisted exploring past losses and as much as possible avoided the work of mourning. I looked for every opportunity to put Yael's feelings about termination into words. Her need to dissociate or minimize the impact of this loss highlighted how difficult it was for her. Yael often regressed during the termination phase by bingeing and being suicidal. She needed me with her to bear this stress. I found myself becoming anxious over the results of our work and wondered if the treatment had been comprehensive enough. Nonetheless, Yael terminated with a sense of joy and an eagerness to move on in her life toward independence. I was happy that she had begun to enjoy life. We shared the experience of delight. I knew, of course, that there was still much work to do, and so I felt some disappointment and sadness that she would be leaving to continue this work in another facility with another therapist.

During the last two months of treatment, Yael worked part-time in a general hospital. She was allowed to leave the hospital each afternoon to exercise in a gym with her tutor and participate in a art history class at a community center located close to the hospital. She went to movies with a friend. She began expressing her curiosity about the staff and wanted to know more about them. She was concerned about the chief nurse, for example, who was sick. She wanted to know the details of the illness but was afraid that by asking her she would hurt the nurse's feelings and destroy the relationship.

As termination came closer, Yael articulated more clearly her feeling of losing her relationship with me. Our relationship had changed. She said that knowing I worked in the outpatient unit was a relief for her, for she would be able to see me here and there around the hospital. That was enough for her to think of me as being available for her. I had arranged for her to see another therapist if she needed one when I was absent, although she did not take up that option.

Yael managed the change in the frequency of sessions with me and continued to improve. Although I considered calling her in my absence, I was aware that I was motivated mostly by my own guilt and did not call. I was happy to hear how well she was managing my absence and was more able to soothe herself. She asked me what I felt about her. I told her that I really liked her and appreciated her courage in her battle with her eating disorder. I added that I would greatly miss her. We had gone together through the stages of her recovery and the shifts in her relationships with her family, staff, and myself.

The final session was painful for both of us. Yael bought me a gift, a hand-made bracelet.

Yael: We both like jewelry. I thought you would like it.
Etty: Yes, I like it very much. [I put the bracelet on my hand.]
Yael: Jewelry always reminds me of you.
Etty: Are there other things that will remind you of me?
     [silence]
Etty: It is painful to say goodbye.
Yael: You know, at first I thought I felt more distance with you than with the staff, but I told you more than I told them. It is weird.
Etty: Probably the distance you are talking about provided you more control and safety. You needed this space between us.

Yael: Where is your military unit?

Etty: This is the first time that you are asking me a personal question.

Yael: I would like to know if your unit is far away from my home.

Etty: You would like to have the option of visiting me.

Yael: Yes.

Etty: I am working in a psychiatric clinic close to Haifa. I will give you my office number, but you will have to call me first so I can arrange for you to get in.

Yael: By the way, you've been here in the hospital almost the same time as I have been. I am sure that you are happy to leave. Are you?

Etty: Yes, I am happy to move on with my career, as you are happy to move on with you life. But I am also sad to leave you. [silence]

Yael: Next Sunday will be my first day in the group home.

Etty: How do you feel about this?

Yael: I assumed that you would ask me about my feelings. I can tell you only that I am confused.

Etty: You are too overwhelmed with different kinds of feelings as you leave this ward after a year of living here.

Yael: I would like to talk only about happy things.

Etty: OK. What do you feel happy about?

Yael: I am happy that I can deal with my binges.

Etty: Yes, you feel that you can now take control over your life. I'm happy to hear that. You have a lot to feel proud of yourself.

Yael left the ward for the residential group home. She had my phone number but never contacted me. I believe that it was soothing enough for her to know she could contact me.

Very few adolescents reach a point of mutually agreed upon termination. The same may also be true for adults, even though the literature suggests otherwise (Novick, 1982). Premature termination is pervasive. With adolescents, however, premature termination is a specific consequence of the conflict of disengagement. For adolescents the very fact of being in treatment is often a concrete reminder of their dependence and immaturity. Often it is extremely difficult to distinguish whether an adolescent's decision to terminate has grown out of conflict and resistance or out of a legitimate need to leave treatment as part of growing up and separating.

Termination can be seen as a result of "adolescent revolt" (A. Freud, 1971, p. 9). Termination is often precipitate, and there is no avoiding the fact that the decision to end is not mutual. I would ask, for whom is the termination premature? Is treatment considered premature because of the therapist's preconception of what constitutes a "complete" therapy? Who needs to have a "complete" termination? Is complete termination possible generally? Is it possible for traumatized patients? Is it even desirable? Is termination considered premature when the patient is the one who decides to terminate? Or is termination a mutual negotiation within the therapeutic dyad to the extent that the patient is able to tolerate the ambiguity of the therapeutic process?

According to Sandler, Kennedy, and Tyson (1980), discussing premature termination with difficult cases like the girls in my group, "both patients and analysts often expect to achieve things which cannot be achieved by analysis. Such unrealistic expectations lead to the idea that treatment has ended prematurely, that the analyst did not do it right or the patient did not cooperate" (p. 253). Ekstein (1983) recommends flexibility during the termination phase with adolescents and cautions against the therapist's overreaction and sense of failure when an adolescent patient imposes the termination of treatment. His focus is on an appropriate "letting go" of the adolescent, based on the therapist's surrender of omnipotent hopes of protecting the adolescent against future risks.

With regard to my therapeutic flexibility, I felt a certain tension between maintaining analytic discipline during this termination phase and being responsive to the girls' needs. Only now the tension was intensified. I tried to pursue what is considered "good termination" and asked the girls to spend a few sessions on termination. That, however, was not possible. Each of the girls, in her own way, chose a traumatic exit—a survival technique to avoid pain and to project her victimized self-representation (projective identification) onto me. The girls' enactments in terminating treatment expressed unconsciously, in action, their inner struggles. Transference and countertransference enactments emerged. The girls were the ones who were abandoning and I was the one who was abandoned, feeling impotent, angry, and helpless. My experience reflected what was so familiar to them. I suspect that this kind of termination is what clinicians have to expect in working with inner-city, multiply traumatized adolescents. Otherwise, therapists risk trauma of their own.

By sharing responsibility for termination, adolescents are less likely than otherwise to be overwhelmed by yet another loss and will be able to negotiate the separation actively and positively. Regrettably, the girls—with the exception of one, Yael—were unable to assume this responsibility. All but Yael terminated abruptly in ways that left me feeling traumatized. I should mention, though, that I had been seeing Yael regularly since her hospitalization and thus had easy access to her. And Yael and I had never had to deal with cancellations or lateness, as was the case with the other girls. Then, too, I saw Yael in intense therapy, three to five times weekly; and both her parents were involved in her life (unlike the parents of the other girls).

The multiple traumas that all the girls had experienced necessitated a different termination process for each. One must recognize realistically the limitations of treatment for severely traumatized adolescents such as these girls, not to speak of the ongoing external impingement on their development. As Brenner (2001) puts it, therapeutic work with these patients should not follow a "psychoanalytic course" (p. 201); termination is necessary even if the goals of psychoanalytic treatment have not been met.

While Yael terminated treatment in an atmosphere of intimacy, the girls of the group terminated abruptly. Laura was the first to leave. She gradually revealed more about her frequent use of drugs and alcohol. During the termination phase we had a discussion about using drugs. Nataline noted that drugs and alcohol had killed her mother, and she did not want to live her life as her mother had. She also talked about how wan her mother had looked even before she got AIDS. Nataline emphasized that she wanted to look pretty and take care of her health.

Michelle described her mother's boyfriend, who used drugs and was cruel and abusive to her. She told us of her fear of him and her decision never to use drugs. Dee and Lisa did not have anything to say. Carmen said that the fact that her father's murder was connected to his drug use and that her mother had contracted AIDS also from drug use would stop her from using drugs. She added that her baby half-sister had died of AIDS (her mother had AIDS when she gave birth to the baby). Carmen added that she would never do this to her own children. When I asked Laura how she felt about what the girls had said, she responded that they did not have enough knowledge about drugs, that she smoked only a little pot each day, and that this did not mean that she was drug addicted.

In the next session, 10 months into the course of treatment, Laura initiated another discussion about her drug use. I already had received phone calls from her teacher, expressing her worries about Laura; Laura was frequently absent from school, at times fell asleep during class, and had become distant from other students. During that session I asked Laura more specific questions about her drug use such how often and how much she used, and I shared with her the information I had received from her teacher. She attributed her absences from school to oversleeping. The other girls looked at me with disbelief and concern in their eyes. I told Laura we were all worried about her.

I raised the possibility of her joining a drug program. Laura announced that I was too worried. Two weeks later she brought in marijuana; sometimes she came to the session high. I said her drug use seemed a very serious situation and she was at risk of hurting herself. I emphasized that she could not bring drugs to the clinic and further suggested she join a drug program. She insisted that she could help herself.

I believed that Laura's presence was destructive to the group and was not therapeutic for her or for the other girls. Witnessing Laura's deterioration under the influence of drugs brought up traumatic memories for the rest of the group. Everyone in the group had an HIV/AIDS parent as a result of drug use. Laura's behavior was destabilizing the group and it was no longer a safe environment. Furthermore, using drugs and the possession of drugs on the clinic premises was prohibited. Following clinic policy, I told Laura that she would have to join a substance abuse rehabilitation program before she could return to the group. I asked Laura how she felt about leaving the group, and she announced that she did not care.

Thus it was I that initiated Laura's termination. It was difficult for me to acknowledge my own limitations, an issue that I struggled with throughout the course of treatment of all these girls and other traumatized patients. In a joint session, I persuaded Laura to tell her mother that she was using drugs and alcohol. The conversation between mother and daughter worked well. Laura was able to tell her mother in detail about her drug use, and her mother was able to listen and appreciate Laura's trust in her.

Laura and I agreed that she would come to the group four more times to say goodbye, but she did not live up to her promise. She called to say that she would not come to the group anymore because she was angry that the girls had not fought for her to remain. I emphasized the importance of saying goodbye and sharing her feelings about the time she had spent with us. I added that the girls had a lot to say to her and that I would like to stay in contact with her. She refused to come but agreed that I could tell the girls about our discussion. The girls expressed sorrow that Laura had not shown up and were upset at hearing what she had said. They were concerned whether or not she would really join the drug program. We discussed termination, and I told them I hoped that they would not leave treatment abruptly as Laura had since it was important to work through their feelings. Nataline and Dee felt guilty because they were the ones who had expressed strong disappointment with their relatives and blamed them for using drugs. Negative transferences toward me were activated. Nataline and Carmen, for example, realized that they had to be careful about what they shared in the group and questioned their trust in me. This termination, though very difficult, provided an opportunity to work through various issues around separation, loss, and individuation.

I was baffled by how differently the girls and I viewed treatment. I hoped they would have a rich and full life in the broadest sense. They wanted only to have some moments of fun in the group, moments they hoped would lead to some modest happiness in the rest of their lives.

Carmen was the second girl to leave the group. After 16 months in therapy, while her mother was hospitalized, Carmen told us that she did not like to stay with her neighbor while her sister stayed with her grandparents. I asked Carmen to explain her difficulties in staying with her neighbor, but she ignored my question. I suggested that we talk with her mother and social worker about other alternatives, but she did not want me to bother her hospitalized mother. Carmen's mother's health was deteriorating rapidly, and Carmen would call her mother at the hospital during sessions. During one phone call, her mother asked Carmen why she had misbehaved with their neighbor. Carmen did not want to explain and asked to stay by herself at home. Her mother agreed.

After Carmen was absent for a session, her mother phoned to tell me that Carmen had damaged the carpeting, furniture, and other possessions in their house with food and alcohol and had had sexual relations with a 20-year-old man. I felt that the mother, suffering from her illness, wanted to be free of Carmen and had unconsciously allowed Carmen to act out. Carmen and her mother had a physical fight; the police were called. In one day, without any discussion or preparation, Carmen's mother sent her to the South, saying that she could never return to New York.

The mother left a phone message telling me that Carmen would not becoming to the group any more. After two weeks of trying to reach the mother by phone, I was finally able to speak with her, twice. She refused to bring Carmen back to New York for a session. I tried to elicit the mother's empathy for her daughter by suggesting that Carmen was probably upset about being away from her. She was enraged that her daughter had had fun while she was in the hospital. She said, "It is too late. I am not going to forgive her." I asked her to give me Carmen's phone number, which she did, but she forbade my giving it to the girls in the group. I offered to help Carmen wherever she was if she needed it. Her mother said that she would think about this, and a week later I received a letter from her. She asked me to write the school psychologist, requesting counseling because of Carmen's emotional and academic problems. The mother also said how sorry she was that Carmen would not talk to her. Carmen was still very angry. Her mother, expressing some regrets, decided to wait until Carmen was ready to talk to her.

In two phone conversations, Carmen told me that she did not want to talk about her mother. She said that her mother expected her to beg to return home, but she was not going to do that, since she felt humiliated enough. She asked me to give her regards to the girls in the group. She knew that her mother had forbidden me to give them her phone number and was upset especially that she could not talk with Nataline, whom she had known for four years.

In a group session, Nataline expressed her sympathy for Carmen but at the same time was angry that Carmen had not called her. I later learned that Carmen's mother did not let her have her address book, so Carmen was unable to contact her friends. In another phone discussion, Carmen said that she was lonely and did not have any friends. "They are prejudiced," she said. She was the only student in her school with "dark skin." She added that she wished she were in our group therapy where she had her only friends.

Not knowing that her mother had no intention of bringing her back to New York, she asked me to arrange a foster parent for her when she returned to New York. The conversation broke my heart. I was overwhelmed with feelings of guilt—I wondered if I mighr have prevented Carmen's acting-out behavior if I had prepared the mother properly to think through arrangements for her children in case she was hospitalized. I also felt uncomfortable at not being able to give the girls Carmen's number and at not giving Carmen the girls' phone numbers. It appeared that it was too late for Carmen and her mother to reconcile. At Carmen's request, however, I called the school counselor and asked to arrange a therapy referral for Carmen. Neither I nor anyone else had a chance to say goodbye in person. Nataline, Carmen's long-time friend, was traumatized by this separation but refused to explore her feelings, "I don't care," she said repeatedly.

Carmen had developed a "cocoon" (Modell, 1986) dynamic configuration as her mother was dying. This cocoon position is a narcissistic defense—nothing leaves and nothing enters. Bromberg (1998) suggests that there is a connection between such a cocoon position and dissociation.

> The cocoon, regardless of what personality style it embodies, is, I feel, an inevitability as soon as dissociation becomes necessary, because consciousness will become inherently a cocoon unless it has access to a sufficient range of self-states to allow authentic interchange with the subjectivity of others [p. 193].

Carmen, who alone asked me not to burden her mother by discussing alternatives about who would take care of her, was also the one person in the group who most burdened her mother. Carmen's cocoon position averted attachment to her mother, who was going to abandon her. In her psyche her mother's anticipated death was dissociated.

After two more months, Dee and Lisa left the group. They had experienced traumatic abandonment by their mother and were trying very hard to please their foster mother so they would not have to move again. They were frustrated and hurt by their foster mother's failure to give them the nurturance they deserved. The sisters complained that I had "forced" them to come. They stated that they had come only because this was a condition set by their social worker for their continued living with their foster mother. Dee talked about finding out if a court had actually ordered them to come to therapy. Lisa said that because they were doing all right in school, they did not need to come to therapy any more.

During another session Dee threatened me, saying that I would be sorry if I did not do what they asked and write a letter to their social worker saying that they did not need to continue therapy. I believe that Dee's dissociations overwhelmed her, and she wanted simply to be silent and deny her feelings. It may be that the intimacy that had been created in the group was profoundly confusing for her. She may have felt that she needed to remove herself from the group in order to preserve her dissociated self.

After the sisters confirmed that therapy was their own choice and not the result of a court order, they decided to leave the group. Lisa, who was conflicted about leaving therapy, could not let herself stay without her sister because doing so would be perceived as a betrayal. I suggested that I meet with the sisters separately, but they refused to discuss their individual conflicts about being in therapy. I said that I appreciated the achievements that they had made, but I would like them to continue therapy because of their continuing worries. In our discussion of the sisters' willingness to terminate, Nataline said, "Michelle and I know that we need help. If Dee and Lisa don't believe they do, they will not be cooperative anyway and will not keep coming." Later I learned that Nataline and Michelle had been fearful of the sisters' aggressiveness and so had tried to push them out of the group.

After Dee and Lisa left the group, Michelle and Nataline gradually became better able to rely on their own psychological resources. It became increasingly possible for me to adopt a more insight-oriented approach. Their hate, envy, rage, and disappointment slowly began to emerge in the transference. They also started to explore their vulnerability relating to their dying parents and traumatic separations from their boyfriends.

During the session when we talked about the man who had raped Michelle, she broke into tears and said, "He destroyed my life." Nataline blamed me for making Michelle cry and became angrier when I asked her how she felt about Michelle's predicament. Before the next session, Nataline left a message that she would not be attending. I called her and encouraged her to express her anger toward me during the session, and she agreed to come. During that session Nataline cursed me, yelled at me, and blamed me for not helping her, not giving her more advice about boys. I told her of my concern about giving advice that might be perceived by Nataline as controlling and intrusive.

Michelle could not tolerate Nataline's anger and shifted the discussion to different issues. Nataline did not let me talk. She repeated that she would not return, and she persuaded Michelle to leave with her five minutes before the end of the session. Once again I felt overwhelmed with guilt, sadness, and helplessness.

I called Nataline before the next session and asked her to come. She said that she wanted to leave the group because it was not fun anymore as we discussed their losses and their being abused physically and sexually. I emphasized that it was important for her to express whatever she felt. She agreed to come. She became angrier as I tried to empathize. She left the session again 10 minutes early and took Michelle with her.

Sometime later, Nataline was hospitalized because of an asthma attack. Michelle said that Nataline called her from the hospital and asked her to visit. They spent the whole day together and had a great time. Michelle tried unsuccessfully to convince Nataline to return to the group, but this time Nataline did not return. I had lost her. Rather than trying to explore her transference enactments, she ran away. She escaped from her positive feelings, although it appeared that she broke off treatment in an overwhelmingly strong negative transference.

I interpreted Nataline's behavior and attitude toward me as grounded in the relational configuration in which she was the deprived child and I was the helpless, dysfunctional parent, unable to help her (and therefore useless, like her mother and grandmother). Thus, her sense of being deprived and badly treated was perpetuated. Nataline terminated therapy when the issues of sexual abuse became too overwhelming. Not infrequently a patient leaves or wants to leave treatment when confronted with memories of abuse (Davies and Frawley, 1994). When a patient begins to remember and share memories of the sexual victimization, the reality of the abuse may hit very hard. Until this point in treatment, the patient has been denying, through dissociation, the reality of the abuse and struggles against the pain of truly knowing about the assaults. Leaving therapy seems preferable to enduring the pain evoked by memories. For Nataline, who was traumatized by Michelle's exploration of her own trauma, leaving therapy was the only way to endure her pain. Her defenses could not protect against uncovering the traumatic memories. Her unstable, dissociated self, which had functioned as an adaptational system so she could regulate her self-experience and move on with her life, broke down.

Michelle left treatment two months later. She had begun to explore the trauma of being raped. At about this time in therapy, Michelle started to date another boy in the clinic and became preoccupied with this relationship. But, just when she and the boy were becoming closer, he suddenly began to ignore her and avoided any contact with her. Her efforts to obtain some explanation for his behavior failed. At this point, she started to speak of terminating therapy because the clinic reminded her of him. I helped her to explore her feelings about others who had abruptly abandoned her. Nevertheless, Michelle came to only one more session rather than the four more she had promised to attend. She did not answer my phone calls. I wrote her a goodbye letter, but I did not see her again. I had lost her too.

Michelle's sudden shift from exploring her traumatic experience—and becoming more attached to me—to leaving treatment created obstacles to her potential growth and the hope for a good relationship as an attainable reality. This abrupt shift in our relationship suggested that her new intimacy with me signaled danger.

On the other hand, abrupt termination may have helped the girls to function more adaptively in the world. Their fragility placed severe limits on the extent to which they could tolerate therapeutic insight and closeness, and escape provided relative safety from the potential repetition of their trauma. Their dissociative states helped them regulate their psychological survival.

The girls' adaptive functioning outside therapy was manifested in different ways. Nataline, after a year and 10 months, terminated therapy as the sexual abuse issues began to overwhelm her. In spite of an apparent lack of trusting communication with me, for almost two years she had managed to deal with and process many of her feelings around the loss of her mother to AIDS. The overall level, frequency, and intensity of her anxiety was reduced so that her daily functioning was enhanced. She also improved dramatically in school; after receiving a scholarship, she transferred to a private school. For the first time in her life she was involved in a serious relationship with a boy, a student her own age.

A year and a half after she terminated treatment with me, Nataline referred herself back for therapy. She told the intake coordinator who took her phone call that she needed therapy because she had a lot of anger inside because of the loss of her mother, grandfather, and others. Clearly, she had achieved awareness about her angry feelings and their origins. In addition, by seeking therapeutic help, she demonstrated hope that therapy could be beneficial, and she was ready to continue the work she began with me.

Carmen stayed in therapy with me for 16 months. While Carmen improved in school, her mother's health continued to deteriorate. Carmen was sent to live with her aunt after she acted out. Carmen was able to express her pain at leaving the girls in the group and asked me to help refer her to therapy. When I asked about the kind of issues she wanted to get help with, she talked of feelings of anger toward her mother. She also accepted responsibility for her behavior. Although she could not forgive her mother, she did ask if she could speak with her mother in the presence of a therapist; she worried that, if she spoke with her mother alone, she would not be able to control herself. I suggested that Carmen contact her school counselor (I assumed that her schoolwork had suffered). She welcomed my suggestion, and I contacted her school counselor and discussed Carmen's crisis and her need for support and help. After achieving some closure with Carmen in telephone sessions, I arranged for her to enter therapy in her new location.

Just as Nataline and Carmen improved in their functioning outside therapy, so did the other girls—with the exception of Laura. Laura agreed to have two individual sessions and stayed in my bereavement group for 10 months. Laura did some good work in the group, even though she had never belonged in the group in the first place because she was very heavily involved in drug use. Unfortunately, this information did not come to light until after nine months of group work. After Laura's termination, her mother continued working with another therapist but dropped out after a short time. Laura did not acknowledge her chemical dependence and could not identify the negative ways her drug use had affected her life. She refused to be admitted to a substance-abuse program.

Lisa stayed in the group for a year. A very talented and creative girl, she attended a school for gifted children. The group therapy encouraged her intellectual gifts and improved her relational conflicts with authority figures. The group gave her a place to work through issues with authority figures through empathy and identification with the other girls. Lisa's grades, quite good to begin with, were showing further improvement at the time of termination.

Dee, like her sister, stayed in the group for a year. In addition, she kept our contract to come to six individual sessions. During those sessions, she told her entire story of the sexual abuse and was able to identify and express the feelings connected to the abuse. She spoke of the traumatic experiences associated with her nightmares and sleeplessness. Unfortunately, she could not tolerate completing this work and resisted having more individual sessions or discussing the sexual abuse during the group sessions. However, she stopped reporting nightmares after three months of group therapy, and she slept better. She displaced a great deal of her anger onto me in the group, which made her less depressed and more energetic. She made new friends and stopped going out with her sister's friends. She interacted socially without excessive fear or anxiety.

Michelle was in therapy in the group for 16 months; she had seen me for six individual sessions before she joined the group. She was the most articulate girl in the group, the one who often expressed her feelings through her pictures and writings. She became more aware of how her upbringing had affected her emotionally and behaviorally. She openly discussed her relationship with her AIDS-stricken father. The school published her poems and granted her a $500 award for her writing. She moved from special education into a regular classroom. She was chosen to attend a writing camp during the summer before she terminated therapy.

Michelle's overall pattern of social anxiety and reluctant involvement in social situations changed. She began to be able to identify how shame affected her relations with others, identified sources of fear of rejection in childhood experiences, and participated verbally in a meaningful way in group therapy. After moving in with her mother, she began family therapy at an agency closer to home.

All the girls were in the group for different durations. Hoping that they might return to therapy in the future, I let them determine how long they could tolerate the therapeutic process. I had to tolerate all the difficulties my girls presented. During this termination phase, I felt defeated, I felt there was nothing more I could do. Like the girls, I felt helpless. And I experienced deep despair. I was not entirely aware of the depth of my despair, for I resisted the idea that I could be affected by the girls. But, in time, I worked through some of my despair.

I watched the girls improve their functioning at home, at school, and with their peers. Their resilience in the face of chaotic lives and multiple traumas has been a constant source of inspiration and hope for me. Altman (2002, personal communication) discusses the delicate balance between maintaining hope in the face of despair when working with traumatized inner-city adolescents. He believes that analysts' surrendering their despair opens new possibilities for patients in dealing with their injured souls. Mitchell (1993), writing on the "analytic crunch," said:

> Some of the most important work done during impasses and stalemates is in the countertransference, in the analyst's struggle to regain his own sense of the meaning and value of his understanding, despite its limitations. By finding again and redefining his own realistic sense of hope, the analyst is more able to find a voice in which to speak to the patient that is different from the voices of the patient's past, offering their perpetually enticing and perpetually disappointing false promises [p. 214].

For fragile adolescents such as those presented in this book, it may be impossible to complete the working-through process of termination and to resolve grief and trauma during a single therapy. Nonetheless, even imperfect termination can still be part of an invaluable therapeutic process.

Epilogue

Thus the analyst's modesty must be no studied pose,
but a reflection of the limitation of our knowledge
—Ferenczi

This book tells the stories of severely traumatized adolescents. In the process, it explores my story of self-discovery as a therapist.

Finding the most appropriate treatment approach for traumatized and impoverished minority adolescents continues to be a source of great controversy in the therapeutic community. Altman (1995, 1996) writes about applying the relational model to the treatment of inner-city patients, including children in public clinics. He advocates change in our way of looking at the problems of patients from economically deprived backgrounds. He makes an important contribution by asking us to look at such patients primarily from the vantage point of the communications that lie behind their apparent ego deficits and that are meant unconsciously to convey to us the object relational deprivation that these patients have experienced. Altman feels, and I agree, that only by entering into a patient's relational world can we hope to make a meaningful connection that will make it possible to do therapeutic work.

This book focuses on an unusually significant group within the larger field of adolescent therapy, namely, multiply traumatized adolescents. Clinical work with multiply traumatized adolescents demands sophisticated care, given the absence of a complete understanding of them. Therapists have to expect the unpredictable and must tolerate uncertainty within the therapeutic setting with these patients so that multiple meanings can be constructed. Hoffman (1992), taking a constructivist approach, suggests:

> The model requires that analysts embrace the uncertainty that derives from knowing that their subjectivity can never be fully transcended. Nevertheless, this very uncertainty frees analysts to "be themselves" within the constrains of the purposes of the analysis [p. 287].

The multiply traumatized adolescents presented in this book illustrate cases for which standard techniques are not applicable. Often we fall back on the familiar when we are at a loss. At these times, we, like our patients, are likely to find ourselves struggling without easy solutions. Because we, along with our patients, are engaged in a process of change, our technique must be continually subject to revision.

Analytical technique has never been, nor is it now, something finally settled.
—Ferenczi

References

Ackerman, N.W. (1958), *The Psychoanalysis of Family Life: Diagnosis and Treatment of Family Relationships.* New York: Basic Books.

Aichhorn, A. (1935), *Wayward Youth: A Psychoanalytic Study of Delinquent Children.* New York: Viking Press.

————— (1964), *Delinquency and Child Guidance: Selected Papers.* New York: International Universities Press.

Aiosa-Karpas, C.J., Karpas, R., Pelcovitz, D. & Kaplan, S. (1991), Gender identification and sex role attribution in sexually abused adolescent females. *J. Amer. Acad. Child & Adolesc. Psychiat.*, 30:266–271.

Ainsworth, M. D. (1980), Attachment and child abuse. In: *Child Abuse: An Agenda for Action,* ed. G. Gerbner, C. J. Ross & E. Zigler. New York: Oxford University Press.

Altman, N. (1995), *The Analyst in the Inner City: Race, Class, and Culture Through a Psychoanalytic Lens.* Hillsdale, NJ: The Analytic Press.

————— (1996), The accommodation of diversity in psychoanalysis. In: *Reaching Across Boundaries of Culture and Class: Widening the Scope of Psychotherapy,* ed. R. Perez-Foster, M. Moskowitz & R. A. Javier. Northvale, NJ: Aronson, pp. 195–211.

American Psychiatric Association (1994), *Diagnostic and Statistical Manual of Mental Disorders* (DSM-III). Washington, DC: American Psychiatric Press.

Amodeo, M. & Drouilher, A. (1992), Substance-abusing adolescents. In: *Countertransference in Psychotherapy with Children and Adolescents,* ed. J. R. Brandell. Northvale, NJ: Aronson, pp. 285–315.

Anastasopoulos, D. (1988), Acting out during adolescence in terms of regression in symbol formation. *Internat. Rev. Psycho-Anal.*, 15:177–186.

————— & Tsiantis, J. (1996), Countertransference issues in psychoanalytic psychotherapy with children and adolescents: A brief review. In: *Countertransference with Children and Adolescents,* ed. J. Tsiantis, A.M. Sandler, D. Anastasopulos & B. Martindale. London: Karnac Books, pp. 1–37.

————— Laylou-Lignos, E. & Waddell, M., eds. (1999), *Psychoanalytic Psychotherapy of the Severely Disturbed Adolescent.* London: Karnac Books.

Aron, L. (1996), *A Meeting of Minds: Mutuality in Psychoanalysis.* Hillsdale, NJ: The Analytic Press.

Atkinson, S. & Gabbard, G. O. (1995), Erotic transference in the male adolescent–female analyst dyad. *The Psychoanalytic Study of the Child*, 50:171–186. New Haven, CT: Yale University Press.

Azima, F. J. C, & Richmond, L. H., eds. (1991), *Adolescent Group Psychotherapy.* Madison, CT: International Universities Press.

Balint, M. (1952), *Primary Love and Psycho-Analytic Technique.* London: Maresfield Library, 1985.

———— (1968), *The Basic Fault*. London: Tavistock.

Benjamin, J. (1988), *The Bonds of Love*. New York: Pantheon.

———— (1991), Father and daughter: Identification with difference—A contribution to gender heterodoxy. *Psychoanal. Dial.*, 1:277–299.

———— (1992), Recognition and destruction: An outline of intersubjectivity. In: *Relational Perspectives in Psychoanalysis*, ed. N. J. Skolnick & S. C. Warshaw. Hillsdale, NJ: The Analytic Press, pp. 43–60.

———— (1996), In defense of gender ambiguity. *Gender & Psychoanal.*, 1:27–43.

Berkovitz, I. H. (1972), *Adolescents Grow in Groups*. New York: Brunner/Mazel.

Berman, M. S. (1986), Transference love and love in real life. *Internat. J. Psychoanal. Psychother.*, 11:27–45.

Bernstein, I. & Glenn, J. (1988), The child and adolescent analyst's emotional reactions to his patients. *Internat. Rev. Psycho-Anal.*, 15:225–241.

Bigras, J. (1990), Psychoanalysis as incestuous repetition: Some technical considerations. In: *Adult Analysis and Childhood Sexual Abuse*, ed. H. B. Levine. Hillsdale, NJ: The Analytic Press, pp. 174–196.

Blos, P. (1962), *On Adolescence: A Psychoanalytic Intervention*. New York: Free Press.

———— (1963), The concept of acting out in relation to the adolescent process. *J. Child Psychiat.*, 2:118–136.

———— (1979), *The Adolescent Passage*. New York: International Universities Press.

Blum, H. (1973), The concept of the erotized transference. *J. Amer. Psychoanal. Assn.*, 29:61–76.

Boesky, D. (1982), Acting-out: A reconsideration of the concept. *Internat. J. Psycho-Anal.*, 53:39–55.

Bok, S. (1983), *Secrets: On the Ethics of Concealment and Revelation*. New York: Vintage Books.

Bolton, F., Morris, L. & MacEachron, A. (1989), *Males at Risk: The Other Side of Child Sexual Abuse*. Newbury Park, CA: Sage.

Bowen, M. (1978), *Family Therapy in Clinical Practice*. New York: Aronson.

Bowlby, J. (1988), *A Secure Base: Parent–Child Attachment and Healthy Human Attachment*. New York: Basic Books.

Brabant, E., Falzeder, E. & Giampieri–Deutsch, P., eds. (1993), *The Correspondence of Sigmund Freud and Sándor Ferenczi, Vol. 1, 1908–1914* (trans. P. T. Hoffer). Cambridge, MA: Belknap Press/Harvard University Press.

Brandell, J. R. (1992), *Countertransference in Psychotherapy with Children and Adolescents*. Northvale, NJ: Aronson.

Brandes, N. S. (1973), *Group Therapy for the Adolescent*. Northvale, NJ: Aronson.

———— (1977), Group therapy is not for every adolescent: Two case illustrations. *Internat. J. Psychother.*, 27:507–510.

Brenneis, C. B. (1996), Multiple personality: Fantasy proneness, demand characteristics, and indirect communication. *Psychoanal. Psychol.*, 13:367–387.

Brenner, I. (2001), *Dissociation of Trauma: Theory, Phenomenology, and Technique*. Madison, CT: International Universities Press.

Briere, J. (1996), *Therapy for Adults Molested as Children: Beyond Survival*. New York: Springer.

Bromberg, M. (1996), *Standing in the Spaces: Essays on Clinical Process, Trauma, and Dissociation*. Hillsdale, NJ: The Analytic Press.

Buchholz, E. & Mishne, J. (1994), *Group Interventions with Children, Adolescents, and Families.* Northvale, NJ: Aronson.

Chodorow, N. J. (1978), *The Reproduction of Mothering.* Berkeley: University of California Press.

Chused, J. F. (1990), Neutrality in the analysis of action-prone adolescents. *J. Amer. Psychoanal. Assn.,* 38:679–704.

———— (1991), The evocative power of enactments. *J. Amer. Psychoanal. Assn.,* 39:615–640.

Cohen, E. (1997a), Traumatized and Impoverished Minority Female Adolescents Facing Parental Loss through AIDS: Theoretical and Clinical Considerations. Unpublished doctoral dissertation, New York University. Ann Arbor, MI: University Microfilms.

———— (1997b), "I am the master of the nuts of the whole world." Dialogues on the unconscious: Enactments in the treatment of a latency age boy. *Psychoanal. Psychother.,* 14:189–220.

———— guest ed. (2001), *American Journal of Psychoanalysis.* 61(1).

Cohen, Y. (1991), Gender identity conflicts in adolescents as motivation for suicide. *Adolesc.,* 26:19–29.

Compact Oxford English Dictionary (1971). New York: Oxford University Press.

Courtois, C. A. (1998), *Healing the Incest Wound.* New York: Norton.

Crowder, A. (1995), *Opening the Door: A Treatment Model for Therapy with Male Survivors of Sexual Abuse.* New York: Brunner/Mazel.

Davies, J. M. (1996), Dissociation, repression, and reality testing in the countertransference: The controversy over memory and false memory in the psychoanalytic treatment of adult survivors of childhood sexual abuse. *Psychoanal. Dial.,* 6:189–219.

———— (1997), Dissociation, therapeutic enactment, and transference–countertransference processes: A discussion of papers on childhood sexual abuse. *Gender & Psychoanal.,* 2:241–257.

———— (1998), Multiple perspectives on multiplicity. *Psychoanal. Dial.,* 8:195–206.

———— (1999), Getting cold feet, defining "safe-enough" borders: Dissociation, multiplicity, and integration in the analyst's experience. *Psychoanal. Quart.,* 68:184–208.

———— & Frawley, M. G. (1994), *Treating the Adult Survivor of Childhood Sexual Abuse: A Psychoanalytic Perspective.* New York: Basic Books.

Derrida, J. (1976), *Of Grammatology* (trans. G. Spivak). Baltimore, MD: Johns Hopkins University Press.

———— (1978), *Writing and Difference* (trans. A. Bass). Chicago: University of Chicago Press.

Dimen, M. (1995), The third step: Freud, the feminists, and postmodernism. *Amer. J. Psychoanal.,* 55:303–319.

Ehrenberg, D. B. (1992), *The Intimate Edge.* New York: Norton.

Ekstein, R. (1983), The adolescent self during the process of termination of treatment: Termination, interruption or intermission. In: *Adolescent Psychiatry,* 9:125–146. Chicago: University of Chicago Press.

Elizur, J. (1999), "Inside" systems consultation in the IDF's installation for treating combat reactions facing a tradition of denial. *SIHOT—DIALOGUE,* 13:188–205.

Epstein, L. (1988), The therapeutic function of hate in the countertransference. In: *Essential Papers on Countertransference,* ed. B. Wolstein. New York: New York University Press, pp. 213–234.

Evans, M. (1990), Brother to brother: Integrationg concepts of healing regarding male sexual assault survivors and Vietnam veterans. In: *The Sexually Abused Male, Vol. 2,* ed. M. Hunter. Lexington, MA: Lexington Books, pp. 57–78.

Fairbairn, W. R. D. (1944), Endopsychic structure considered in terms of object-relationship. In: *Psychoanalytic Studies of the Personality.* London: Routledge & Kegan Paul, 1952, pp. 82–136.

———— (1952), *Psychoanalytic Studies of the Personality.* London: Routledge & Kegan Paul.

Fast, I. (1984), *Gender Identity: A Differentiation Model.* Hillsdale, NJ: The Analytic Press.

Fenichel, O. (1945), *The Psychoanalytic Theory of Neurosis.* New York: Norton.

Ferenczi, S. (1913), Stages in the development of the sense of reality. In: *First Contributions to Psycho-Analysis,* ed. M. Balint (trans. E. Mosbacher). London: Karnac Books, 1994, pp. 213–240.

———— (1915), Psychogenic anomalies of voice production. In: *Further Contributions to the Theory and Technique of Psycho-Analysis,* ed. J. Richman (trans. J. Suttie). London: Karnac Books, 1994, pp. 105–109.

———— (1920), The further development of an active therapy in psychoanalysis. In: *Further Contributions to the Theory and Technique of Psycho-Analysis,* ed. J. Richman (trans. J. Suttie). London: Karnac Books, 1994, pp. 198–217.

———— (1928), The elasticity of psychoanalytic techniques. In: *Final Contributions to the Problems and Methods of Psychoanalysis,* ed. M. Balint (trans. E. Mosbacher). London: Karnac Books, 1994, pp. 87–101.

———— (1929), The unwelcome child and his death-instinct. In: *Final Contributions to the Problems and Methods of Psychoanalysis,* ed. M. Balint (trans. E. Mosbacher). London: Karnac Books, 1994, pp. 102–107.

———— (1931a), On the revision of the interpretation of dreams. In: *Final Contributions to the Problems and Methods of Psychoanalysis,* ed. M. Balint (trans. E. Mosbacher). London: Karnac Books, 1994, pp. 238–243.

———— (1931b), Child analysis in the analysis of adults. In: *Final Contributions to the Problems and Methods of Psychoanalysis,* ed. M. Balint (trans. E. Mosbacher). London: Karnac Books, 1994, pp. 126–142.

———— (1932), *The Clinical Diary of Sándor Ferenczi,* ed. J. Dupont (trans. M. Balint & N. Z. Jackson). Cambridge, MA: Harvard University Press, 1988.

———— (1933), Confusion of tongues between adults and the child. In: *Final Contributions to the Problems and Methods of Psychoanalysis,* ed. M. Balint (trans. E. Mosbacher). London: Karnac Books, 1994, pp. 156–167.

Fraiberg, S., Adelson, E. & Shapiro, V. (1987), Ghost in the nursery. In: *Selected Writings of Selma Fraiberg,* ed. L. Fraiberg. Columbus: Ohio State University Press, pp. 100–136.

Frankel, J. (1993), Collusion and intimacy in the analytic relationship. In: *The Legacy of Sándor Ferenczi,* ed. L. Aron & A. Harris. Hillsdale, NJ: The Analytic Press, pp. 227–248.

Freedman, R. (1994), More on transformation: Enactments in psychoanalytic space. In: *The Spectrum of Psychoanalysis,* ed. A. R. Richards & A. D. Richards. Madison, CT: International Universities Press, pp. 93–110.

Freud, A. (1936), *The Ego and the Mechanisms of Defense.* New York: International Universities Press, 1946.

———— (1958), Adolescence. In: *The Writings of Anna Freud, Vol. 4*. New York: International Universities Press, pp. 136–166.

———— (1971), The infantile neurosis-genetic and dynamic consideration. In: *The Writings of Anna Freud, Vol. 7*. New York: International Universities Press, pp. 189–203.

———— (1974), A psychoanalytic view of developmental psychopathology. In: *The Writings of Anna Freud, Vol. 8*. New York: International Universities Press, pp. 57–74.

Freud, S. (1912), Recommendations to physicians practicing psychoanalysis. *Standard Edition*, 12:109–120, London: Hogarth Press, 1958.

———— (1914), Remembering, repeating, and working through. *Standard Edition*, 12:147–156. London: Hogarth Press, 1958.

———— (1915), Instincts and their vicissitudes. *Standard Edition*, 14:117–140. London: Hogarth Press, 1957.

———— (1917), Mourning and melancholia. *Standard Edition*, 14:243–258. London: Hogarth Press, 1957.

———— (1920), Beyond the pleasure principle. *Standard Edition*, 18:7–64. London: Hogarth Press, 1955.

Furman, E. (1957), Treatment of under fives by way of parents. *The Psychoanalytic Study of the Child*, 12:250–262. New Haven, CT: Yale University Press.

———— (1974), *A Child's Parent Dies*. New Haven, CT: Yale University Press.

Gabbard, G.O. (1994), Commentary on papers by Tansey, Hirsh, and Davies. *Psychoanal. Dial.*, 4:203–213.

Gabriel, A. (1939), An experiment in group therapy. *Amer. J. Orthopsychiat.*, 9:593–602.

———— (1944), Group therapy for adolescent girls. *Amer. J. Orthopsychiat.*, 14:593–602.

Gardner, F. (1999), A sense of all conditions. In: *Erotic Transference and Countertransference: Clinical Practice in Psychotherapy*, ed. D. Mann. New York: Routledge, pp.139–149.

Gartner, A. (1985), Countertransference issues in the psychotherapy of adolescents. *J. Child & Adolesc. Psychother.*, 2:187–196.

Gartner, R. B. (1999), *Betrayed as Boys: Psychodynamic Treatment of Sexually Abused Men*. New York: Guilford Press.

Gibbs, J. T. (1989), Black American adolescents. In: *Children of Color: Psychological Interventions with Minority Youth*, ed. J. T. Gibbs & L. N. Huang. San Francisco: Jossey-Bass, pp. 179–224.

Gil, E. (1996), *Treating Abused Adolescents*. New York: Gail Ford Press.

Gilgun, J. (1990), Factors mediating the effects of childhood maltreatment. In: *The Sexually Abused Male, Vol. 1*, ed. M. Hunter. Lexington, MA: Lexington Books, pp. 177–190.

Gill, M. M. (1982), *The Analysis of Transference, Vol. 1*. New York: International Universities Press.

Giovacchini, P. (1974), The difficult adolescent patient: Countertransference problems. In: *Adolescent Psychiatry, Vol. 3: Development and Clinical Studies*, ed. S. Feinstein & P. Giovacchini. New York: Basic Books, pp. 271–288.

———— (1985), Countertransference and the severely disturbed adolescent. In: *Adolescent Psychiatry, Vol. 12*, ed. S. Feinstein & P. Giovacchini. New York: Basic Books, pp. 449–467.

Goldner, V. (1991), Toward a critical relational theory of gender. *Psychoanal. Dial.*, 1:249–272.

Goldstein, E. G. (1994), Self-disclosure in treatment: What therapists do and don't talk about. *Clin. Soc. Work J.*, 22:417–433.

Gordon, R. M., Aron, L., Mitchell, S. A. & Davies, J. M. (1998), Relational psychoanalysis. In: *Current Theories of Psychoanalysis*, ed. R. Langs. Madison, CT: International Universities Press, pp. 31–58.

Gorkin, M. (1985), Varieties of sexualized countertransference. *Psychoanal. Rev.*, 72:421–440.

———— (1987), *The Uses of Countertransference*. Northvale, NJ: Aronson.

Green, A. H. (1983), Dimensions of psychological trauma in abused children. *J. Amer. Assn. Child Psychiat.*, 22:231–237.

———— (1994), Impact of sexual trauma on gender identity and sexual object choice. *J. Amer. Acad. Psychoanal.*, 22:283–297.

Green, V. (2000), Therapeutic space for re-creating the child in the mind of the parents. In: *Work with Parents: Psychoanalytic Psychotherapy with Children and Adolescents*, ed. J. Tsiantis, S. B. Boethious, B. Hallerfors, A. Horne & L. Tischler. London: Karnac Books, pp. 25–46.

Greenacre, P. (1950), *Trauma, Growth, and Personality*. Madison, CT: International Universities Press.

Greenberg, J. R. (1995), Self-disclosure: Is it psychoanalytic? *Contemp. Psychoanal.*, 31:193–205.

Greenson, R. R. (1967), *The Technique and Practice of Psychoanalysis*. New York: International Universities Press.

Gutheil, T. G. & Havens, L. L. (1979), The therapeutic alliance: Contemporary meanings and confusions. *Internat. Rev. Psycho-Anal.*, 6:467–481.

Haley, J. (1976), *Problem-Solving Therapy*. San Francisco: Jossey-Bass.

Harley, M. (1970), On some problems of technique in the analysis of early adolescents. *The Psychoanalytic Study of the Child*, 25:99–121. New Haven, CT: Yale University Press.

Harris, A. (1991), Gender as contradiction: A discussion of Freud's "The psychogenesis of a case of homosexuality in a woman." *Psychoanal. Dial.*, 1:197–224.

Herman, J. L. (1992), *Trauma and Recovery*. New York: Basic Books.

———— & Shatzow, E. (1984), Time-limited group psychotherapy for women with history of incest. *Internat. J. Group Psychother.*, 34:605–610.

Herzog, J. M. (2001), *Father Hunger: Explorations with Adults and Children*. Hillsdale, NJ: The Analytic Press.

Hoffer, A. (2000), Neutrality and the therapeutic alliance: What does the analyst want? In: *The Therapeutic Alliance*, ed. S. T. Levy. Madison, CT: International Universities Press, pp. 35–54.

Hoffman, I. Z. (1992), Expressive participation and psychoanalytic discipline. *Contemp. Psychoanal.*, 28:1–15.

———— (1998), *Ritual and Spontaneity in the Psychoanalytic Process: A Dialectical-Constructivist View*. Hillsdale, NJ: The Analytic Press.

Horovitz, M. J. (1985), *Stress Response Syndromes*. New York: Aronson.

Hunter, M. (1990), *Abused Boys: The Neglected Victims of Sexual Abuse*. Lexington, MA: Lexington Books.

Imber-Black, E. (1998), *The Secret Life of Families*. New York: Bantam Books.

Jacobs, T. J. (1986), On countertransference enactments. *J. Amer. Psychoanal. Assn.*, 34:289–307.

——— (1991), *The Use of Self.* Madison, CT: International Universities Press.

Jacobson, E. (1957), Denial and repression. *J. Amer. Psychoanal. Assn.,* 5:61–92.

James, B. (1989), *Treating Traumatized Children: New Insights and Creative Interventions.* New York: Lexington Books.

Josselyn, I. (1972), Prelude—adolescent group therapy: why, where and a caution. In: *Adolescents Grow in Groups,* ed. H. Berkovitz. New York: Brunner/Mazel, pp. 1–5.

Kihlstrom, J., Gliski, M. & Anguiulo, M. (1994), Dissociative tendencies and dissociative disorders. *J. Abn. Psychol.,* 103:117–124.

Kohut, H. (1977), *The Restoration of the Self.* New York: International Universities Press.

Kymissis, P. & Halperin, D. A. (1996), *Group Therapy with Children and Adolescents.* Washington, DC: American Psychiatric Press.

Lansky, M. R. & Bley, C. R. (1995), *Posttraumatic Nightmares: Psychoanalytic Explorations.* Hillsdale, NJ: The Analytic Press.

Layton, L. (1998), *Clinical Practice Meets Postmodern Gender Theory.* Northvale, NJ: Aronson.

Lester, E. P. (1985), The female analyst and the erotized transference. *Internat. J. Psycho-Anal.,* 66:283–293.

Lewis, H. J. (1992), *Trauma and Recovery.* New York: Basic Books.

Levenson, E. A. (1972), *The Fallacy of Understanding.* New York: Basic Books.

——— (1983), *The Ambiguity of Change.* New York: Basic Books.

——— (1996), Aspects of self-revelation and self-disclosure. *Contemp. Psychoanal.,* 32:237–248

——— (2000), An interpersonal perspective on dreams: Commentary on paper by Hazel Ipp. *Psychoanal. Dial.,* 10:119–125.

Lidz, T. (1946), Nightmares and combat neuroses. *Psychiat.,* 19:37–49.

Loewald, H. W. (1951), Ego and reality. In: *Papers on Psychoanalysis.* New Haven, CT: Yale University Press, 1980, pp. 3–20.

Lynn, D. J. (1997), Sigmund Freud's psychoanalysis of Albert Hirst. *Bull. Hist. Med.,* 71:69–93.

Lynn, D. J. & Vaillant, G. E. (1998), Anonymity, neutrality, and confidentiality in the actual methods of Sigmund Freud: A review of 43 cases, 1907–1939. *Amer. J. Psychiat.,* 155:163–171.

MacLennay, B. W. & Dies, R. R. (1992), *Group Counseling and Psychotherapy with Adolescents.* New York: Columbia University Press.

Mahler, M. S., Pine, F. & Bergman, A. (1975), *The Psychological Birth of the Human Infant.* New York: Basic Books.

Markman, H. (1997), Play in the treatment of adolescents. *Psychoanal. Quart.,* 66:190–218.

Maroda, K. (1994), *The Power of Countertransference.* Northvale, NJ: Aronson.

Masterson, J. (1972), *Treatment of the Borderline Adolescent: A Developmental Approach.* New York: Wiley.

McLaughlin, J. (1987), The play of transference: Some reflections on enactment in the psychoanalytic situation. *J. Amer. Psychoanal. Assn.,* 35:557–582.

Meeks, J. & Bernet, W. (1990), *The Fragile Alliance: An Orientation to the Psychiatric Treatment of the Adolescent,* 4th ed. Malabar, FL: Krieger.

Meissner, W. W. (1996), *The Therapeutic Alliance.* New Haven, CT: Yale University Press.

Minuchin, S. (1974), *Families and Family Therapy.* Cambridge, MA: Harvard University Press.

Mishne, J. (1984), Criteria for selecting treatment interventions with adolescents. *Child & Adolesc. Soc. Work,* 1:219–234.

———— (1986), *Clinical Work with Adolescents.* New York: Free Press.

Mitchell, S. (1993), *Hope and Dread in Psychoanalysis.* New York: Basic Books.

———— (1997), *Influence and Autonomy in Psychoanalysis.* Hillsdale, NJ: The Analytic Press.

Modell, A. H. (1986), A narcissistic defense against affects and the illusion of self-sufficiency. In: *Essential Papers on Narcissism,* ed. A. P. Morrison. New York: New York University Press, pp. 293–308.

Neubauer, P. (1960), The one-parent child. *The Psychoanalytic Study of the Child,* 15:286–309. New York: International Universities Press.

Novick, J. (1982), Termination: Themes and issues. *Psychoanal. Inq.,* 2:329–365.

———— (1992), The therapeutic alliance: A concept revisited. *Child Anal.,* 3:90–101.

Offer, D. & Vanderstoep, E. (1975), Indications and contraindications for family therapy. In: *The Adolescent in Group and Family Therapy,* ed. M. Sugar. New York: Brunner/Mazel, pp. 145–160.

Pearce, J. W. & Pezzot-Pearce, T. D. (1997), *Psychotherapy of Abused and Neglected Children.* New York: Guilford Press.

Pearlman, L .A. & Saakvitne, K. W. (1995), *Trauma and the Therapist.* New York: Norton.

Pérez-Foster, R. (1998), *The Power of Language in the Clinical Process: Assessing and Treating the Bilingual Person.* Northvale, NJ: Aronson.

Pines, M. (1985), Psychic development and the group analytic situation. *Group,* 9:60–73.

Pizer, S. A. (1992), The negotiation of paradox in the analytic process. *Psychoanal. Dial.,* 2:215–240.

————(1996), Negotiating potential space: Illusion, play, metaphor, and the subjunctive. *Psychoanal. Dial.,* 6:689–712.

———— (1998), *Building Bridges: The Negotiation of Paradox in Psychoanalysis.* Hillsdale, NJ: The Analytic Press.

Price, M. (1995), Knowing and not knowing: Paradox in the construction of historical narratives. In: *Sexual Abuse Recalled: Treating Trauma in the Era of the Recovered Memory Debate,* ed. J. L. Alpert. Northvale, NJ: Aronson, pp. 289–311.

Prior, S. (1996), *Object Relations in Severe Trauma: Psychotherapy of the Sexually Abused Child.* Northvale, NJ: Aronson.

Rachman, A.W. (1995), *Identity Group Psychotherapy with Adolescents.* Northvale, NJ: Aronson.

———— & Ceccoli, V. C. (1996), Analyst self-disclosure in adolescent groups. In: *Group Therapy with Children and Adolescents,* ed. P. Kymissis. & D. A. Halperin. Washington, DC: American Psychiatric Press, pp. 155–174.

Racker, H. (1957), The meanings and uses of countertransference. *Psychoanal. Quart.,* 26:303–357.

Rangell, L. (1992), The psychoanalytic theory of change. *Internat. J. Psycho-Anal.,* 73:415–428.

Rauschenberger, S. & Lynn, S. (1995), Fantasy proneness, DSM-III-R Axis 1 psychopathology, and dissociation. *J. Abn. Psychol.,* 104:373–380.

Reiser, M. & Kushner-Goodman, S. (1972), A drop-in group for teen-agers in a poverty area. In: *Adolescents Grow in Groups,* ed. I. H. Berkovitz. New York: Brunner/Mazel, pp. 149–152.

Renik, O. (1994), Countertransference enactment and the psychoanalytic process. In: *Psychic Structure and Psychic Change*, ed. M. Horowitz, O. Kernberg & E. Weinshel. Madison, CT: International Universities Press, pp. 135–157.

Sandler, J., Dare, C. & Holder, A. (1973), *The Patient and the Analyst: The Basis of the Psychoanalytic Process*. New York: International Universities Press.

———(1976), Countertransference and role responsiveness. *Internat. Rev. Psycho-Anal.*, 3:43–47.

Sandler, S., Kennedy, H. & Tyson, R. L. (1980), *The Technique of Child Psychoanalysis: Discussions with Anna Freud*. Cambridge, MA: Harvard University Press.

Schafer, R. (1992), *Retelling a Life*. New York: Basic Books.

Scharff, D. E. & Scharff, J. S., eds. (1987), *Object Relations Family Therapy*. Northvale, NJ: Aronson.

——— ———(1994), *Object Relations Therapy of Physical and Sexual Trauma*. Northvale, NJ: Aronson.

Scheidlinger, S. (1982), *Focus on Group Psychotherapy*. New York: International Universities Press.

———(1994), An overview of nine decades of group psychotherapy. *Hosp. & Community Psychiat.*, 45:217–225.

Selvini Palazzoli, M., Boscolo, L., Cecchin, G. & Prata, J. (1980), Hypothesis—circularity—neutrality: Three guidelines for the conductor of the session. *Fam. Proc.*, 19:3–12.

Shane, M. (2000), The therapeutic alliance. In: *The Therapeutic Alliance*, ed. S. T. Levy. Madison, CT: International Universities Press, pp. 109–124.

Siegler, A. L. (1983), Group work with single mothers. In: *Group Interventions with Children, Adolescents, and Parents*, ed. E. S. Buchholz & J. M. Mishne. Northvale, NJ: Aronson, pp. 95–111.

Singer, M. (1974), Comments and caveats regarding adolescent groups in a combined approach. *Internat. J. Group Psychother.*, 24:429–438.

Skolnick, N. J. & Davies, J. M. (1992), Secrets in clinical work: A relational point of view. In: *Relational Perspectives in Psychoanalysis*, ed. N. J. Skolnick & S. C. Warshaw. Hillsdale, NJ: The Analytic Press, pp. 217–238.

Slavson, S. R., ed. (1943), *An Introduction to Group Therapy*. New York: International Universities Press.

Spence, D. P. (1988), *Narrative Truth and Historical Truth: Meaning and Interpretation in Psychoanalysis*. New York: Norton.

Spitz, R. A. (1959), *A Genetic Field Theory of Ego Formation*. New York: International Universities Press.

Stebbins, D. (1972), Playing it by ear: In answering the needs of a group of black teenagers. In: *Adolescents Grow in Groups*, ed. I. H. Berkovitz. New York: Brunner/Mazel, pp. 126–133.

Steele, B. (1980), Psychodynamic factors in child abuse. In: *The Battered Child*, ed. C. H. Kempe & R. E. Helfer. Chicago: University of Chicago Press, pp. 49–85.

Stein, R. (1997), Analysis as a mutual endeavor—What does it look like? *Psychoanal. Dial.*, 7:869–880.

Stern, D. B. (1985), Some controversies regarding constructivism and psychoanalysis. *Contemp. Psychoanal.*, 21:201–208.

——— (1996), Dissociation and constructivism: Discussion of Davies and Harris. *Psychoanal. Dial.*, 6:251–266.

——— (1997), *Unformulated Experience: From Dissociation to Imagination in Psychoanalysis*. Hillsdale, NJ: The Analytic Press.

Stern, D. N. (1995), *The Motherhood Constellation: A Unified View of Parent–Infant Psychotherapy*. New York: Basic Books.

Sugar, M. (1975), *The Adolescent in Group and Family Therapy*. New York: Brunner/Mazel.

——— ed. (1999), *Trauma and Adolescence*. Madison, CT: International Universities Press.

Sullivan, H. S. (1940), *Conceptions of Modern Psychiatry*. New York: Norton.

——— (1953), *The Interpersonal Theory of Psychiatry*. New York: Norton.

Terr, T. (1990), *Too Scared to Cry: Psychic Trauma in Childhood*. New York: Basic Books.

Tylim, I. (1978), Narcissistic transference and countertransference in adolescent treatment. *The Psychoanalytic Study of the Child*, 33:279–292. New Haven, CT: Yale University Press.

van der Kolk, B .A., ed. (1987), The role of the group in the origin and resolution of the trauma response. In: *Psychological Trauma*. Washington, DC: American Psychiatric Press, pp. 153–172.

Weisberger, E. (1983), Mother guidance groups: An aid in the ego development of pre-school children. In: *Group Interventions with Children and Adolescents*, ed. E. S. Buchholz & J. M. Mishne. Northvale, NJ: Aronson, pp. 81–94.

Weiss, J. & Sampson, H. (1993), *The Psychoanalytic Process: Theory, Clinical Observation, and Empirical Research*. New York: Guilford.

White, R. S. (1992), Transformations of transference. *The Psychoanalytic Study of the Child*, 47:329–348. New Haven, CT: Yale University Press.

Winnicott, D. W. (1947), Hate in the countertransference. In: *Collected Papers: Through Paediatrics to Psycho-Analysis: Collected Papers*. New York: Brunner/Mazel, 1992, pp. 194–203.

——— (1956), The antisocial tendency. In: *Through Paediatrics to Psycho-Analysis: Collected Papers*. New York: Brunner/Mazel, 1992, pp. 306–315.

——— (1958), The capacity to be alone. In: *The Maturational Process and the Facilitating Environment*. New York: International Universities Press, 1965, pp. 29–36.

——— (1960), The theory of the parent-infant relationship. In: *The Maturational Process and the Facilitating Environment*. New York: International Universities Press, 1965, pp. 37–55.

——— (1962), Ego integration in child development. In: *The Maturational Process and the Facilitating Environment*. New York: International Universities Press, 1965, pp. 56–63.

——— (1969), The use of an object and relating through identification. In: *Playing and Reality*. London: Tavistock, 1971, pp. 101–111.

——— (1971), *Therapeutic Consultations in Child Psychiatry*. New York: Basic Books.

Wolfe, D. A., McMahon, R. J. & Peters, R. D., eds. (1997), *Child Abuse: New Direction and Treatment Across the Lifespan*. Thousand Oaks, CA: Sage.

Index